# RESEARCH 2.0 AND THE FUTURE OF INFORMATION LITERACY

T0383227

CHANDOS
ADVANCES IN INFORMATION SERIES

Series Editors: David Baker
(Email: d.baker152@btinternet.com)
Wendy Evans
(Email: wevans@marjon.ac.uk)

Chandos is pleased to publish this major Series of books entitled Chandos Advances in Information. The Series editors are Professor David Baker, Professor Emeritus, and Wendy Evans, Head of Library at the University of St Mark & St John.

The series focuses on major areas of activity and interest in the field of Internet-based library and information provision. The Series is aimed at an international market of academics and professionals involved in digital provision, library developments and digital collections and services. The books have been specially commissioned from leading authors in the field.

New authors - we would be delighted to hear from you if you have an idea for a book. We are interested in short practically orientated publications (45,000+ words) and longer theoretical monographs (75,000–100,000 words). Our books can be single, joint or multi author volumes. If you have an idea for a book please contact the publishers or the Series Editors: Professor David Baker (d.baker152@btinternet.com) and Wendy Evans (wevans@marjon.ac.uk)

# Research 2.0 and the Future of Information Literacy

By

**TIBOR KOLTAY**

**SONJA ŠPIRANEC**

**LÁSZLÓ Z. KARVALICS**

AMSTERDAM • BOSTON • CAMBRIDGE • HEIDELBERG
LONDON • NEW YORK • OXFORD • PARIS • SAN DIEGO
SAN FRANCISCO • SINGAPORE • SYDNEY • TOKYO
Chandos Publishing is an imprint of Elsevier

CHANDOS
PUBLISHING

Chandos Publishing is an imprint of Elsevier
80 High Street, Sawston, Cambridge, CB22 3HJ, UK
225 Wyman Street, Waltham, MA 02451, USA
Langford Lane, Kidlington, OX5 1GB, UK

ISBN: 978-0-08-100075-5 (print)
ISBN: 978-0-08-100089-2 (online)

**British Library Cataloguing-in-Publication Data**
A catalogue record for this book is available from the British Library

**Library of Congress Cataloging-in-Publication Data**
A catalog record for this book is available from the Library of Congress

For information on all Chandos Publishing publications
visit our website at http://store.elsevier.com/

# CONTENTS

# ABOUT THE AUTHORS

**Tibor Koltay**, PhD, is Professor at the Department of Information and Library Studies of Szent István University, Hungary. In 2010, he published *Abstracts and Abstracting: A Genre and Set of Skills for the Twenty-first Century* with Chandos Publishing.

**Sonja Špiranec**, PhD, is an Associate Professor at the Department of Information and Communication Sciences, University of Zagreb, Croatia. She is the co-founder of the European Conference on Information Literacy and served as the editor of the book *Worldwide Commonalities and Challenges in Information Literacy Research and Practice*.

**László Z. Karvalics** is an Associate Professor at the Department of Cultural Heritage and Human Information Science of the University of Szeged, Hungary. He was the founding director of BME-UNESCO Information Society Research Institute and founding editor of *Információs Társadalom*, a Hungarian language quarterly that addresses the issues of information in society.

All three authors have published several papers on information literacy and related topics both internationally and in their native languages.

# INTRODUCTION

Information literacy (IL) is alive and well, as it should be (Cowan, 2014, p. 30). By affirming this, Suzanna Cowan argues for a reform of IL that may include changing its name and not leaving it in the hands—at least not exclusively—of librarians. She adds to this that we should be brave enough to find innovative ways of fostering IL.

There is a significant and notable trend in the development of IL, materializing in the expansion of views that we should devote effort to caring for research and researchers. A number of documents are witness to this. For instance, Auckland (2012) is of the opinion that IL is gaining importance as the infrastructure of research continues to evolve and researchers must be accustomed to the resulting new environment. This is affirmed also by the expert panel that examined key trends, challenges, and emerging technologies for their impact on academic and research libraries (NMC, 2014).

All these opinions substantiate our belief that a shift in IL toward research is inevitable and necessary. This shift involves breaking innovative paths and setting new accents. However, we must put it through without losing sight of the educational role of the library.

While we argue for a shift, novelty has to be treated with caution. Our related story begins in 2008, when Peter Godwin urged readers to "discuss the social aspect of networks enabled through Web 2.0 which are so readily embraced by the Internet generation and which can be the key for librarians and academic staff seeking to reach them" (Godwin, 2008).

This was obviously only one example and Godwin was not the only one who adopted these ideas enthusiastically. However, in 2012, in the first chapter of the book *Information Literacy Beyond Library 2.0*, Godwin (2012, p. 3) noticed that the general enthusiasm about Library 2.0 "has died down and scepticism about its merits has surfaced, we need to examine what it was all about in the first place and how it has turned out in practice."

It is important to note that his writing is a kind of review, in which he enumerates the upsides and downsides of Library 2.0, while indicating that it signals important changes in the thinking of the profession.

Somewhat earlier, Roy Tennant used hard words against Library 2.0, when he nominated the term for the dustbin of history, never to be seen again (Tennant, 2011). No doubt there was over-enthusiasm, with institutions feeling that they should have a blog or a Facebook site. Sometimes this meant that services were set up without thoroughly examining the evidence that the users required these tools or would even use them. Social media have been used in order to be "current" rather than "useful" and the concepts of 2.0 were just unfocused buzzwords (Lankes, 2011).

As regards differentiating academic from research libraries, we share the opinion that research libraries fall into the same definition as academic (and university) libraries. This is supported by the definition of research libraries as "libraries that support research in any context: academia, business and industry or government" (Maceviciute, 2014, p. 283).

Obviously, the mission of academic libraries is not limited to aggregating research resources and services, and communicating them to the research community. They also support the education at any given higher education institution. Taking this into account, we will use mainly the expression *academic library* throughout this book to denominate these two types of libraries.

# CHAPTER 1

# Shifting Research Paradigms Toward Research 2.0

Until the end of the last century, the role of technology in formal scholarly (scientific) communication and the resulting *scholarly record* was the same as in any other type of print-based communication (Aalbersberg et al., 2013). This was changed by the widespread use of Web 2.0, which—as a term— has now been replaced by *social media* (Godwin, 2012). The scholarly record can be defined in the words of Lavoie et al. (2014, p. 6) as "the curated account of past scholarly endeavour."

Obviously, the boundaries of the scholarly record are fluid, not least because they also depend on the perspective that particular groups of stakeholders bring to bear on it. The same young faculty member might view the scholarly record in one way when focusing on obtaining tenure and through different glasses when looking at it when acting as a researcher. The former role includes concentrating on establishing credentials, while the latter includes materials that are useful for research interests.

A publisher or a library also may view the scholarly record from a different angle. Consequently, we have to ask how to distinguish the scholarly record from the cultural record, especially if we want the boundaries of the former to remain distinct enough to avoid including everything in it. Let us add that the scholarly record is in close connection with scholarly communication that can be understood as the process of sharing and publishing research works and outcomes which have been made available to a wider academic community and beyond (Gu & Widén-Wulff, 2011).

According to another definition, scholarly communication is the system through which research and other scholarly writings are created, evaluated for quality, disseminated to the scholarly community, and preserved for future use. This system includes both formal means of communication and informal channels (ACRL, 2003).

The appearance of the Research 2.0 paradigm was thus brought about by numerous technological innovations resulting from the abundance of social media. Research 2.0 denotes a range of activities that reflect on and are required by *eScience*, a subsystem of networked and data-intensive science, as described by Hey and Hey (2006).

Furthermore, Taylor (2001) refers to "global collaboration in key areas of science, and the next generation of infrastructure that will enable it." This definition implies that eScience comprises not only tools and technologies, but also depends on pooling resources and connecting ideas, people, and data. It has to do as much with information management as with computing. Therefore, the concept Research 2.0 is complementary to the idea of eScience and may be defined as a means for realizing its principles.

The strong presence and popularity of social media that characterizes the Research 2.0 environment may lead to transformations that will change the principles underlying research activities. Having this in view, when explaining the nature of Research 2.0, we will highlight factors that hinder its wider uptake. We will also try to show that information literacy (IL) is changing in some of its aspects as a result of developments in the Research 2.0 domain, regardless of the fact that it is not widely adopted.

The consequences resulting from the transformations analyzed in IL are of the utmost importance for academic and research libraries, the content of their instructional activities, and future conceptualizations of information literacy.

In the relevant literature, there is a general acceptance of statements such as that the globalization of science has accelerated, that modes of knowledge production are emerging which follow new patterns, or that the rapid build-out of the new cyber-infrastructure of science introduces radical changes in the methodologies of numerous scientific fields.

There is, however, a considerable divergence of opinions concerning the depth of the challenge that research faces. Opinions differ on how a comprehensive framework might be produced to interpret the respective changes.

On the one hand, there is no doubt that research has changed and metamorphosed through the use of information and communications technologies (ICTs), as numerous authors have noted so far (Arms & Larsen, 2007; Borgman, 2007; de Sompel et al., 2004; Nentwich, 2003; Odlyzko, 2009; Waldrop, 2008). However, deeper and more radical transformations that potentially could cause changes in the configurations of the principles of research activities have resulted from technological innovations brought about by Web 2.0 (Lievrouw, 2011; Luzon, 2009; Odlyzko, 2009; Procter et al., 2010; Waldrop, 2008).

Given the social and communicative nature of scientific inquiry, it is little surprise that many researchers have become active participants in this new Web, often using services and tools created specifically for research (Priem & Hemminger, 2010). If we follow the actual developments in the world of research, it is becoming clear that the scholarly record is evolving in a direction where it becomes different from its previous, print-based version.

As Lavoie et al. (2014) outline it, the scholarly record is shaped by various evolutionary trends, including the well-known shift from being print-centric to becoming digital to an ever greater extent; and its extension to a variety of materials, including data sets. (About research data, see the section on data-intensive science.)

By virtue of its transition to digital formats, the scholarly record is much more changeable and dynamic than it used to be in the past. It is available through a blend of both formal and informal publication channels, and its boundaries may expand, driven by, among other issues, an increased emphasis on the replicability of scholarly outcomes, and by expectations for a greater ability to integrate seamlessly previously published material into new work. This involves issues of citation and referencing.

Even though the scholarly record becomes digital, selection remains an important issue. In this respect, there is no difference from the world of print resources. For successful selection, researchers need clearly established priorities. As we will also see in the section on data management and data curation, stewardship models for the evolving scholarly record are needed to secure its long-term persistence. (Consulting the section on data-intensive science, mentioned above, again may be useful.)

The traditional importance attributed to formal communication via journal articles and monographs published by established scholarly publishers has come under pressure as informal modes are increasingly becoming visible with the use of digital technologies.

In comparison to smaller audiences and limited distribution after months-long blind peer-review procedures that characterize the traditional mode of formal communication, we can see intellectual priority registered first on a blog or in a video posted online (Tatum & Jankowski, 2012).

There may be changes in the exclusivity of science. The academic world has been as selective as possible in its membership, thus it imposed isolation on itself to some extent. While we can lament that this may change or be enthusiastic about it, we can also avoid these extremities by choosing a moderate and balanced position, based on a SWOT (strengths, weaknesses, opportunities and threats) analysis of the most used digital technologies. This analysis should include acknowledging the fact that Research 2.0 is a response to challenges induced by changes in technology, while being in many respects a return to centuries-old principles of open science, consequently not entirely new and revolutionary (Borgman, 2007; Dinescu, 2010).

The promise of social media is to enable researchers to create, annotate, review, reuse, and represent information in new ways and make possible a wider promotion of innovations in the communication practices of research, e.g., by publishing work in progress and openly sharing research resources (Procter et al., 2010). The term *Research 2.0* expresses exactly these substantial changes.

The analysis of several definitions shows that both terms refer to new approaches in research that promote collaborative knowledge construction, rely on providing online access to raw results, theories and ideas, and focus on the opening up of the research process (Luzon, 2009; Ullmann et al., 2010). According to Weller et al. (2007), the potentials of coupling Web 2.0 tools and services with research processes may be differentiated into several dimensions. It is the generation and management of collective knowledge that creates new structures and systems of scholarly communication.

The prevalence of the digital, mentioned above, also allows new models of public interaction in the field of research activities through the use of blogs, podcasts, etc. All these features and dimensions differentiate traditional research activities from Research 2.0. The traditional forms of research, sometimes labeled as *Research 1.0*, are dominated by a text- and document-centric paradigm.

In contrast, research in the Web 2.0 environment revolves around people and communities that have now become the new central focus of research processes. In their search for data and information, researchers have always been relying on their peers, professional communities, and networks. This did not change.

However, how they do it is changing; and the changes are obviously not just technological and process-based in nature, but are more substantial and have a significantly deeper epistemological impact that could be described as shifting (Dede, 2008), disruptive (Cope & Kalantzis, 2009a), or even distorting (Schiltz, Truyen, & Coppens, 2007). Dede describes the "seismic shift in epistemology" resulting from Web 2.0 by drawing on distinctions between classical perceptions of knowledge and approaches to knowledge within Web 2.0 environments.

According to these distinctions, in the classical perspective "knowledge" consists of firmly structured interrelationships between facts, which are based on unbiased research that produces compelling evidence of systemic causes. Epistemologically, a single right answer is believed to underlie each phenomenon, while in the context of Web 2.0 "knowledge" is defined as a collective agreement on the description of a particular phenomenon that may combine facts with other dimensions of human experience such as opinions, values, and spiritual beliefs.

While some authors perceive such disruptive forces as an opportunity for overcoming flaws in scholarly communication (Cope & Kalantzis, 2009a), others question the ever-present mantra of the growth of knowledge through information sharing. For example, Schiltz, Truyen, and Coppens (2007) state that the mere distribution of information does not directly and necessarily amount to the growth of knowledge, since knowledge and information are two different things. Information is something that can lead to knowledge, but the sheer availability of information does not necessarily result in the increase of knowledge.

In a wider (information literacy) context, we also might give a heed to the words of Bundy (2004b), p. 14), who asserts that "the sheer abundance of information and technology will not in itself create more informed citizens without a complementary understanding and capacity to use information effectively." This may prove true in the Research 2.0 environment if we do not control processes, especially through appropriate forms of information literacy.

Following the ideas that James Beniger set out in his work *The Control Revolution*, we can assert that ICTs support the broad establishment of new and effective control structures (Beniger, 1986). Yet, insofar as the very processes whereby information is interpreted and evaluated for control purposes are not successfully subjected to repeated regulation by the use of adequate methods, the feedback weakens and the system runs into new forms of control crisis.

When Beniger applies this to science, as a system constructed par excellence from the streaming of information flows, he perceives almost everywhere the indications of a growing control crisis. He finds the primary threat in the large-scale presence of new systems of ICTs, which disturb, or with their excessive radicalism even disorganize, the accustomed flow patterns of already produced knowledge, because they abandon the paper-based world. Thereby they further weaken the functioning of the most important feedback mechanism, the citation system.

Notwithstanding this, Beniger (1988, p. 26) is mistaken when he has fears for scientific reports, the publishing of specialized journals, or the publication of conference proceedings in their capacity as feedback mechanisms, on account of their exposure to information challenges.

Modern sciences, with their up-to-date information technology parks, are producing output data in quantities already so staggering as to make them incapable of being overviewed in a properly interpretive manner by the scientific community, which—to make things worse—is continually perfecting its capacity to produce and store even more new information and data. (The growing importance of data will be discussed in the section on the data-intensive paradigm of research and also in relation to data literacy.)

Yet, researchers are aware of the control crisis. They all have the bitter experience that their efforts to build new models and come up with pioneering connections and hypotheses are constrained by the small capacity of the analytic personnel available for handling lower-level, supportive transformational tasks. These tasks include surveys of measurement data, of elementary objects, or of relevant singular events; the testing of map structures; or confirming and verifying masses of elementary correlations.

Any successes achieved in automating the analysis of the raw data will face a burden at the next higher analytic level by the support personnel not being able to cope with the mass of transformational tasks. In the past, researchers had met this experience only when surveying the literature and running into the limits of the library services or the reference, abstracting, and search systems.

However, by now, the capacity limit shows up in relation to the output of each researcher's own data, so the control crisis cannot be managed by traditional approaches. The reason for this is that until now the preferred tool of control revolutions was the automation (computerization) of the kind of human intellectual effort that could be translated into appropriate algorithms, just as the computer itself had replaced human computations done by pencil and paper (Grier, 2005).

Technology easily crosses over the boundaries between categories. Levels two and three are brought into each other's proximity by science centers, and the process toward integration clearly will not stop at the boundaries of level one and level four. Levels three and four are also strongly drawn to each other. Level one and level two "shift into" the collective category of peta-scale scientific data management because of the analogue nature of the challenges they face and the large number of hardware and software elements they have in common. Distances have been reduced. Now it is not at all surprising when a researcher at level four needs level one sensor data which they can receive within a short span of time, thanks to the capacity of interconnected systems.

The data intensity of the sciences (which we will discuss in the section that addresses the data-intensive paradigm of scientific research) is not only increased by the big machines but also by the digitization of human culture, as well as the millions of measurement sensors.

We support Paul A. David's thesis, according to which the starting point for the evaluation of the new digital tools must be that they profoundly alter the ways in which "ordinary" scientific programs are organized (David, 2000). More than that, the team of authors of the document *Towards 2020 Science*, released in 2006, goes as far as stating that merging information technology with individual disciplines has exceeded the infrastructure revolution, resulting in the profound transformation of science itself. Computers, networks, and digital equipment with software and applications no longer contribute to future science at the meta-level and in a service-oriented way, but rather at the object level. Information technology not only helps in solving problems but its terminology, methodology, and principles are organically built into the tissue of studying a given field of science, thus creating new qualities (Microsoft, 2006).

Since there is little hope at the moment of changing the interest, control, and financing structures that developed in the industrial era, the international scientific community has moved in two directions. On the one hand, it has started to include players outside the sciences in ongoing research projects, move which has reached staggering proportions since the turn of the millennium.

On the other hand, researchers working in various fields of science have started to increasingly turn toward each other and form new problem communities without establishing new disciplines. These so-called scientific clusters weld together individual areas of research and bring researchers closer together in an unprecedented way, creating new synergies, knowledge hubs, and knowledge junctions between the natural and social sciences as well as the humanities (EC, 2009).

The question is whether the new kind of science, i.e., Research 2.0 really means a paradigm change. Have the structural, control, and operational mechanisms of modern science, that is, control structures, been replaced by the qualitatively different forms characteristic of the information society? Perhaps one of the answers will be that, while we are not experiencing a sudden revolution in the development of the scholarly record, new trends of an evolutionary path are on the horizon. They promise to transform our view of the nature and scope of the scholarly record, as well as the configuration of stakeholders' roles associated with it (Lavoie et al., 2014).

Let us round up this section by adding that the idea of *second-order science* has also surfaced which stresses reflexive knowledge by including the observer in scholarly thinking. It therefore contradicts the key assumption that the purpose of science is to create objective descriptions (Müller & Riegler, 2014). In other words, second-order science differs from Research 2.0 while at the same time complementing it, because the latter addresses the growing potential for scientific cooperation with the tools and instruments of Web 2.0 (Umpleby, 2014).

## RESEARCHERS' SKILLS AND ABILITIES

No one would deny that researchers are central figures in research, be it traditional research or research embedded in the Research 2.0 paradigm. It therefore goes without saying that we have to examine their skills and abilities, even though we do not intend to be exhaustive on this topic. Being a researcher encompasses a number of permanent aspects that are unlikely to change with the transformation of the information environment, while the developments in scholarly communication are unlikely to leave it untouched.

Becoming a researcher involves a complex of socialization issues, identity formation, and skills development. Librarians interested in reaching researchers absolutely must ensure that their understanding of research is up-to-date to avoid being disconnected from the researchers' world. Behaving in this way is also an act that fosters information literacy among researchers (Exner, 2014). Research—as we will also explain later—is often coupled with teaching, that is, researchers are in many cases members of the teaching staff (i.e., faculty members to use the American term).

We can move on from here by contemplating a set of the vital skills that characterizes any worker, as identified by Davies, Fidler, and Gorbis (2011), but can be adapted to fit researchers as well. Accordingly, the ideal researcher is principally characterized by *novel and adaptive thinking*, that is, finding solutions and responses beyond mechanical, rote, or rule-based answers.

Researchers are able to manage their cognitive load properly, filter information based on importance, and use a variety of tools and techniques.

All this must be accompanied by a specific type of mindset that allows these tools and techniques to be used in work processes aimed at the desired outcomes.

*Sense-making* is also absolutely essential, as there is no serious research without the ability to determine the deeper meaning of what is being expressed at face value. Davies, Fidler, and Gorbis (2011, p. 8) add to this issue the following: "As smart machines take over rote, routine manufacturing and services jobs, there will be an increasing demand for the kinds of skills machines are not good at. These are higher level thinking skills that cannot be codified. We call these sense-making skills, skills that help us create unique insights critical to decision making."

*Social intelligence*, that is, the ability to connect to others in a way that allows sensing and stimulating reactions and desired interactions, is also required.

*Data-based reasoning* is typical in a number of research settings, coupled with the ability to translate large amounts of data into abstract concepts. *Computational thinking* provides a framework for these abilities because research is largely determined by computing. *Social networking* skills are gaining importance, with differences across different contexts.

Furthermore, owing to globalization and a growing international cooperation between researchers, *cross-cultural competency* is gaining importance, and can be defined as the ability to operate in different cultural settings by adapting ourselves to these settings.

*Networking skills* are also surfacing as more and more significant. Despite undeniable technological and social changes, it is networking where we experience continuity with past practices as researchers have always participated in meetings and conferences in order to share their preliminary work with colleagues and to gather feedback from them (Donovan, 2011). As Davies, Fidler, and Gorbis (2011) also point out, networking is often brought about virtually, often using social media tools. This fact may justify the extension of networking to collaboration and allow us to speak of *virtual collaboration*.

For many research activities, a *design mindset* is required, which allows the use of tools and techniques in work processes applied to address desired outcomes. Design-based research combines research, design, and practice into one process and results in usable products that are supported by a theoretical framework; thus, it can be valid in library and information science research (Bowler & Large, 2008), which—as pointed out earlier—provides the main theoretical framework for information literacy.

Design is also underlined as a key part of the digital humanities (DH) scholarship. Burdick et al. (2012, p. 24) state that it is a creative practice, which harnesses "cultural, social, economic, and technological constraints in order to bring systems and objects into the world." In dialog with research, it is simply a technique that becomes an intellectual method when used to pose and frame questions about knowledge. The DH comes into the picture here because—as a relatively new discipline—it exemplifies the approaches, characterizing Research 2.0 to a substantial extent, so it will be included in our argument.

*Project management skills* are also necessary in research, especially when it involves funding. Funding is an important framework to consider when planning instructional outcomes for researchers. Including the practical considerations of funding may serve as an example of speaking the audience's language, i.e., addressing researchers properly in information literacy education (Exner, 2014). *Time-management* is of the utmost importance, especially as researchers are often time-stressed. For example, as a survey of Slovenian researchers shows, most often they seem to have enough time for a quick review, but not enough time for thoroughly reading, writing, and organizing the information in their personal archives (Vilar, Južnič, & Bartol, 2012).

Looking at these skills from the viewpoint of information literacy, we see a number of relevant features. As the chapter on the nature of information literacy will show, filtering information, employing a variety of tools and techniques, including sense-making, may sound familiar and are germane.

The theory of sense-making developed by Dervin (1998) is strongly connected to various forms information management, including personal information management (PIM), that we will treat as a "borderline" field of information literacy. More importantly, sense-making, in its use as a tool for discovering deep meanings and deciding if content is relevant to a particular user or not, is a subprocess of information behavior (Spink, 2010).

Time management is closely tied to PIM, while computational thinking will be explored as part of the computational turn, addressed in the section that considers the turns of library and information science on page 81.

We should not forget that many of today's problems are extremely complex and cannot be solved by one specialized discipline. This implies that there is a need for *transdisciplinarity* (Davies, Fidler, & Gorbis, 2011). Shenton and Hay-Gibson (2011) describe four assumptions related to this concept:

- phenomena that are of relevance across different subject fields;
- the application of essentially acontextual skills and attitudes, i.e., skills that are not determined by and not conforming to any particular context, while these qualities can be put to use across different subjects;
- collaborations across different fields in order to accomplish mutually desired outcomes. This is the reason why transdisciplinarity is often discussed in terms of research partnerships between researchers, who work in different areas.
- the use of techniques, ideas, or viewpoints associated with one field in order to realize aims that lie in another. This latter feature is the most intellectually demanding and conceptually ambitious, especially if the "aims" may appear fairly abstract.

Beyond being an important general framework for research, the use of transdisciplinary approaches offers for IL the potential to raise its overall status and profile. As Shenton and Hay-Gibson (2011, p. 172) affirm, transdisciplinary work

> may involve demonstrating the wide ranging utility of what is covered in IL programmes, in terms of both facilitating the acquisition of material on different subjects and providing a basis for wider life skills and attitudes, as well as involving other professionals, such as teachers. In addition, use of material from related disciplines, such as education and psychology, not only helps to ensure that IL programmes remain truly relevant to the needs and situations of learners; it also demonstrates to teaching colleagues who may already be familiar with these frameworks that information specialists have a sufficient theoretical grounding to be considered genuine educators.

Examining *self-regulation* provides a distinct point of view because it comprises a universal set of skills and abilities that characterize not just researchers. Nonetheless, researchers have to be aware of its importance.

Without giving a comprehensive psychological analysis of research processes, we intend to indicate the activities and strategies that are usually discussed under the umbrella of self-regulation. Self-regulation is directed toward cognitive processes within ourselves, utilizing skills and strategies with volition, carrying out tasks with a specific purpose in mind (Wolf, 2007).

Self-regulation is closely related to and is often used synonymously with *meta-cognition*, that is, thinking about someone's own thinking. In other words, it is reflecting on and evaluating someone's own thinking processes (Granville & Dison, 2005). The two complementary components of this broader notion are *meta-cognitive knowledge* and *meta-cognitive strategies*.

Meta-cognitive knowledge refers to information that learners acquire about their learning. Meta-cognitive strategies are general skills, through which learners manage, direct, regulate, and guide their learning. Meta-cognitive knowledge also plays a role in reading comprehension and writing. It can be deliberately activated when conscious thinking and accuracy are required (Wenden, 1999).

The ability to think meta-cognitively is essential for undertaking higher-order tasks (Granville & Dison, 2005) like abstracting (to be discussed in the section on reading and writing (Page 71)).

Self-regulation fits well with information literacy (see also the section on the nature of information literacy). For instance, the *Information Literacy Competency Standards for Higher Education*, conceived by the Association of College and Research Libraries (2000), directs our attention to a framework for gaining control over how someone interacts with information. This is achieved by sensitizing learners to the need to develop a meta-cognitive approach to learning that makes them conscious of the explicit actions required for gathering, analyzing, and using information.

A somewhat different role fulfilled by researchers is related less to the above skills and abilities. Nonetheless, it has to be mentioned as it is an everyday occupation for many—teaching.

Researchers—especially those who are also involved in teaching activities—should teach students not just content but also the conventions of a particular *discourse community*. Discourse communities provide ordered and bounded communication processes that take place within the boundaries of a given community (Hjørland, 2002). The problem is that these researchers often have a graduate, master's, and doctoral degree in the same discipline, which often makes them prone to believe that learning and adopting the ways of scientific communication is possible without explicit instruction.

This feeling is reinforced by their specialization in ever narrower fields of knowledge which, while in other circumstances a desired objective, hinders an understanding of their students' needs. Being focused on a given discipline and immersed in its particular discourse can hinder their ability to make visible and to explain how this discourse is different from the discourses of other fields. Academic librarians involved in either student instruction or helping research activities—many having subject specialties—can play an important educational role here, among others, as they have an interdisciplinary perspective.

This educational aspect is based to a substantial extent on genre theory. Traditionally, the term *genre* was used to refer to literary forms. Later, its meaning was extended in linguistics, communication studies, and education to textual patterns. These patterns can be interpreted as those that originate from pragmatic, social, political, and cultural regularities of discourse, i.e., are rhetorical actions that evolve in response to recurring situations. Teaching genres of this understanding could help in the teaching of the established conventions of academic work (Holschuh Simmons, 2005).

## OPEN SCIENCE

According to some forecasts, scholarly communication is heading toward openness (Lewis, 2013). This means that sharing research results in the wide sense comes to the foreground. This is explained in the 2012 report of the Royal Society as follows:

> *Open inquiry is at the heart of the scientific enterprise. Publication of scientific theories – and of the experimental and observational data on which they are based – permits others to identify errors, to support, reject or refine theories and to reuse data for further understanding and knowledge. Science's powerful capacity for self-correction comes from this openness to scrutiny and challenge.*
>
> **Royal Society (2012, p. 7).**

The report outlines the potential to create novel social dynamics in science, and differentiates between *data-intensive science*, which is science that involves large or massive data sets, and *data-led science*, which can be defined as the use of massive data sets to find patterns as the basis of research. An important concept is data as described by a unique identifier, but also containing identifiers for other relevant data called *linked data*.

Data–led science is a promising new source of knowledge. Through the deeper integration of data across different data sets, linked data have the potential to enhance automated approaches to data analysis, thus creating new information.

Last, but not least, *open data* are data that meet the criteria of intelligent openness by being accessible, useable, assessable, and intelligible. The proposed, emerging, and to some extent materializing changes mean and bring about much more than the setting of requirements to publish or disclose more data. They demand a more intelligent openness, which presupposes that data are accessible and can be easily located, intelligible through reliability and usability. Data also must be accompanied by metadata.

In the future, all research literature and all data will be online and the two will be interoperable (Royal Society, 2012). These are the ideas and principles that stand behind the open data movement.

However, as Stuart (2011) explains, open data is driven not by a single, idealistic movement, but by numerous individuals and organizations interested in data being made publicly available for both selfish and selfless reasons. Nonetheless, large-scale openness of data seems to be too ambitious at this moment in time, as there are a number of impediments in the way (Zuiderwijk et al., 2012).

First of all, we have to be aware of the legitimate boundaries of openness set by commercial interest, the protection of privacy, safety, and security. The barriers to openness have to be scrutinized carefully, in order to limit prohibition to cases where research could be misused to threaten security, public safety, or health (Royal Society, 2012).

Ethical issues of collaboration in Research 2.0 environments are identical to those for traditional research and include respect for people and justice. However, considerations of how to maintain these ethical principles cause additional difficulties. In addition to possessing virtues that are closely related to ethical practice, researchers must be ethically informed and sensitive about the norms, values, and regulations that might emerge in the virtual research context. Privacy may be threatened by the fact that collaboration in the digital environment is translucent and transparent, which in itself can be also seen as beneficial (Saat & Salleh, 2010).

The best-known aspect of open science is *open access* to scientific publications (OA). The idea to allow the delivery of scientific publications on the Internet without fees or restrictions appeared in the 1990s, initially as a small-scale voluntary effort by individual and groups of scholars to enhance scholarly communication.

The first successful OA implementation, the *arXiv*[1] repository for preprints in high-energy physics and related fields, started in 1991. Some early peer-reviewed OA journals started in the same era still exist. For example, *First Monday*[2] that has been publishing research concerning the Internet exists since 1996 (Björk & Paetau, 2012).

OA can be defined as a mode of publication and distribution of research results that limits or removes payments, fees, licensing, or other barriers to readers' access to scholarly literature, primarily journal articles

---

[1]http://arxiv.org.
[2]http://firstmonday.org.

(Palmer & Gelfand, 2013). According to Suber (2012, p. 4), it covers scholarly literature which is "digital, online, free of charge, and free of most copyright and licensing restrictions."

As electronic publishing has not reduced journal prices and as the rather absurd economics of the commercial sector have begun to penetrate the consciousness of researchers, the idea that OA may better suit the essence of scholarly communication goals is emerging in resistance to profit-making logic (Maceviciute, 2014).

Although many of the best-known discussions of OA focus on research in the (natural) sciences, technology, and medicine, an examination of the *Directory of Open Access Journals* (DOAJ)[3] shows that OA publishing covers all subject areas, i.e., it includes the social sciences and the humanities. This directory fulfills a mission in proving the practical usefulness of OA in providing access to free scholarly content of controlled quality.

We must not forget that many researchers agree that this trustworthy research information should be made accessible in countries where journal subscriptions cannot be afforded (Jamali et al., 2014a).

OA was formally defined by the Budapest Open Access Initiative (BOAI, 2002) as follows:

> ...free availability on the public internet, permitting any users to read, download, copy, distribute, print, search, or link to the full texts of these articles, crawl them for indexing, pass them as data to software, or use them for any other lawful purpose, without financial, legal, or technical barriers other than those inseparable from gaining access to the internet itself. The only constraint on reproduction and distribution, and the only role for copyright in this domain, should be to give authors control over the integrity of their work and the right to be properly acknowledged and cited.

OA is rooted in the very nature of academic publishing, i.e., publications are written by scholars for other scholars, and their understanding depends on highly specialized knowledge (Atkinson, 1996). Since the 1990s, there has been a growing dissatisfaction with the path that scientific communication has taken as many researchers think that, due to their high costs, many journals no longer serve their community of researchers. Okerson (1991) was already pleading for universities to publish their own research. The title of her paper ends with a question mark. It reads "Back to Academia?" This can be substituted most definitely by an exclamation mark: "Back to Academia!"

---

[3]http://doaj.org/.

Six years later, Morton (1997) highlighted the main ethical issue of the traditional scientific publishing system by asking if it is ethical that scholars, who do research based mainly on public subsidies, give away the ownership of the fruits of their intellectual labor to profit-driven enterprises. While he may not have been the first to direct attention to this, unfortunately he is not the last.

Duckett and Warren (2013, p. 42) cite a similar view put in the form of a question:

> How is it possible that much of the research published in these journals was published by taxpayers' money through federal grants yet publishers make it almost impossible for those same taxpayers to have access to the research they helped fund?

As explained by Harnad (1995), in the paper-based world, this was the consequence of a "Faustian bargain," according to which authors trade the copyright of their works in exchange for having them published. However, in the digital world, this bargain would not be necessary. As Suber (2003) indicated, this bargain causes an ongoing journal pricing crisis, an important consequence of which is that prices limit access, and intolerable prices limit access to an intolerable degree. He also mentions another issue that may be called a permission crisis. It is the result of raising legal and technological barriers to limit use. Suber argues that OA will solve them both.

OA journals are free of charge to everyone. This solves the pricing crisis. The copyright holder has consented in advance to unrestricted reading, downloading, copying, sharing, storing, printing, searching, linking, and crawling. This solves the permission crisis (Björk, 2004).

Free access is achieved in two ways. One of them is called *green OA*, which means that authors can reserve in their publication agreements the right to post their manuscripts in an OA repository, including the authors' or their institutions' Web sites and subject-specific repositories. Green OA publications often appear as preprints or postprints as the majority of scientific journal publishers explicitly allow green OA in their copyright agreements, but usually not for the final published versions (Fruin & Rascoe, 2014).

In more recent times, the decision about determining how widespread and popular OA may become is often given over to authors of manuscripts submitted to peer-reviewed journals. Authors have three choices. If the journal to which they submit the manuscript is OA, there is nothing more to do. If the journal is not OA but gives the opportunity to choose between paying an article processing charge (APC) in order to publish the paper OA, authors can opt for it. If not, the paper will be published along with the remaining articles for which green OA is in force (Björk & Paetau, 2012). Assessing APCs is an established business model adopted by a number of publishers. In the United States, the usual sums range from $200 to $5000, with $904, as the average.

Research grants can be used to cover these fees, but can be overwhelming for graduate students or junior faculty without grant funding, especially in the humanities. To respond to this need, many institutions have established OA publishing funds as a means of covering some or all of these costs (Fruin & Rascoe, 2014; Monson, Highby, & Rathe, 2014).

In contrast to the green way, Gold OA means that the journals themselves are open access (Fruin & Rascoe, 2014). According to Björk and Paetau (2012), gold OA has been less successful than the green model.

However, Beall (2014) does not see the green OA model as a solution to the problems of gold OA. OA mandates on researchers are not legitimate as they take the freedom away from researchers to publish research in the way they regard to be appropriate. Among others, this is a sign that the ongoing debate about OA is full of controversies. According to Beall (2014), with the existence of the gold OA model, there is a built-in conflict of interest, i.e., the more papers a journal accepts, the more money it makes, taking into consideration that APCs are charged to authors. As a consequence, gold OA threatens the existence of scholarly societies, especially those in the arts and humanities, as they are largely funded by library subscriptions to their journals and will be on the losing side if these fall by the wayside.

Beall (2014, p. 83) stringently points out the controversies in the ongoing debate on OA as follows:

> There is a lot at stake, and each stakeholder wants the future of scholarly communication to suit his or her best interests. Representatives of megajournals, such as PLoS one, tout their products effectively using the Internet, perhaps leading many to believe the journal is more successful than it really is. Predatory publishers (and some other publishers) use spam email to solicit articles (and their accompanying fees) and editorial board memberships.

He uses strong words when emphasizing the following:

> …there are many who are content with the traditional system of scholarly publishing, many who have no problem with signing over their copyright to someone who can manage it for them better than they can, and many who really do not want their work to be accessible by the ever increasing number of lonely pseudoscientists on the Internet. (83)

According to him, the appearance of *predatory* publishing is also one of the consequences of gold OA. Predatory (i.e., fake) OA journals (about which we can read in Beall's blog and his *List of Predatory Publishers*[4]) damage the reputation of the OA system, among other things, because they are a hotbed of author misconduct that goes as far as committing outright plagiarism.

Beall (2014) goes on to provide an inventory of problems. However, there is neither a need, nor enough and appropriate space in this book, to discuss these issues in their entirety. Instead, we will restrict our argument to agreeing with Beall in underlining the importance of *scientific publishing literacy*, which is a type of scientific literacy (on page 89). Publishing literacy furnishes researchers with an awareness and knowledge of the differences between publishers which behave ethically and those that do not. This aspect of OA has a direct interface with our main topic, i.e., information literacy and related literacies.

As Mehrpour and Khajavi (2014) underline, predatory journals may even discourage researchers from using OA. More details about detecting predatory journals can be found in the section on literacies that go beyond information literacy.

Among the researchers studied by Nicholas et al. (2015), there was a clear hostility toward predatory OA journals that claim to but do not perform peer review. However, this hostility seemed to be based more on suspicion that real knowledge of the peer-review systems of these journals.

Despite the controversies, an important driver behind the idea of OA is that the majority of academic publications are based on research that is funded by taxpayers' money. We have already touched upon this issue, which is not just a purely ethical question. In practice, if the public sector funded the research, then it should have the right of OA to the resulting publications. Accordingly, research funders and universities gradually began to require that researchers who are funded or employed by them to make their publications available through OA channels (Björk & Paetau, 2012).

Over 300 research funders and institutions now have some form of OA mandate. Notable among these are the National Institutes of Health and the Howard Hughes Medical Institute (in the United States), Research Councils UK (RCUK), the Medical Research Council, and the Wellcome Trust (in the United Kingdom), the Australian Research Council and the National Health and Research Council (in Australia).

---

[4]http://scholarlyoa.com.

According to some estimates, more than 16% of articles are published OA, not including self-archived manuscripts. The growth of OA publication seems to be inevitable, and there is evidence that heightened online accessibility is significantly associated with doubling the number of full-text downloads of research articles. This involves that OA articles can become particularly interesting means for measuring research output with alternative metrics (Mounce, 2013).

Among the main barriers to a wider permeation of OA is the reward system for teaching staff and researchers. A cornerstone of this system is that most universities intend to use an objective process for evaluating teaching staff. The easiest way to do this is to apply mechanical processes in which publication in peer-reviewed journals is central and on which promotions are based (Arms, 2002) (see also the section on alternative metrics that begins on page 31).

In most fields, it is an outstanding publication record in prestigious peer-reviewed journals that brings rewards (Harley et al., 2010). Academic appointment and grant committees rank the output of academics following the indicators in citation indexes. As Björk (2004) indicated, this generates high rewards for publishing in journals that are regarded the most important by the fact that citation indexes regularly monitor them. In contrast to this, primary publishing in relatively unknown OA journals is a very low priority.

No doubt, to achieve OA takes more effort than was originally imagined, especially as academic traditions and attitudes, lifelong habits, and the work overload on researchers inhibit full exploitation of the repositories (Maceviciute, 2014).

The empirical investigation by Nicholas et al. (2014) mentioned above shows a lack of knowledge among researchers about OA, including a significant confusion about the difference between OA and Open Source.

One of the most common misunderstandings is rooted in the existence of predatory OA publishers. Generalizing predatory behavior to the whole of OA, researchers believe that OA journals are produced by new publishers which cannot be trusted, because among other reasons they do not have proper peer-review systems, while in fact many traditional publishers have OA journals, often with rigorous peer review in force. There is also a perceptible unease among some researchers regarding the payment of APCs.

One important role that can be taken by libraries in fostering OA is the creation and maintenance of institutional repositories. For academic libraries, opening access to full text seems to be a logical extension to pulling together bibliographic data on local research output, not to mention the economic situation in libraries that makes them question commercial models of publishing and look for alternatives (Maceviciute, 2014).

In recent decades, an increased demand has emerged for public scrutiny of research. In addition to this, the divide between professionals and amateurs is becoming blurred by the participation of members of the public in research programs, so-called citizen scientists. However, many areas of science demand levels of skill and understanding that are beyond the grasp of most people, including researchers working in other fields. Accordingly—as said before—data made open to the wider public has to be intelligible, assessable, and usable for nonspecialists, which requires much greater efforts than in the case of researchers.

We have to be aware that making data open is only part of the public engagement with science (Royal Society, 2012).

## THE DATA-INTENSIVE PARADIGM OF SCIENTIFIC RESEARCH

As is well known, every other year the ACRL Research Planning and Review Committee identifies the top trends in academic libraries. The 2014 list of these trends contains data-related issues, indicating the following:

> Increased emphasis on open data, data-plan management, and "big data" research are creating the impetus for academic institutions from colleges to research universities to develop and deploy new initiatives, service units, and resources to meet scholarly needs at various stages of the research process.
>
> **ACRL (2014a, p. 294).**

We have already mentioned the NMC Horizon Report (2014). Among other important trends, this report also singled out the growing importance of research data management for libraries. This trend figures in the list of fast-moving trends, the impact of which will materialize in the next year or two.

While this is true, many of the related issues are not new at all. In their book entitled *Information Architects*, Bradford and Wurman (1996, p. 235) wrote the following:

> There is a tsunami of data that is crashing onto the beaches of the civilized world. This is a tidal wave of unrelated, growing data formed in bits and bytes, coming in an unorganized, uncontrolled, incoherent cacophony of foam.

We know that the *data deluge*, as this phenomenon is often called, can be qualified as prevalent (Borgman, 2012). There are high bandwidth networks that have the capacity to store massive amounts of data. These and other components of the highly developed ICT infrastructure are beginning to bring with them changes to the nature and practice of research and scholarship (Carlson et al., 2011).

There is interest in research data in the natural sciences, social sciences, as well as the arts and humanities (Boyd & Crawford, 2012). Beyond the world of research, data are also beginning to dominate different kinds of businesses.

One of the consequences of these developments is the potential availability of research data and other data-related activities, such as data sharing, data quality, data management, data curation, and data citation, are becoming central. Some of the main related concepts are defined vaguely or are still emerging, sometimes showing continuity, other times discontinuity with existing concepts.

The vast amounts of data allow researchers to ask new questions in new ways, and—at the same time—also pose a wide range of concerns for access, management, and preservation (Borgman et al., 2011). To name just a few of the pertinent issues, we can say that making data accessible requires the development of appropriate technical and organizational infrastructures for storage and retrieval.

Incentives and policies for researchers to share data are also indispensable (Kowalczyk & Shankar, 2011). Last but not least, data literacy, which carries the potential of motivation, is one of the essential elements of this infrastructure.

In his insightful paper, Lynch (2009) characterizes the fourth paradigm of science. He follows the ideas of Jim Gray and explains that Gray's fourth paradigm, introducing the idea of "data-intensive science," provides an integrating framework that allows the first three frameworks to interact and reinforce each other. To understand the effects of data-intensive science, it is necessary to examine the nature of the scientific (scholarly) record. This record is stored in a highly distributed fashion across a range of libraries, archives, and museums worldwide. Lynch's discussion of the data-intensive paradigm is limited to science, despite the fact that data-intensive scholarship is not so limited but also applies to the humanities and the social sciences.

The scientific record worked well during the dominance of the first two scientific paradigms. It had to face the complicated, sophisticated, and technologically mediated nature of experimental science, as well as the sheer scale of the scientific enterprise, which manifested itself the enormous growth of the literature. The challenge was in developing appropriate tools and practices to manage it with the tools, given by the print-based system.

Computational technologies brought in the third paradigm. In the era of data-intensive computing, the scientific record can be approached *in the small*, i.e., reading papers in the traditional way, than using computational tools that allow them to engage the underlying data more effectively.

In contrast to this, we can engage the scientific record *in the large* by using text corpora and interlinked data resources with the help of a wide range of new computational tools. This latter pattern is used by the digital humanities when applying *distant reading*, to which we will come back in the section about the DH.

There is also a fresh idea about the data universe, conceived by Tim Berners-Lee, the father of the World Wide Web. It is linked data, which is about a structured, interlinked, and searchable "microverse" of previously isolated data sets, using basic web technologies (Berners-Lee, Bizer, & Heath, 2009). From another point of view, following the enormous growth in institutional (government, corporate, and scientific) data production and storage, linked data presents a strong signal to identify the unstoppable birth of a new system level. This *global data space* (Heath & Bizer, 2011) or new *data ecosystem* marks a great leap forward, very similar to the revolution ushered in by the WWW 20 years ago.

The aforementioned changes will result in the eradication of *data silos*, with their unstructured, loose content, and the continuous redesign of the inter-data space, also influencing even private databases. Multi-linked crosspoints called *data hubs* will emerge, in line with the creation of *data compendiums* (the seamless, project-like integration of data sets serving special goals).

From this point in time, *data asset* means the full holdings of this new data space, vivified by millions of small knowledge operations. At the same time, it may be a common good for humanity, and a more and more valuable form of capital for data owners called *data equity*, which expresses the economic value of high-performance analytical tools, supporting immediate decision-making for business advantages (Mohamed & Ismail, 2012).

There is also a need in high-level command and control mechanisms for *global data governance* (Ladley, 2012) creating a more comprehensive level over the corporate data culture and the data management practice of international organizations.

On the corporate organizational level, the familiar data warehouse and data mining model will mobilize the expanding datasets. However, in the new data space, there is a new, more important place for *data deduplication* (a rational reduction and compression), since in the jungle of copies and places of safe-keeping, every transmission and recording operation has an importance.

Technology should follow the transaction types, supporting the increasing needs. This is the reason why *data portability* becomes determinant besides its *accessibility*.

We can also see a new kind of megatechnology with the latest generation of giant *data centers*, specializing in the management of the data mass that has grown, in terms of occupied places, the size of the works, the number of machine components per square meter, the number of automated processes, the volume and innovativeness of the energy solutions (cooling, electricity needs, etc.), and so on.

The linked data space provides a new lease of life for data packs considered useless or valueless. The reuse of data in secondary, repeated, or multiple appropriations can fertilize the circulation of data in several ways. When there is time and energy to find links to seemingly dead *data trashes*, carefully elaborated *data recycling* can also become meaningful. Nonetheless, this does not justify a moral panic about *data smog*.

The new data space works effectively directing the real data trash into *data puddles* (previously in the corporate environment *cemeteries* of unnecessary, redundant, excrescent *data*).

Data-intensive research made its impact on scientific communication. For a long time, despite extensive technological developments in scientific publishing, the scientific article remained almost unchanged. While distributed in an electronic form (mainly PDF), it still resembled print.

The new development in this field is that the role of technology in the scientific article has changed. For instance, we can add value to articles by providing supplementary material in nontraditional formats (Aalbersberg et al., 2013). Such enhanced publications usually consist of a mandatory narrative part containing the description of the research conducted, supplemented, and enhanced by related elements such as data sets, images, and workflows (Bardi & Manghi, 2014).

Our discussion of a data-intensive paradigm requires that we determine what data is and what constitutes big data. *Data* can be defined as "any information that can be stored in digital form, including text, numbers, images, video or movies, audio, software, algorithms, equations, animations, models, simulations, etc." (NSB, 2005, p. 9).

Data comes in several varieties, such as observational, computational, and experimental. One of the distinct varieties of data is records, i.e., records of government, business, public, and private life (Borgman, 2007). We suggest that data also comes from works of art and literature and artifacts of cultural heritage (Nielsen & Hjørland, 2014).

What constitutes data is determined by the given community of interest that produces the data. However, an investigator may be part of multiple, overlapping communities of interest, each of which may look differently at data (Borgman, 2012).

*Research data* is the output from any systematic investigation that involves a process of observation, experiment or the testing of a hypothesis. All researchers use and produce data, regardless of whether they work in the sciences, the social sciences or the humanities (Pryor, 2012).

*Big data* is an emergent and important, though not exclusive facet of the data-rich world. It is about the capacity to search, aggregate, and cross-reference large data sets, and it is conditioned by the interplay of cultural, technological, and scholarly phenomena (Boyd & Crawford, 2012).

Big data is not only big, but it is fast, unstructured, and overwhelming (Smith, 2013). From this point of view, it is of note that it exceeds the processing capacity of conventional database systems in capturing, storing, managing, and analyzing (Gordon-Murnane, 2012).

We do not know enough about the *ethical use* of big data. This is especially true if social media is used as the source of data. We should ask, among others things, if it is allowable to take data of someone's blog post out of context and analyze in a way that the author never would have imagined. The answer to this question is that we have to get a clear picture of whether it is ethical to analyze someone's data without their informed consent.

Obviously, there are answers as well. For instance, that content is publicly accessible does not mean that it is meant for consumption by anyone. It is reasonable to think that some of those who created messages in the highly context-sensitive spaces of social media applications possibly would not give permission for their data to be used elsewhere, not least because researchers were not meant to be their audience (Boyd & Crawford, 2012).

In addition, we have to be aware of the fact that a substantial part of this data is in private hands, a circumstance that raises several questions once more about the potential unethical use of these data (Lynch, Greifeneder, & Seadle, 2012).

The data-intensive paradigm of research relies heavily on *data management* and *data curation*, which do not seem to be clearly separated from each other. Nonetheless, we will concentrate on data curation. As Giarlo (2013) notes, digital curation aims to make selected data accessible, usable, and useful throughout its life cycle. It subsumes digital preservation and provides context by supplying documentation, descriptive metadata, or both.

As stated by Erway (2013), data curation poses, among others, the following questions:

- Who owns the data?
- What requirements are imposed by others (such as funding agencies or publishers)?
- Which data should be retained?
- For how long should data be maintained?
- How should it be preserved?
- What are the ethical considerations related to it? (How will sensitive data be identified and contained? Are there access restrictions that have to be enforced?)
- What sort of risk management is needed?
- How is data accessed?
- How open should it be?
- How should the costs be borne?
- What alternatives to local data management exist?

An intriguing facet of data curation is the *disposal* of "unnecessary" data. Decisions about data disposal have to take account not only of changes in the potential long-term value of data sets but also any legislation governing the length of time that certain types of data must be preserved. The nature of some data may influence this. For example, confidentiality may even dictate the use of secure destruction methods.

The costs of curating data also dictate that we periodically review what to keep and what to dispose of, not forgetting the migration of data in order to ensure its immunity to hardware or software obsolescence (Pryor, 2012).

Digital (data) curators need competences in the following fields:

- the data structure of different digital objects;
- the ways to assess the digital objects' authenticity, integrity, and accuracy over time;
- storage and preservation policies, procedures, and practices;
- relevant quality assurance standards;
- the risks of information loss or corruption of digital entities;
- requirements of the information infrastructure in order to ensure proper access, storage, and data recovery;
- the need to keep current with international developments in digital curation and understand the professional networks that enable this.

Digital curators can be involved in the following activities:

1. planning, implementing, and monitoring digital curation projects;
2. selecting and appraising digital documents for long-term preservation;
3. diagnosing and resolving problems to ensure continuous accessibility of digital objects;
4. monitoring the obsolescence of file formats, hardware, and software and the development of new ones;
5. ensuring methods and tools that enable interoperability of different applications and preservation technologies among users in different locations;
6. verifying and documenting the provenance of the data to be preserved;
7. elaborating digital curation policies, procedures, practices, and services;
8. understanding and communicating the economic value of digital curation to existing and potential stakeholders;
9. establishing and maintaining collaborative relationships with various stakeholders;
10. organizing personnel education, training, and other support for the adoption of new developments in digital curation;
11. organizing and managing the use of metadata standards, access controls, and authentication procedures;
12. observing and adhering to all applicable legislation and regulations when making decisions about preservation, use, and reuse of digital objects (Madrid, 2013).

The spirit of open science requires more and more open data, the foundation of which is given by data sharing. Data sharing is the release of research data for use by others (Borgman, 2012). The problem with data sharing is that it raises several significant questions for both researchers and librarians (information professionals).

These questions concern research itself in the public and the private sectors, citizen participation in the scientific process, and the proper distribution of research results, while being at the intersection of storage, retrieval, preservation, management, access, and policy issues.

Several factors can motivate researchers to share their data. Sharing data may be a condition of gaining access to the data of others, and may be a prerequisite for receiving funding, as set out by different funding agencies with varying degrees of rigor. In the majority of cases, this incentive appears in the form of requiring the provision of data management plans.

It is also clear that researchers have a number of reasons not to share their data. Documenting data is extremely labor intensive. However, the main reason is the lack of interest, caused by the well-known fact that in most fields of scholarship the rewards come not from data management, but from publication (Borgman, 2010).

Each discipline has its own "data culture," and data from "big science" is typically more uniform and therefore more easily transferable, while data generated by smaller research teams in more idiosyncratic formats are not easily transferable beyond a given team. Notions of security and control play a role here. Greater openness requires researchers to shift from perpetual proprietary control to forgetting fears of misuse or misinterpretation (MacMillan, 2014).

In addition, there are some distinct "natural" barriers to data sharing. In order to overcome them, we have to:

1. Discover if a suitable dataset exists.
2. Identify its location.
3. Examine the copy to see if it has deteriorated too much and/or is too obsolete to be usable or not.
4. Clarify whether it is permissible to use.
5. Ascertain its interoperability, i.e., if it is standardized enough to be usable with acceptable effort.
6. Judge if its description is clear enough to indicate what the given dataset represents.
7. Ascertain trust.
8. Decide if it is usable for someone's purpose.

There are no simple answers to these questions, which form a chain, i.e., the existence of any of these barriers may prevent the use of the data (Buckland, 2011).

A survey and interview study on publication sharing practices gives an interesting insight into the nature of sharing, which can also be useful in promoting research data sharing. Two main types of sharing appeared among participants of the study. The most common way was sharing a citation or link to an article. Some researchers also send full text, most often as a PDF files, and usually their own work. Those who share their own full texts also upload their work into repositories. Researchers share material for a variety of reasons. After all, sharing publications to further scientific and academic discovery is regarded to be a natural part of scholarship (Tenopir et al., 2014).

Paramount to achieving the goals of efficient data-intensive research is data quality. The problem is that the appraisal of data requires deep disciplinary knowledge. In addition to this, manually appraising datasets is very time consuming and expensive, and automated approaches are in their infancy (Ramírez, 2011).

Notwithstanding this, the quality of the data is one of the cornerstones in the data–intensive paradigm of scientific research. It is determined by multiple factors. The first is trust. This factor is complex in itself.

According to Buckland (2011), the elements of trust include the lineage, version, and error rate of data and the fact that they are understood and acceptable. Giarlo (2013) mentions that trust depends on subjective judgements of authenticity, acceptability, and applicability of the data, and is also influenced by the given subject discipline, the reputation of those responsible for the creation of the data, and the biases of those who are evaluating the data. It is also related to cognitive authority, about which we will present details in the section that describes digital literacy as one of the literacies closely related to and supplementing information literacy.

The next factor of data quality is authenticity, which measures the extent to which the data are judged to represent the proper ways of conducting scientific research, including the reliability of the instruments used to gather the data, the soundness of underlying theoretical frameworks, and the completeness, accuracy, and validity of the data. In order to evaluate authenticity, the data must be understandable.

The presence of sufficient context in the form of documentation and metadata allows an evaluation of the understandability of data. To achieve this, data have to be usable. To make data usable, data have to be discoverable and accessible, and be in a usable file format. The individuals judging data quality need to have at their disposal an appropriate tool to access the data which has to show sufficient integrity to be rendered. Integrity of data assumes that the data can be proven to be identical, at the bit level, to some previously accepted or verified state. Data integrity is required for usability, understandability, authenticity, and thus overall quality (Giarlo, 2013).

According to Miller (1996), other dimensions of data quality include:
- relevance to user's needs;
- accuracy;
- timeliness;
- completeness;
- coherence;
- proper format;
- physical and logical security;
- validity.

The latter, i.e., validity is related to other dimensions, like accuracy, timeliness, completeness, and security.

Besides data quality, there is another decisive factor: *data citation*, which is of the utmost importance (Carlson et al., 2011) as it allows the identification, retrieval, replication, and verification of data underlying published studies, even though there are no standard formats to cite data as yet. Standardized forms of data citation could be of the utmost importance as they provide a motivation for researchers to share and publish their data, by the potential of becoming a tool of reward and acknowledgment for them (Mooney & Newton, 2012).

As data citation is closely associated with data sharing, there is a need for the recognition of data as a significant contribution to the scholarly record. However, the environment is not yet beneficial and—despite several positive developments—there is also a lack of community for data citation.

This situation may change through initiatives such as DataCite[5] or the DataVerse Network[6] (Mooney & Newton, 2012). Thomson Reuters, a major information provider, also sees the importance of data citation. Their Data Citation Index appears to be heavily oriented toward the natural sciences, and contains three document types, i.e., datasets, data studies, and repositories. Datasets can be defined as single or coherent sets of data or data files provided by a repository as part of a collection, data study, or experiment. Data studies describe studies or experiments held in repositories with the associated data which have been used in the data study (Torres-Salinas, Martín-Martín, & Fuente-Gutiérrez, 2014).

It is worth examining a heavily data-intensive research paradigm: the digital humanities, as well. As we already pointed out in the introductory part of this chapter, Research 2.0 concerns not only research in the hard sciences but also research in the social sciences and humanities. In addition, it also includes the new paradigm of the humanities, i.e., the DH.

Perhaps the most characteristic feature of the DH is that it "explores a universe in which print is no longer the exclusive or the normative medium in which knowledge is produced and/or disseminated" (Schnapp & Presner, 2009). With this, it can be qualified as a genuinely new approach toward research, i.e., a representative of Research 2.0.

A key concept of the DH is *distant reading*, which is defined by Moretti (2005) as using graphs, maps, and trees instead of reading concrete, individual works, applying deliberate reduction and abstraction, and concentrating on fewer elements that will allow us to find a sharper sense of their overall

[5]http://www.datacite.org/.
[6]http://thedata.org/.

interconnection. This would not be possible without a highly developed computing infrastructure, mentioned above. Text can also become data and it is used as data in research.

No doubt, the DH is deeply interested in text (Schreibman, Siemens, & Unsworth, 2004), and shows an evident preference for textual material and the inclination to interpret written documents (Alvarado, 2012).

A founder of DH, Busa (2004) approached the discipline from the humanities computing side, stating that it is "precisely the automation of every possible analysis of human expression", therefore it is humanistic activity, in the widest sense of the word. While emphasizing the high degree of heterogeneity in the DH, Svensson (2012) also points toward the foundational role of the epistemic traditions of humanities computing. Schmidt (2011) sees the importance of using technology to create new objects for humanistic interrogation. Frischer (2011) affirms this, and identifies the humanities' basic tasks as preserving, reconstructing, transmitting, and interpreting the human record. Piez (2008) turns toward the "media consciousness" of the digital age, which is "a particular kind of critical attitude analogous to, and indeed continuous with, a more general media consciousness as applied to cultural production in any nation or period." He adds that critique may imply refiguration and reinvention, i.e., DH should go beyond studying digital media and be concerned with designing and making them.

We know that digital information prevails in our world. Evens (2012) explains that the source of this prevalence is abstraction, which leads to a stage where the essence of the digital can be boiled down to the discrete code, typically a binary one. The digital side of the DH is strongly informed by a narrative of technological progress, while the humanities side has strong roots in a humanities sensibility. However, this equilibrium may be questioned (Flanders, 2009).

Taking into account that research is increasingly being mediated through digital technology, Berry (2011) speaks about a computational turn. The idea of this turn was conceived for the DH and the social sciences. Apparently, it can be imported into the general thinking about scientific research. As library and information science (LIS) that underlies information literacy pertains to the social sciences, the computational turn may find its place among the turns and paradigms of LIS. We outline these in the section that explains the contexts of information literacy.

As regards the DH, Berry proposes looking at its digital component "in the light of its medium specificity, as a way of thinking about how medial changes produce epistemic changes" (Berry, 2011, p. 3). He adds that this can

be done by "problematizing computationality, so that we are able to think critically about how knowledge in the 21st century is transformed into information through computational techniques, particularly within software."
More concretely, he stated the following:

> To mediate an object, a digital or computational device requires that this object be translated into the digital code that it can understand. This minimal transformation is effected through the input mechanism of a socio-technical device within which a model or image is stabilised and attended to. It is then internally transformed, depending on a number of interventions, processes or filters, and eventually displayed as a final calculation, usually in a visual form.
>
> **Berry (2011, pp. 1–2).**

There seems to be an agreement about the importance of computationality. For instance, Frabetti (2011) is of the opinion that it should include engaging with software as a problem of reading and writing, adding that the textual aspects of software make the concept of the document more than a simple metaphor.

Even though the digital tools of interpretation are core epistemological resources of the DH, we can agree with the following statement of Dalbello (2011, p. 482).

> the humanities fields are struggling to develop criteria to guide the use of technology to maintain the ideals of humanistic endeavour, and understand the effects of a growing digital infrastructure as a system for knowledge production in the humanities.

While this is true, it seems to be important that the ways of using computers as tools for modeling humanities data should not be the same as using the computer for modeling the typewriter (Unsworth, 2002).

Last but not least, we should not forget that the DH appears among the top 10 trends in academic libraries, identified by the ACRL Research Planning and Review Committee, and already mentioned in this book. The ACRL experts state that the DH can be understood as an intersection, where traditional humanities research methodologies and digital technologies meet. They add that academic libraries can play a key role in supporting it (ACRL, 2014a).

The appearance of *alternative metrics* of scientific output is a feature of Research 2.0. The availability and accessibility of big quantities of textual material, in particular full texts of journal papers and books, makes it technically possible that we go beyond traditional measures of scientific output. All this is in accordance with open science and data-intensive research.

Notwithstanding this, we have to be aware that the ready existence of technology does not mean that alternative approaches become easily institutionalized and accepted by the communities of researchers or other stakeholders in the research field such as funders, institutions (universities and research centers), learned societies, or publishers.

The main impediments of accepting alternative measures are rooted in the need to filter scholarly information. These major hindrances are recognition and trust. This filtering of information for credibility, quality, and reliability has become utterly complicated in the last decade because, among other reasons, the efficiency of the main filters used in research publications is constantly being questioned (Priem et al., 2010). As the Web matures and researchers' works are published on the Web, the criteria and methodologies for measuring the impact of research may change (ACRL, 2014a).

In this section, we are going to take a snapshot of these issues, as the relationship between Research 2.0 and information literacy cannot be explored properly without paying attention to them. However, this short review is not intended to be exhaustive or comprehensive.

Among them, already mentioned future trends in academic librarianship, identified by the ACRL Research Planning and Review Committee, we find altmetrics, with the following comment:

> The expanding digital environment drives changes in the criteria for measuring the impact of research and scholarship. As the web matures and the researchers' works are referred to or published on the web, it is important to have a method for tracking the impact of their work in these new media.
>
> **ACRL (2014a, p. 298).**

As is well known, the only major international multidisciplinary citation indexes were the *Science Citation Index*, the *Social Sciences Citation Index*, and the *Arts & Humanities Citation Index*. They were devised and started in 1975 by Eugene Garfield, offered originally by the Institute for Scientific Information, then united under the name *Web of Science* (WoS),[7] by Thomson Reuters.

In 2004, Elsevier's *Scopus*[8] became the second subscription-based database of this kind. Since then, *Google Scholar* (GS)[9] has joined as a citation service provider which collects its data partly by automatically crawling the Web.

---

[7]http://thomsonreuters.com/thomson-reuters-web-of-science/.
[8]http://www.scopus.com/.
[9]http://scholar.google.com/.

Whatever sources they come from, citation counts have long been the exclusive measure of academic research impact. Publishing articles in prestigious journals and citing articles that appeared in other prominent journals still open the doors to prestige and tenure. This dominant way of determining impact was developed in the 1960s, and has not changed to the same degree as collecting and disseminating information (Buschman & Michalek, 2013; Torres-Salinas, Cabezas-Clavijo, & Jimenez-Contreras, 2014).

In disciplines where journal articles have been the dominant format of research output, classic citation analysis remained more valid. In fields where books and book chapters are the main form of publishing (especially in the humanities), it is more difficult to impose this model (Buschman & Michalek, 2013).

WoS mainly indexes academic journals, even though, more recently, Thomson Reuters has included citation databases for conference proceedings, books, and monographs. Scopus has a larger number of publication sources than WoS, including book series and conference proceedings, but operates only with citation data from 1996.

GS has broader coverage and a wider variety of sources than WoS and Scopus (Mas Bleda et al., 2014). Criticisms of GS are mainly related to the fact that it processes citations with automated tools. Analysts indicate incomplete or inaccurate metadata, inflated citation counts, lack of usage statistics, and inconsistent coverage across disciplines (Asher, Duke, & Wilson, 2013).

Citation analysis is a useful but incomplete measure as not all influences are cited in an article (Priem et al., 2010; Priem, Groth, & Taraborelli, 2011), and because such analyses, among other reasons, omit informal influences or cite reviews instead of the original work. Moreover, some unread papers are cited, while some relevant articles are not (Mas Bleda et al., 2014). The Matthew effect, that is, the phenomenon in which the rich get richer, also distorts citation practices, as authors tend to cite well-cited material from well-cited journals, while ignoring other work (Buschman & Michalek, 2013). The strong and growing strain of criticism also includes deprecating the inappropriate use of bibliometrics—especially the journal impact factor (IF)—as measures of performance. Nevertheless, these criticisms often imply acceptance of the need for competitive evaluation of research outputs, as competition is not an aberration but a fundamental and intrinsic part of the research environment (Jubb, 2014).

For a relatively long time, IFs have been the single metric that indicates the quality of an academic journal. Recently, the *Journal IF* that appears in the *Journal Citation Report* (JCR), which is also a product of Thomson Reuters, came under fire. The JCR measures the frequency with which the "average article" in a journal has been cited in a given period of time. Criticisms raised against the factor include that it is often incorrectly used and its exact details are kept a trade secret (Priem et al., 2010). Besides citation counts, impact is often represented by other bibliometric measures, such as the *h-index* (Weller, 2011) which, being a citation-dependent and journal-level metric, should be supplemented by other metrics (Priem, Groth & Taraborelli, 2011).

With the increasing presence and importance of online scholarly communication, a number of new indicators have become available, which are both a product and tool of the Web (ACRL, 2014a). A substantial part of these new metrics is called *altmetrics*, a term derived from the first part of *alternative* and *metrics* (Piwowar, 2013).

Being a social Web metric for measuring academic output (Južnič, Vilar, & Bartol, 2014), altmetrics denote the study and use of scholarly impact measures based on activities in online tools and environments, and have also been used to describe the metrics themselves (Priem, Groth, & Taraborelli, 2011). The term *metric* itself denotes a quantifiable standard of measurement, which can be applied consistently in different situations to allow comparisons between similar objects of investigation (Stuart, 2011). To distinguish the latter meaning from the first, Južnič, Vilar, and Bartol (2014) even suggest we should name it a "set of new altmetrics." In any case, altmetrics is citation-independent.

Altmetrics can be regarded not only as a subset of scientometrics but also of webometrics. Nonetheless, instead of investigating the web more generally, it focuses on scholarly influence, measured in online environments, with the help of online tools (Priem, Groth & Taraborelli, 2011).

Using altmetrics is a radical move away from measuring citations and from metrics based on the academic article (Weller, 2011). One of the reasons for this is that the proportion of highly cited papers coming from high-impact journals is steadily decreasing. Behind this tendency, we find the increasing habit of readers to find articles through search engines (Lozano, Larivière, & Gingras, 2012).

Altmetrics also strive to provide a nuanced understanding of research impact by indicating the effect of reading, discussing, saving, and recommending. It reflects the impact on diverse audiences, which include not only scholars but also practitioners, clinicians, educators, and the general public (Piwowar, 2013).

The number of article downloads seems to be the most obvious new measure though it is by no means the only one. It is not the same as the Journal IF. However, it is a viable alternative to assess a journal's influence (Bawden, 2013).

Metrics based on usage also include library circulation and course readings. Another category of impact comes from published and informal reviews and comments (Buschman & Michalek, 2013).

On a more fine-grained level, citation counts can be filtered by the type of citation, that is, citations in editorials and citations in review articles. Article-level metrics have been pioneered by the OA publisher, *Public Library of Science* (PLoS). This means that metrics are collected on a *per article* and not a *per journal* basis and are complemented by real-time data from the social Web (Fenner & Lin, 2014).

Article-level metrics measure both the *immediacy* and the *socialization* of an article by drawing data from a variety of traditional and new data sources. They are also a toolkit of heterogeneous data points that can be mixed and matched in order to enhance our ability to measure a wide variety of ways in which research may reach and affect its audience (SPARC, 2014)[10]. The list of these metrics goes on and their variety undoubtedly grows.

Citations take time to accumulate, so their impact may only be seen a few years after publication (Južnič, Vilar, & Bartol, 2014). This is why perhaps one of the common advantages of the new metrics is that they may prove to be quicker than traditional metrics, the slowness of which impedes effective scholarly communication (Mas Bleda et al., 2014; Sugimoto et al., 2014).

Altmetrics can not only evaluate impact in a much shorter time period than conventional measures but can also help to identify the works that are influential but not cited, or point toward work and impact from sources that are not peer-reviewed.

Bibliometricians see some value in altmetrics, especially download metrics, and there is already evidence that a range of altmetrics correlate with traditional citation counts. There are now some Web sites, such as Altmetric[11] and ImpactStory,[12] that provide a range of altmetrics for publications (Mas Bleda et al., 2014).

An interesting facet of altmetrics is their use in someone's curriculum vitae (CV). Ambitious scholars have been including altmetric indicators in their CVs for years, for example by indicating papers that were recommended by other researchers and faculty members.

[10]http://www.sparc.arl.org/initiatives/funds.
[11]http://www.altmetric.com/.
[12]https://impactstory.org/.

Altmetrics also raise the issue of negative research results. While the current system of promotion does not encourage the publication of negative research results, both positive and negative results help advance science, and not sharing negative results can lead to unnecessary duplication and incomplete understanding of positive results (Buschman & Michalek, 2013).

Piwowar and Priem (2013) comment on this as follows:

> As tools improve, we can anticipate these early-adopters will begin to incorporate a much wider range of altmetrics on a much wider range of products. However, if we expect these early adopters to be joined by their more cautious peers, scholars will need a clearly articulated case for value. What are the benefits that will stand the test of time and that should motivate early and ongoing action? Librarians can help in this process.

Potentially usable data is available in large quantities. Nonetheless, achieving robust measurements with alternative metrics is still some way off (Weller, 2011). The relationship between classic bibliometric indicators and the new metrics has to be investigated. The correlation between altmetrics and the number of citations remains to be convincingly demonstrated. Although there is some evidence of an association between highly cited or frequently downloaded and highly tweeted articles, this impact has not been properly determined. Altmetrics offer an additional, complementary point of view when measuring the visibility of papers in the widest sense. Altmetrics have their limitations, first of all because they work with sources, which are evanescent by their nature. For example, if an article has been reviewed in a blog, it is questionable whether the comments should be added to the article's original impact (Torres-Salinas, Cabezas-Clavijo, & Jimenez-Contreras, 2014).

An investigation by Schloegl et al. (2014) led to the conclusion that citations, downloads, and readership metrics are not substitutes for each other. Rather, they are complementary as they represent different aspects of scholarly communication, not to mention disciplinary differences.

Establishing a digital scholar's footprint beyond the academic paper across different digital services is difficult as people use different tools, so there is no standard unit of measurement (Weller, 2011). Another core challenge to collecting altmetric data is that the same research artifact can appear in many separate digital locations. For example, the same article can be found in a preprint repository, on the publisher's Web site or as a postprint on the researcher's homepage. All these appearances have to be taken into account (Buschman & Michalek, 2013).

As Priem et al. (2010) point out, altmetrics can point toward crowd-sourcing peer review. This might give speed to the process of measuring impact. On the other hand, altmetrics could crowdsource other measures of the reward system. However, such moves could make researchers, who want to rely on trust, suspicious (see the wisdom of the crowd).

Accordingly, we can state that the goal of altmetrics, through the use of social media and by crowdsourcing peer review, is to determine impact, to learn about new applications, and to solicit and use feedback and assessment on the scholarly information provided (Palmer & Gelfand, 2013).

Perhaps the most strongly organized and cross-disciplinary critique on the prevalence of "traditional" metrics can be found in the manifesto known as *DORA: San Francisco Declaration on Research Assessment*.[13] The DORA declaration calls for placing less emphasis on publication metrics and becoming more inclusive of non-article outputs. The 82 original signatories of DORA included scientific societies from around the world. Editorial boards of well-known journals, prestigious research institutes and foundations, and providers of new metrics also support it. As of late January 2014, DORA had more than 400 supporters among organizations, and more than 10,000 individuals had signed the declaration. To decrease their reliance on journal-based metrics, DORA asks that members of the scientific community commit to reformulating their definitions of research quality, including their criteria for hiring, tenure, and promotion. Additionally, institutions and funding agencies are urged to consider research outputs other than articles (Bladek, 2014).

There is a temptation to see altmetrics as a passing fad, qualifying them as interesting but premature, or simply not serious enough (Buschman & Michalek, 2013). If we want altmetrics to be a proper way of measuring impact, correlations should be found between altmetrics and existing measures. Predicting citations from altmetrics and comparing altmetrics with expert evaluation would be also instrumental (Priem et al., 2010).

In summary, altmetric data are compiled from the usage, recommendations, shares and reuse of a common document, which is identified by its DOI, URL, or other ID. Many activities can be a source of altmetrics; however, one type of data cannot necessarily be equated with another as different kinds of data have very different characteristics. For instance, the intention of a person uploading a paper to Mendeley (a free reference

---

[13]http://am.ascb.org/dora/.

manager, PDF organizer, and academic social networking tool promoted by Elsevier[14]) is not the same as that of someone writing a newspaper article or a blog post.

Similarly, different platforms also have different characteristics, including discipline bias. This is the reason why there is no canonical source of altmetric data. It is not a single indicator as, for example, the *h*-index. To describe altmetrics as one thing is impossible. In a similar way to traditional measures of scholarly impact, altmetrics can be manipulated, so with the growing importance of altmetrics, the likelihood of cheating is also increasing. Overall, more research is needed in this field (Taylor, 2014).

A slightly different alternative is offered by post-publication comments that can also contribute to researcher evaluation in terms of the individual's contribution to post-publication discussions of others' work, as well as by evaluations of the researcher's own work by their peers. As nontraditional (but in principle also measurable) scholarly outputs, data are valuable and important research outputs (Khodiyar, Rowlett, & Lawrence, 2014) (see the chapter on the data-intensive paradigm of science).

*Semantometrics*, proposed by Knoth and Herrmannova (2014), is a new class of metrics for evaluating research. Contrary to the existing metrics (including the alternative metrics), it is not based on measuring the number of interactions in the scholarly communication network, but built on the premise that full-text is needed to assess the value of a publication.

Semantometrics are based on the process of how research builds on existing knowledge in order to create new knowledge. Accordingly, the hypothesis is that the added value of publication $p$ can be estimated based on the semantic distance from the publications cited by $p$ to the publications citing $p$.

Altmetrics are at an early stage in their development leaving many questions unanswered. On the other hand, in the evolution of scholarly communication, the speed and richness of altmetrics make them worth investigating (Priem et al., 2010). Indeed, Južnič, Vilar, and Bartol (2014) suggest that a very cautious approach should be adopted toward using specific tools and indicators, not only across all disciplines but also in different national environments. As regards the societal impact of research, it is unlikely that

---

[14]http://www.mendeley.com/.

any indicators will be found that can be measured easily, that are based on uniform principles, and that can be employed across most disciplines and institutions.

Alternative metrics are still evolving and we can agree with Jubb (2014), who sees a bewildering array of metrics surrounding journal articles that is growing and consists of various citation scores.

As with new developments in scholarly communication encouraged by advances in technology, the reception of altmetrics is mixed. Altmetrics can also be qualified therefore as a "technology of narcissism" (Mounce, 2013). Only time will prove whether such a statement is true or false. However, the real issue is whether altmetrics are accepted among researchers or not, and if yes, to what degree. For the moment, as Torres-Salinas, Cabezas-Clavijo, & Jimenez-Contreras (2014, p. 60) affirm,

> the only definite conclusion seems to be that altmetrics is here to stay, to enrich the possibilities and dimensions of impact analysis, in all fields of scientific research, and to illuminate from a new perspective the relationship between science and society.

Whether we like it or not, the academic reward system that includes hiring and grant funding is still based on quantifiable data, so it is difficult to foresee if it will change and whether it needs to change or not. The actual system has persisted for five decades and will continue to evolve. However, it is not certain whether these changes will require more holistic measurements (Buschman & Michalek, 2013).

Academic libraries have a long-standing tradition of collaborating with researchers in demonstrating the impact of their scholarship. Librarians anticipate that this role will continue by providing access to, and instruction in, the appropriate use of altmetric information that is already incorporated into resources for scholarly communication, impact, and citation management (ACRL, 2014a).

The results of an empirical study, presented by Nicholas et al. (2014), show that altmetrics (in the wider sense) are not familiar to most researchers; moreover, many showed a degree of skepticism of it.

The beliefs and norms of professional communities may change. In accordance with this, we can ask along with Tsou, Schickore, and Sugimoto (2014) if it is possible that much scholarly work remains unpublished, not because of its lack of value, but because it does not fit in with the current publishing paradigm. Their survey of 2535 faculty members at Indiana University, followed by in-depth interviews, indicates that academic discourse would benefit from the formal dissemination of papers that included inconclusive or null results, as well as replication and refutation studies. The results of this investigation show that negative results, even if not directly contributing to a field's body of knowledge, are still useful, primarily as they have the potential to prevent other researchers from pursuing unfruitful avenues of research.

Despite this, most respondents were not optimistic about the prospects of publishing negative results, although some interviewees did indicate that publishing "negative results" would not be problematic in their discipline.

These results are in accordance with the finding of another survey that indicated that there was no general editorial policy concerning the publishing of negative results, null results, or replication studies. However, there are journals dedicated to publishing negative results, such as the *Journal of Negative Results*, the *Journal of Negative Results in BioMedicine*, and the *Journal of Pharmaceutical Negative Results*, as well as an archive of replication attempts in experimental psychology.[15]

Nonetheless, such sources are generally not very well known, nor are they necessarily relevant to all researchers. As a consequence, the overall proportion of negative results papers has been on a steady decline. To admit that errors have been found in their field is difficult for many researchers, and journal editors are often reluctant to admit that a flawed study went through their supposedly rigorous quality filters.

Tsou, Schickore, and Sugimoto (2014) suggest that we need to distinguish between research outcomes unpublished for good reasons and materials that are unpublishable though worthy of publication. The technological environment and the spirit of Research 2.0 may mean that we make a step forward in this direction.

Besides metrics, *peer review* also has to be mentioned, fist of all because discussions of the future of scholarly communication are almost unimaginable without doing so (Acord & Harley, 2013). Peer review is undoubtedly at the heart of the scientific process as a quality-control and certification filter, necessitated by the vast scale of research material available today.

This is underlined by Nentwich (2003), among others, who asserts that quality control is an essential element in the modern system of scientific research. Without it, no one would know where to start, what is worth reading, and what to build one's own further research upon (Harnad, 1999).

---

[15]http://psychfiledrawer.org.

On the other hand, there are indications that the peer-review process has become an end in and of itself (Harley et al., 2010).

Empirical evidence presented by Nicholas et al. (2014, 2015) clearly shows that peer review is perceived as the central pillar of trust. Peer review shows that someone has put effort into a given work. It is a familiar, reliable, and traditional practice that provides a degree of certainty about the quality of a publication, showing that it has been validated by a community of scholars.

There are additional merits to peer review as well. It is organized by publishers; moreover, it is regarded by many to be *the* really important role for publishers. While in some cases researchers feel that their ideas have been misunderstood during the process, suggestions from top-quality referees often improve an article, even if it is rejected.

Researchers want to be published in journals that have robust peer review and feel secure in citing other peer-reviewed material. On the other hand, they do not blindly trust in peer review, as there are problems with the way it is undertaken. Peer review has many shortcomings. The most frequent and well-known criticisms are that reviewers are biased, the system is not transparent enough so it may be abused, and it is slow.

Nonetheless, it is apparent that there is no consensus about viable ways to improve peer review. Many share the opinion that editors should function as a relief valve for the peer review process. In any case, researchers think that the crowd is certainly not to be trusted in this respect (see the wisdom of the crowd).

There have been several attempts to find better methods, one of which is the introduction of *open peer-review*. It may add value to the peer review process, but (among other reasons) lack of time prevents its widespread adoption, and it is mainly lack of time that causes difficulties in recruiting competent reviewers.

This is an issue despite the fact that peer reviewing is considered to be an important part of a researcher's activities, thus they receive credit for it (Acord & Harley, 2013). The results of a randomized controlled trial by the *British Medical Journal* imply that open peer review does not lead to higher quality opinions, nor does it lead to poorer ones (Smith, 1999).

Should open comments on preprints or published work become more widespread, it will be important to assess who is offering the comments (i.e., what portion of such open comments come from "friends"), what costs occur, and whether these costs exceed the normal levels of traditional informal and formal peer review (Acord & Harley, 2013). Besides this, imposing traditional methods of peer review on digital publishing might help more traditionally minded researchers to see electronic and print scholarship as equivalent in value (Weller, 2011).

## FACTORS INHIBITING A WIDER UPTAKE OF RESEARCH 2.0

Among the factors of scholarly communication that influence the uptake of Research 2.0, we find the following:
- adherence to existing practices;
- the predominance of well-established channels;
- the distinctive role of specific purposes and particular stages of research;
- lack of trust.

Adherence to existing practices and the predominance of well-established channels are two closely related issues that build a contrast to a wide-ranging take-up of social media, which has played a decisive role in the emergence of Research 2.0.

Social media can be defined as "a group of Internet-based applications that build on the ideological and technological foundations of Web 2.0, and that allow the creation and exchange of user-generated content" (Kaplan & Haenlein, 2010, p. 61).

Despite interesting possibilities of applying social media technologies in research, a review of published literature shows that the use of Web 2.0 in academic research has not become widespread to date. Research evidence also suggests that Web 2.0 will not prompt any radical changes in scholarly communications in the short or medium term.

Borgman (2007) asserted this at a more generalized level:

> While information technology has radically altered the means by which scholars communicate publicly and privately, the underlying processes and functions of communication have changed little over the last few decades. Innovations in scholarly communication are more likely to be successful if they work with, rather than against, the social aspects of the system.

The research findings by Procter et al. (2010) demonstrate that only Web 2.0 services experienced rapid uptake, which built upon existing practices. The reason for this may be that new technologies are often not sufficiently good replacements for older practices.

As regards the details, another study by Procter, Williams, and Stewart (2010) indicated that social media tools are used, at least occasionally, for purposes related to their research: for communicating their work; for developing and sustaining collaborations; or for finding out what others are doing.

However, frequent or intensive use was rare and some researchers regarded using social media as a waste of time or even dangerous. The key question of using social media for research was the benefit that it brings. How these tools fit with established services was also decisive. Researchers who did use some tools did not regard them as comparable to or substitutes for other channels and means of communication. Their importance seemed to have a distinctive role for specific purposes and at particular stages of research. Consequently, frequent use of one kind of tool did not imply frequent use of others as well.

The well-established channels of communication, including scholarly journals, conference proceedings, and monographs, remained the most highly esteemed for publishing work, and these channels offered the highest recognition and rewards.

It was also found that—contrary to the widespread and stereotypical perception about the use of social media among the younger generations—the differences between various demographic groups were relatively small. This means that high usage was positively associated with older age groups and those in more senior positions.

Newman and Sack (2013) found that everyone uses e-mail frequently and a few interviewees stated that they use e-mail more frequently than in the past. On the other hand, no one reported heavy use of social media tools for work, while several interviewees emphasized the importance of conferences, seminars, and other face-to-face communication.

Acord and Harley (2013) point out one of the reasons, why social media is less accepted among researchers than by the general public. The essence of this barrier is that researchers avoid disorder caused by mixing traditionally separate spheres of activity. Researchers oppose mixing strictly scholarly contents (in a wide sense) with nonscholarly ones that characterize social media. This situation is somewhat similar to the experiences with digital native children and young people, who do not necessarily expect or want to use technology in school settings in the same manner as they do at home (Selwyn, 2009).

In their interview study—similarly to the findings of Procter, Williams, and Stewart (2010)—Acord and Harley (2013) demonstrate that researchers use social media tools to locate and access scholarly resources and collaborate. On the other hand, there is much less use of the same technologies to share and disseminate results.

While there is widespread agreement among researchers that new digital technologies have made scholarly communication much faster, the same tools are seen by many as enabling the proliferation of junk and noise. The usual advice given to beginning researchers is to focus on publishing in the right venues and avoid spending too much time on competing activities, including developing Web sites and blogging. Among other reasons, this has its roots in the conviction that there is an important distinction between experimenting with the new tools and using the well-established channels of scholarly communication (Acord & Harley, 2013). As Nentwich (2003) suggests, while it is somewhat unlikely that academia would be totally "virtual," the impact of computer-mediated communication on science is likely to result in a diminution of the importance of physical space and a consequent increase in the importance of such things as the reliability of the technological infrastructure. In other words, discussions and experimentation with new technologies should be framed by the integrity of research (Procter et al., 2010).

Accordingly, some researchers exploit social media if its use does not deviate from their existing priorities and principles. As Collins (2013, p. 89) put it, they "use social media only where it mimics or reinforces their existing behaviours."

The extent of using social media tools is also discipline-specific. It is most prominent in those disciplines which already had a tradition of working in extended collaborations and sharing draft papers.

Massive reliance on informal communication has always characterized scholarship. For instance, Kroll and Forsman (2010) affirmed that researchers' productivity "continues to be built on a foundation of direct human connection, researcher to researcher" (Kroll & Forsman, 2010, p. 5). Thus, it is not surprising that social media are often used as a tool to support the conversations between researchers. On the other hand, there is no evidence that social media would function as an alternative way of formally publishing research findings.

Overall, then, social media are not yet shifting the nature of scholarly communications. They are extending the reach and ease of use of traditional scholarly functions such as finding, sharing, and organizing information, but they have failed to break through the long-standing academic attachment to conventions including formal journal articles and blind pre-publication peer review.

Academic conventions have been built up over hundreds of years, so it is not realistic to expect them to alter overnight in the ways in which people can communicate. Only time will tell whether the kinds of novel usage outlined in this chapter represent a new road for scholarly communications, or an academic cul-de-sac (Collins, 2013).

The apparent contradiction between tradition and supposedly innovative tools reminds us that we have to be cautious with the rhetoric that surrounds technology. This is true not only generally, but sober assessment is also needed when discussing Research 2.0 (Weller, 2011). As Collins (2013, p. 89) points out, "social media have been hailed as a significant opportunity for scholarly communications, offering researchers new and effective ways to discover and share knowledge." However, the reality lies behind the idea that online tools will revolutionize scholarly communication by enabling a wider range of people to participate in scientific enterprise (Weller, 2011). Time may change this. Nonetheless, the 2 years that elapsed between the appearance of Weller's book and Collins' paper did not bring a substantial shift with them.

Judging trustworthiness by the reputation of the researcher or of the journal in a researcher's speciality is a long-established tradition (Becher & Trowler, 2001; Rieh, 2002). This means that trust is determined by personal inspection and judgement, which is not always feasible due to lack of time and the abundance of material.

In particular, trust possesses two layers. The first is institutional or academic trust, which is determined by traditional metrics, such as the journal IF. The second one is personal trust, which may be in conflict with academic trust. A paper may have appeared in a highly prestigious journal but nevertheless individual researchers may not trust its content. For example, a number of researchers are of the opinion that prestigious journals do not allow for innovation and creativity. While feeling that this diminishes their trust, they still feel pressure to publish in the top-tier journals of their discipline in order to advance their career.

Lozano, Larivière, & Gingras (2012) are of the opinion that by using OA repositories, scholars will find publications in their respective fields and decide if they are worth reading and citing. This would mean that the relationship between IFs and articles' citations is weakening. However, research by Nicholas et al. (2015) found evidence of the IF losing its legitimacy as an indicator of journal quality. On the contrary, IFs clearly have a major role in determining what to cite and where to publish. (With regard to publishing in prestigious journals, see the chapter on open science).

The comments above do not suggest that trustworthiness would be perceived by researchers as a pressing issue, not even in the circumstances of a massive digital transition and considerable socio-technical disruption. They simply use metrics, journal, or author reputation to judge the quality of content, without thinking that these were not perfect measures and without being pleased by the fact that their citing or publishing decisions were based on tenure or university policy pressures. Nonetheless, that is the world for which they have been trained and to which they are accustomed. Differences in function, e.g., users of the literature, authors or editors, do not influence greatly researchers' related perceptions (Nicholas et al., 2014).

As regards trust, we can outline an important aspect of the Research 2.0 environment as follows. Information exchange, which is the heart of scholarly research activities, has been based on long-established, trusted channels and sources. As a consequence of the transformations to the digital environment, the Internet, being now at the center of scholarly communication, has substantial potential for the abuse of trust. Even though the traditional scholarly environment has never been free from research misconduct, the digital environment with its diversity of information sources, such as social media, can complicate the situation. In their large-scale survey, Jamali et al. (2014a) looked at factors that influence how academic researchers (both as producers and consumers of information) decide what to read, what to cite, where to publish their work, and how they assign trust when making these decisions. For us, the results of this study are a point of interest, not in the geographical differences that were emphasized by the authors of the study but in the factors that are listed below.

The top decisions on actions to decide what to read can be presented in decreasing level of perceived importance. Among internal factors, we find:
1. checking if the arguments and logic presented in the content are sound;
2. checking to see if a paper is peer reviewed;
3. checking the figures and tables;
4. checking to see if the data used in the research are credible.

The importance of the main external factors is judged in following order:
1. checking the name of the publisher;
2. checking the name of the author;
3. checking to see if the paper has been disseminated or published by a subscription journal, an OA journal, a repository, a blog, etc.

As regards the agreement with statements on the quality and trustworthiness of information sources, the "best performing statement" among them was "Peer reviewed journals are the most trustworthy information source," followed by the importance of being recommended by a colleague.

The third place under trustworthiness does not seem to cause surprise to anyone. It is to be welcomed, though it is not self-explanatory, that open access publications are judged to be trustworthy if they are peer reviewed. The fifth place is taken by the importance of the journal's IF.

A substantial number of researchers do not have problems citing articles published in OA journals if they have been properly peer reviewed, or are from a reputable publisher. Many of them regard mentions and likes on social media as indications of popularity only, not quality. Similarly, they often think that usage metrics are not indications of quality, but show popularity.

Researchers prefer to publish in journals and books that are highly relevant to their field and are peer reviewed. There are other influencing factors as well. To mention but one example, the existence of both an online and a print version of the publication influences decisions to a lesser degree.

Publishing in international journals is slightly more preferred than publishing in high IF journals. At the other end of the spectrum, writing a blog or tweet about someone's research has extremely low prestige (Jamali et al., 2014a). Blogging by researchers is often viewed as unprofessional and a worthless pastime, as it does not fit into traditional formats of research and publication. Notwithstanding this, there are examples that demonstrate its value. On the other hand, those blogs, which advocate inaccurate or unscientific viewpoints, contribute to the perception that blogs cannot be trusted by the scientific community (Putnam, 2011).

As already mentioned, when reviewing the above findings, we deliberately disregarded the geographical differences specified by the authors. Nevertheless, we should not lose sight of the fact that these differences influence researchers' behavior to a substantial extent.

Researchers are often reluctant to share professional information with a wide and uncontrolled audience. In order to build their academic careers, researchers must publish their work in books and scholarly journals, so social media cannot serve as a wholesale replacement for those channels (Collins, 2013). A cornerstone of the reward system is that most universities intend to use an objective process for evaluating teaching staff. The easiest way to do this is to apply mechanical processes in which publication in peer-reviewed journals is central (Arms, 2002). (See also the section on alternative metrics of research output.)

In principle, publishing in OA online-only journals (see OA) has made it easier for researchers to share their findings with a wider circle of readers. Nonetheless, publication in such journals is still far less rewarding than in their more traditional counterparts (Procter et al., 2010). In most disciplines, it is an outstanding publication record in prestigious peer-reviewed journals that brings (academic) acknowledgment (Harley et al., 2010). Academic appointments committees rank academic research output by following citation indicators. As Björk (2004) indicates, publications in the leading or most influential journals—which owe their status to being included in citation indexes—bring the highest rewards. In contrast to this, publication in relatively unknown OA journals is not equally acknowledged. Similar arguments may be used when predicting the future of Research 2.0. Much like OA publishing, Research 2.0 is based on principles of openness and free access to research and research results. Therefore, the same reluctance to publish research results outside the already established and valued channels of scholarly communication may be expected.

Apart from the fact that research published through social media services is not rewarded and therefore is not motivating, another factor that prevents social media from becoming an equally accepted alternative mainstream channel for publishing academic research is a lack of trust among its (potential) users.

On a more general level, dealing with Research 2.0 trends reveals a substantial amount of holding back among researchers when it comes to the actual use of social media for research purposes due to two major hindering factors: recognition and trust (Wanser, 2014). An investigation into trust in scholarly communications indicated that the presence of technological changes did not change the measures of trust and authority, and in general, researchers have become more skeptical about a source's trustworthiness (Nicholas et al., 2014).

As regards recognition, we cite Mabe (2010, p. 141):

> *Modern authors publish to establish their personal reputations and to register their priority and ownership of ideas. The third-party date-stamping mechanism of the journal marks their paper as received and accepted at a certain date, while the reputation of the journal becomes associated with both the article and by extension the author. As authors publish in more and better journals, they, in turn, become regarded as more prolific and better authors. In other words: they associate with known high quality brands and this leads to their own names becoming high quality brands in their own right.*

As Calvi and Cassella (2013) put it, even if the consolidation of social media technologies in scholarly communication is increasing, it is still difficult to understand whether or not this remains a niche phenomenon if we take generational and disciplinary biases into consideration. It is somewhat unclear whether the social media bring any benefits to the research workflow, and if so, what kind of benefits they will be in the long run.

An empirical investigation by Nicholas et al. (2015) shows that, while the lack of interest in social media could be partly explained by the problems with trust and validity, there are other reasons as well. First and foremost, researchers feel that the current higher-education climate favors peer review and citation indices. In addition to this, they are aware that—in contrast to traditional content—there are no generally accepted measures to evaluate social media-based content. Nor are there are any career benefits that result from using social media.

Using new tools, the social media, in particular, directs our attention toward informal communication, which is the continuous exchange of ideas between researchers by correspondence. It has remained important to this day though letters have been replaced by e-mails. While this is true, formal publication prevails. The norms and cultures of disciplinary communities vary, but communicating results by sending working papers and drafts beyond a relatively small group of colleagues—especially before the publication of a formal paper in a journal—is as yet far from the norm in many disciplines. While there is a growing recognition that the traditional format of journal articles is not the most effective means of communication beyond a small group of specialists in the field, most researchers have been slow to adopt innovative means of communication. Moreover, many of them express suspicion about the use of these means, primarily the social media. One of the reasons is to be found in a contradiction. On the one hand, in today's highly competitive research environment, most researchers strive to be collaborative and are—indeed—collaborative. On the other hand, they know that they are competing for recognition and status in their field. Universities, research institutions, charities, and public bodies that fund research do not behave any differently (Jubb, 2014). This is probably why asserting that the introduction of digital technology is a revolution akin to the invention of writing, for instance by Harnad (1991), is often contested and qualified as an overstatement arising from naive notions of technological progress, as noted by Mabe (2010).

If we direct our attention to a particular group of disciplines, Collins and Jubb (2012) offer a picture of the humanities. Although their findings cannot be taken as representative of the humanities as a whole, the cases that they present show the diversity of practice and illustrate how researchers are engaging with the new technologies. This is true, despite the fact that they themselves indicate that the cases were taken from among technologically well-informed researchers. They found that collaboration is relatively common within the humanities, although not necessarily formally organized, and there are noticeable differences between subject fields. For instance, philosophers say that collaborating to collect and analyze data is not encouraged in their field. Researchers from other humanistic disciplines were more enthusiastic, using the Web to share their data in a reasonably open way among a community of interested peers. Using social media to communicate research findings is often not a new practice made possible by the Web, but a continuation of a long tradition in which pre-publication happened face-to-face at conferences or with the help of e-mail discussion forums. Most researchers surveyed by Collins and Jubb (2012) continue to use e-mail lists to share and edit work in progress with their collaborators.

Researchers think and act pragmatically, so they adopt new technologies where these technologies enhance existing practices. Where new technologies do not satisfy all needs, there is a continuing demand for print and hybrid approaches may also play a role. As Procter et al. (2010) affirmed, researchers are likely to accept new methods if they improve the research outcomes and do not threaten the reputation that is associated with research.

Collins and Jubb (2012) found that philosophers used electronic versions of key texts to search for important words or passages, but turned to the print editions of the same texts to cross-reference page numbers. It is not only their findings, but also our own experience, which show that Google Books is used to skim chapters or sections in order to decide whether it is worth acquiring the full text in print, or simply to look up the correct way to cite the work of others, independently of whether it was found in print or electronic form. Conceived demand for print can be based on both objective judgments about its usefulness and habit.

In any event, researchers made clear assessments of the value of new technology and, where they did not consider it to be useful, would not engage with it for its own sake. This was particularly apparent in the case of social media. The findings by Collins and Jubb (2012) also reveal that some humanities researchers showed concern about the partial and unsustainable nature of digitized versions of source material. Many of these sources are created through project funding, and are thus vulnerable in the longer term due to financial constraints. For the same reason, entire collections are rarely digitized. Overall, humanities researchers behaved in many regards in a similar way to other researchers working in other fields. They recognized the value of engaging with a wider audience through different means, offered by new technologies. At the same time, they also felt that using these tools could become a distraction from their main occupation, i.e., research. The above arguments substantiate why some authors speak about a hybrid scholarly social network in the sense that it both mirrors scholarly and general social networking norms (Thelwall & Kousha, 2014).

Basically, it is not different among those academic librarians who not only serve researchers but also act as researchers, i.e., publish the results of their investigations. A survey of librarians working in one of the member libraries of the Association of Research Libraries (ARL) shows that they make heavy use of Twitter and other social media tools to stay up to date on research and best practices. However, they also noted that their area of scholarship is not the same as their area of practice. As a consequence, the sources they use to keep up to date are those required by their professional occupation rather than research in library and information science (Sugimoto et al., 2014).

From the basic functions of scholarly communication (discovery, interpretation, comparison referencing and acknowledging, selecting appropriate samples, clarifying, elucidating, explaining, and publishing) (Unsworth, 2002), it is discovery that can be easily shared with colleagues and the wider academic community (Weller, 2011). Besides discovery, teaching also plays an important role (Boyer, 1990). Although we have already mentioned teaching activities among the possible occupations for researchers, its analysis, which raises a number of complex issues, falls outside the scope of this book.

Prior to social networks, the range of fellow researchers with whom scholars could share ideas and collaborate was limited to those with whom they could interact regularly, mainly in person. Leaving aside the question of whether online relationships are inferior to those that are face-to-face, and not knowing whether they are different in their nature or are complementary to existing networks, we can say that online social networks allow interaction with a wide group of peers (Weller, 2011). It is thus not by accident that the main incentive for using social networks is *networking*, both for personal and professional goals (James et al., 2009).

The discourses we have mentioned in the section about researchers' skills and abilities are relatively inflexible as is shown by the acceptance of social media tools by researchers. However, researchers might weigh the advice given by Weller (2011) who suggests that instead of resisting or being reluctant to adopt some of the new practices, they could engage with technology and reflect on changing scholarly practice. Resilience—which in this case means adapting themselves to such difficulties—is a useful means of considering their response to the potential impact of new technologies. No doubt, researchers, like anyone, cannot avoid having some anxiety, resistance, or skepticism around the adoption of new technology and related approaches. Nevertheless, we have to strive not to fall into the pitfalls of extremism in these attitudes, by dismissing new developments or, conversely, by surrendering to technology fetishism that lacks critical reflection.

Taking the present state of scientific communication into account, we can say at least that it is a system which is not easy to change, even if it seems to be close to a threshold resulting from the working of external socio-technical forces. As of today, researchers are often reluctant to share professional information to a wide and uncontrolled audience as in order to build their academic careers. Therefore, researchers must publish their work in books and scholarly journals, so social media cannot serve as a wholesale replacement for those channels (Collins, 2013). It is clear that researchers have a hierarchy of journals in mind when they decide where to publish their findings, taking different metrics into consideration (Jubb, 2014).

In spite of being underlain by an open and participative philosophy, Research 2.0 is still a context for a traditional quest for highly specialized, reliable, accurate, and valid information. It is exactly this required standard of research information that turns all the potentials of Research 2.0 into an unstable environment teeming with risks and controversies. The collaborative model of knowledge production, mash-up practices, and anonymity result in the creation of information contexts where authenticity, trustworthiness, authority, and reliability have to be questioned and are subject to continual scrutiny. The global "copy and paste" culture that characterizes many activities in the 2.0 landscape poses considerable risks for researchers: those who put their preliminary findings online risk that others will copy or exploit their work to get credit or even patents, particularly in hypercompetitive fields where patents, promotion, and tenure normally hinge on who first published a new discovery (Waldrop, 2008). The amateurism that so strongly characterizes social media environments, along with issues surrounding privacy, confidentiality, and trust (Yuwei, 2008), may be tolerable for entertainment purposes, but they are not unconditionally acceptable in science.

The main reason for this is that—in contrast to the majority of social media users, who are amateurs—researchers are professionals. Amateurs can be defined as people who love to be engaged in a particular activity. They may be knowledgeable or not, but they lack credentials (Keen, 2007). The perceived value of their activities is participation and self-fulfillment and—at the bottom line—they are motivated to show activities that can be made into a commodity (Cox, 2008). This works rather paradoxically. Amateurs on Web 2.0 undoubtedly produce some kind of content, while there is often no real possibility to provide quality, to pursue esthetic goals, or simply to be critical, even though this is not perceived by the majority of users, who are encouraged to produce anything without giving attention to its value. On the whole, in the value system of everyday social media environments, critical thinking and conscious selection of information do not occupy a prominent place.

This problem in itself should not worry us, if we direct our attention to the issues of differentiating between content generated by amateurs and content produced by and for professionals. Whatever the motivation behind participating in social media activities, amateur contents may be useful or at least tolerable. However, they cannot substitute for content created by professionals for professionals, that is, in our case, by researchers for researchers.

The reason for this is rather self-explanatory because amateur and anonymous production that is characteristic of social media is different in many regards from the production of professional and academic knowledge.

There is a particular question in the midst of these issues that deserves attention. It is the value of social media tools, designed for professionals in general (like LinkedIn[16]) and in particular those meant for researchers (e.g., Academia.edu[17] or Researchgate[18]). At present, it is simply not sufficiently clear whether their existence has fundamentally changed the picture presented above. In any case, more research is needed in this field.

The differences between amateur and professional purpose can be seen first of all in the existence of academic credentials and authorship. This means that the wisdom of the crowd which ranks content according to its popularity is applicable to the production of professional output and especially academic knowledge only to a limited extent and for limited purposes. This is true despite arguments that the logic and logistics of knowledge production based on new media are disruptive of the traditional values of scholarly work (Cope & Kalantzis, 2009a).

The discourse about the disruptive nature of new media in regard to professional contents is somewhat similar to the discourse about digital natives. The different discussions about empowerment and disempowerment of digital natives are often based on informal observation and anecdote, but not on representative empirical studies (Selwyn, 2009). The latter give

[16]https://www.linkedin.com/.
[17]http://www.academia.edu/.
[18]http://www.researchgate.net/.

us a more balanced picture, indicating for example that children use technology in institutional settings and at home differently (Lohnes & Kinzer, 2007). Why should we believe in a general transformation that influences all spheres of our life to the same extent, if different spheres are really different? Obviously, all this does not entirely negate the possibility of crowdsourcing some functions of scientific communication, primarily the use of altmetrics, provided that the "crowd" consists of qualified professionals who are relevant to the given professional community. While the wisdom of the crowd may be used for certain purposes, people who have gathered together somewhere are not necessarily wiser than the individuals that constitute the crowd. The irresponsibility and lack of expertise causes the lack of ability to correct errors and mistakes by themselves and by others. Consequently, there is no guarantee that it is possible to filter out rubbish, misinformation, and erroneous interpretations of reality if the participants are incompetent.

The approaches of amateur users of social media and researchers toward agreement, cooperation, and shared knowledge are different from those of academia. For users of social networks, for those who do social bookmarking and tagging, agreement is in fact not needed. They may influence each other, but may also function independently. Despite the desire to be similar to the majority or choose what is popular, they may not take the opinion of other users into consideration. Academia is different also in this regard. It is well known for its epistemological richness and diversity. It would be thus usually difficult to reach agreement among researchers on the epistemological status of their domain (Yuwei, 2008). This is true, even if general principles of scholarship apply, at least within a given scientific paradigm.

Grand et al. (2012) refer to issues of trust by arguing that "public spats in the blogosphere will jeopardise science's position in society" and suggesting that "by exposing the argument, dissent, and speculation natural to the scientific process, trust will be eroded." However, the same authors believe that the opposite could happen: "Practising science in the open, facilitating access to information, processes, and conjecture as well as to data, results, and conclusions, could sustain trust through increased transparency and greater completeness. By showing all the workings in the margins and making clear the foundations – or lack of – on which conclusions rest, more people will be enabled to make independent judgments of those conclusions' validity."

Content creation is easier than ever because the same technology can be readily used for sending and receiving messages, thus many are already content producers. As a consequence, we have witnessed not only an explosive growth of online publishing but also an increasing number of writers (Beeson, 2005). In this environment, writers have to realize that they are reaching a much wider and more varied audience that comprises both specialists and lay people (Chan & Foo, 2004).

The role of trust is different in the case of an intermediate category that can be placed between professionals and amateurs. It is called *self-trained experts* or *professional amateurs* (Pro-Ams), identified by Leadbeater and Miller (2004). Pro-Ams, also often referred to as *educated amateurs*, are investigators who, making use of the Internet, are producing significant innovations and discoveries in a wide range of fields to the mutual benefit of both professional researchers and themselves. They may be involved in science from astronomy to medicine, often making fundamental and lasting contributions. Another example is local history, which later developed into local studies: as it is too sophisticated to generate mass popularity but not sophisticated enough to be removed entirely from the popular realm, it has been the pursuit of educated amateurs since the nineteenth century (Reid & Macafee, 2007).

Following the above line of thought, we can add that *superficiality* is also a challenging issue and a frequent source of objections to and reservations against digital scholarship (Weller, 2011). Superficiality is deeply intertwined with the issue of trust. At least, the value system of research shows this. Our approach in this book is no different in this regard. The noun *trust* and the adjective *trustworthy* appear in our writing with high frequency, and not by accident.

The social media often foster superficiality because commercial social networks usually do not encourage or even impede the critical comparing and contrasting of different views, thus discretion and selectivity does not characterize them because of the very nature of their business model (Friesen, 2010). This raises the question of whether we can use the same techniques for deeper (i.e., professional) tasks, including research.

In addition to all that, the above issues provoke the following questions asked by Weller (2011):

- If we use social media, do we move beyond superficiality?
- Does understanding quality mean not restricting ourselves to maintaining current quality, but appreciating when different levels of quality can be used?

- Does managing online identity compromise our professional identity?
- How much of scholarly discourse and activity do we give over to social media?
- Do the benefits of their widespread use outweigh the potential risks?

Still, we can see that—due to the hindering factors described above—a rapid adoption of social media services is not expected among researchers. In general, we can state that researchers are risk averse (Carpenter et al., 2010). Let us add that research evidence and opinions are somehow contradictory in this regard. For example, longitudinal data show indications that active or passive use of some social media and networking tools in research is slightly on the increase among Generation Y doctoral students (Carpenter et al., 2010). This is consistent with the findings of Arms and Larsen (2007) who predict a more intensive uptake and identify younger researchers as early adopters of innovations such as Web search engines, GS, Wikipedia, and science blogs. Some authors also refer to evidence that many postgraduate and postdoctoral researchers are changing the ways in which they acquire and share research information and are using social media technologies to "pre-publish" research papers (Procter, Williams, & Stewart, 2010).

Elsewhere, while there were no marked differences found between different generations of doctoral students in using social media (Carpenter et al., 2010), established scholars seem to enjoy more freedom in the choice of publication channels than their younger, untenured colleagues. Some authors indicate that it is not the younger, but the established researchers who are more willing to experiment with new technologies and forms of information and data dissemination. The situation is rather strange as younger researchers are encouraged to be conservative while the reinterpretation of practice and exploration is left to their established colleagues (Weller, 2011). As mentioned earlier, the advice given to young researchers is to focus on publishing in the right venues.

At the bottom line, younger researchers do not seem to be counteracting traditional publishing practices (Harley et al., 2010). This obviously contradicts the assumption that younger researchers are more at home with new technologies (Carpenter et al., 2010). Nicholas et al. (2014, p. 133) do not see any significant change in this regard. They write:

*Early career researchers are particularly conscious of rankings and very careful in regard to what they used, cited, and published. As academic apprentices they exhibit the concerns of someone starting their profession and not wanting to put a foot wrong. This is only to be expected, of course.*

Overall, researchers use new tools in conjunction with the traditional ones, and try to find appropriate and more effective uses for them (Weller, 2011). There is little evidence that the extended use of social media services will lead in the short or medium term to radical changes in scholarly communications. These services are beginning to make their mark on research, but not yet in any sustained or systematic way. Researchers are gradually adopting some social media tools where they see advantages in doing so, while at the same time other participants in the system of scholarly communication are responding to these developments by providing some social media functionality as part of their services (Collins, 2013). In other words, social media supplements rather than replaces the established channels (Procter et al., 2010).

This is verified by a recent empirical investigation on the use of online communities by researchers, carried out by Jamali et al. (2014b). Its findings show that—despite a shift in widespread acceptance of the idea of creating online communities—in reality not much is actually going on. In a similar way to the results of earlier studies we also referred to, the results show that a majority of researchers is making at least occasional use of one or more social media tools for purposes related to their research, i.e., for communicating their research activity, for developing and sustaining personal networks, and for collaboration. The differences are mainly according to the researchers' subject, and not much by age or other demographic factors. Those who are accustomed to collaboration in their research are more likely to join online communities, usually benefiting from the services of generic, public platforms like Facebook, Twitter, and Skype, and established e-mail lists.

Although at this point of analysis it seems like social media services will never entirely replace the established media and information channels in research, the power of social media services and technologies should not be underestimated. Social media services have already brought new qualities to research processes and will therefore at least supplement the traditional processes in many aspects. Let us add that technological solutions are evolving much faster than the development of our understanding of the effects of technologies. This is especially true in regard to researchers who work in different disciplines. As a consequence, it is extremely difficult to approximate their impact on research (Maceviciute, 2014).

On a more fundamental level, we should not leave general criticisms of social media out of consideration. As Golumbia (2013, p. 2) puts it, we witness exaggerated claims for the transformative power of digital media, simply because communicative practices that in earlier times were not located (or not observed) in formal media sites today occur there. He adds that the contemporary emphasis on the consumer as producer, especially in social media, seems to be unconvincing, or at least notably over-emphasized. Let us point out, without going into a detailed discussion, that this phenomenon is rooted in a new type of economy, where commercial social media applications are free to users, as they generate profit by attracting as many users as possible by selling advertisement space to third parties. The more users are recruited, the more profit can be generated (Fuchs, 2009). Overall, we must see that the Web 2.0 ideology simply strictly filters all statements for applicability to the market (Scholz, 2008). Services based on this philosophy may not prove conducive for research in the long run. Presumably, researchers can also be convinced of this.

The assumptions of Procter, Williams, and Stewart (2010, p. 8) seem to be valid today, as well. According to them, those services are most likely to succeed.

*where researchers are actively involved in uncovering, exploring and exploiting new capabilities, and adapting them to their own purposes, in accordance with the broader cultures and contexts in which they undertake their work. The processes of discovery and negotiation are likely to be protracted, and may lead to fundamental changes in how tools and services operate and are used.*

According to Procter et al. (2010), many researchers are discouraged from making use of new forms of scholarly communication because they are unable to put their trust in resources that have not undergone traditional peer review. Similar research results have been documented in other studies (Carpenter et al., 2010; Harley et al., 2010). Thus, it may be said that Research 2.0 opens up exciting possibilities for improving research processes, but simultaneously creates a zone of risk. When talking about social media technologies, analyses of risks and benefits should always include different contexts. While risks in the contexts of everyday life, entertainment, or public discourse may produce less distress, they are of paramount importance in domains such as education, health, or research.

The reliability of social media-generated content is often questioned due to *disintermediation*. The evolution of end-user services loosened the historically close and strong connections between researchers and academic librarians and led to disintermediation (Nolin, 2013). This can be described as a process that empowers and enables users and creators of content to sidestep the intermediary (e.g., librarians, or health professionals and travel agents to name but a few in other fields) and access and even create information or services directly. As a result of that, and in contrast to what happens in information environments that are managed and structured centrally, information not stewarded by traditional information gatekeepers enters the research process. This allows users to bypass the expert intermediary in both creating and using content, i.e., to both create and be exposed to unfiltered information, which raises issues of credibility, quality, and reliability of information (Eysenbach, 2008). As Badke (2004) pointed out, the apparent loss of gatekeepers, such as reviewers, editors, librarians, and others, forces readers themselves to fulfill gatekeeping functions, that is, exercise information literacy.

In the opinion of Herman and Nicholas (2010), present-day information seekers consistently demonstrate characteristic patterns of unproductive information behavior, which would require reintermediation. Kwanya, Stilwell, and Underwood (2012) argue in a similar vein, declaring that libraries could act as *apomediators*. This would not be intermediation in the classic sense. Nonetheless, users would neither be left alone to deal with raw information, nor be prevented from venturing forth on their own.

# CHAPTER 2

# The Nature of Information Literacy

It is rather obvious that researchers are or should be informed citizens, not only in their everyday life but also in their professional work. This means that relying on a number of literacies is foundational to the work of today's researcher. To gain a more accurate picture of the nature of these literacies, we can consider them from a bird's-eye view. Such a perspective reveals three levels of literacy:

- conceptual competencies that include innovative thinking, problem-solving, and critical thinking;
- human competencies: social networking skills, self-management, and cross-cultural interaction skills;
- practical competencies: including learning skills and information literacy (Lee, 2013).

The best-known literacy from among practical competencies is information literacy.

## DEFINITIONS, DECLARATIONS, AND FRAMEWORKS

The terms *information literacy* and *information literate* were coined by Zurkowski (1974) to refer to people who are able to solve their information problems by using relevant information sources and applying relevant technology. As Pinto, Cordón, and Diaz (2010) point out, information literacy has stimulated considerable, long-standing interest throughout the second half of the twentieth century, and more significantly from the 1980s onward. This is shown by the number and variety of publications, regularly reviewed by Johnson et al. (2012), among others.

Zurkowski's work was the formative moment for information literacy. His approach logically perceived information literacy as a programmatic aim, and placed libraries and librarians at the core of this effort. The advent of bibliographic databases ushered in a new era of research. Early databases required significant additional technological know-how, often possessed by librarians only. This decisive intermediary role diminished with the appearance of CD-ROMs in the 1980s and finally vanished with the arrival of social media tools.

Zurkowski and other early writers on the topic were undoubtedly right to see that the changes in the research landscape would result in a situation in which researchers would be left without knowledge of the technologies of searching. These new methods of searching were indispensable, and without them researchers would have remained practically functionally illiterate in seeking academic information. Naturally, this required education.

When databases became searchable and usable by non-experts, the role of librarians as teachers of research skills was well established. The meaning of information literacy as a theory as well as a practice had yet to be clearly articulated. The appearance of the ACRL Competency Standards in 2000 was an important step forward, as it could be used to show information literacy in all its complexity, laying out achievable objectives. Information literacy became a full-fledged practice with theoretical backing.

In the meantime, information seeking has become a daily activity as "googling" is employed with unbelievable frequency. However, this does not question the validity of information literacy. The question is whether we should "refocus our efforts on the educational, cultural, and technological shifts in which 'information literacy' *per se* becomes a somewhat arbitrary label for the very stuff of learning and information discovery in today's academic (and larger) world" (Cowan, 2014, p. 28).

In a more general context, we can say that the increase in available materials not only caused changes in collection management practices, but also drove the need for information literacy (Palmer & Gelfand, 2013).

Definitions and descriptions of information literacy (IL) can be summarized as referring to

1. the use of information and communication technologies (ICTs) to retrieve and disseminate information;
2. the competences to find and use the information in information (re)sources;
3. the process of recognizing information need, and finding, evaluating, and using information to acquire or extend knowledge.

The third option is the most comprehensive and most useful, as it includes both the use of ICT and the information (re)sources concept (Boekhorst, 2003).

Perhaps the best known and widely accepted *definition* of IL says that information literate people are able to recognize when information is needed. They are also able to identify, locate, evaluate, and use information to solve a particular problem (ALA, 1989). This definition has been widely used and further developed by other definitions.

In their foundational work, Johnston and Webber (2003, p. 336) provide the following definition of information literacy:

> Information literacy is the adoption of appropriate information behaviour to obtain, through whatever channel or medium, information well fitted to information needs, together with critical awareness of the importance of wise and ethical use of information in society.

They identify four major goals for information literacy in the information society:

- information literacy for citizenship, including engagement in development by freedom of access to and critical use of data and information;
- information literacy for economic growth that stimulates the development of new and existing enterprises by intensive and creative use of information and knowledge;
- information literacy for employability;
- information literacy for personal growth and creativity, which cuts across and contributes to achieving all the above goals (Webber & Johnston, 2000).

Our previous discussion has demonstrated that all four goals are valid in the research environment. Obviously, the weight of these goals differs to some degree. If we take the role of the researcher as a citizen, we have to say that there is no room in this book for outlining this issue in its entirety and we do not intend to do so. Nonetheless, we have already pointed toward this role and mentioned developments to achieve citizen science and open science or open access, just to name a few. Critical use of information and data is crucial for information literacy and thus has found its place in this book and plays a major role in it. Without wanting to be exhaustive again, there is hardly any doubt that research contributed to economic growth and development in general. Intensive and creative use of information and knowledge is very much the essence of research. IL may not influence employability directly, but writing this book would make little sense if we did not believe in its importance. The relevance of personal growth and creativity is unquestionable, especially as they affect all the goals above.

IL education emphasizes critical thinking (appearing in several places throughout this book, especially in the section about reading and writing) and the necessity of being able to recognize the quality of a given message. It is firmly positioned among other literacies despite a certain amount of (occasionally well-founded) skepticism, which in itself highlights the fact that information literacy and especially its lack has always been of greater importance to academic librarians than to any other group of "players" in the information and education arena (Bawden & Robinson, 2009).

Different *models* approach information literacy from different viewpoints. The *Seven Faces of Information Literacy in Higher Education*, conceived by Christine Bruce in 1997, concentrates on experiencing information literacy (Bruce, 1997). From a different point of view, we will come back to this model.

Using Vannevar Bush's vision of the technologically connected and enabled researcher who plays key role in the information society, Johnston and Webber (2005) propose information literacy as a soft applied discipline. They contrast this approach to the characterization of information literacy as a personal attribute. As we will demonstrate, they are not the only ones directing attention to the importance of information literacy aimed at research and researchers.

From among the numerous conceptual *models* of IL, we will take the approach that differentiates between three levels, that is, macro, micro, and meso, and places culture on the macro-level. The meso-level is composed of different information subcultures, and the micro-level represents the so-called individual playground. The meso-level materializes in concepts such as the information culture of individual organizations. The micro-level is entirely individual.

There are also several process models that address information literacy on a general level in the educational and library environment, as indentified by Wai-yi (1998) and Uribe Tirado and Castaño Muñoz (2012).

Markless and Streatfield (2007) offer a model that consists of three elements:
- connecting with information (orientation, exploring, focusing, locating);
- interacting with information (thinking critically, evaluating);
- making use of information (transforming, communicating, applying).

The Big Six model (Eisenberg & Berkowitz, 1990) contains the following six stages of problem-solving with two substages under each:
1. Task definition
   1.1. Defining the information problem
   1.2. Identifying information needed
2. Information seeking strategies
   2.1. Determining all possible sources
   2.2. Selecting the best sources
3. Location and access
   3.1. Locating sources (intellectually and physically)
   3.2. Finding information within sources

4. Use of information
   **4.1.** Engaging (e.g., read, hear, view, touch)
   **4.2.** Extracting relevant information
5. Synthesis
   **5.1.** Organizing from multiple sources
   **5.2.** Presenting the information
6. Evaluation
   **6.1.** Judging the product (effectiveness)
   **6.2.** Judging the process (efficiency).[1]

Coming from the world of different literacies more or less closely connected to IL, there are some higher order abilities and activities that can be used when thinking about information literacy, especially in the world of research. These skills broaden the models of IL by adding several new dimensions to them. Information literate people thus are required to effectively communicate verbal and visual information in oral and written form, in their native language and in a second (foreign) language (AACU, 2002; Bundy, 2004a, 2004b).

The activities required from information literate people are as follows:

- choosing a communication medium and format that best supports the purposes and the intended audience;
- using a range of information technology applications in creating the product or performance;
- incorporating principles of design and communication;
- communicating clearly and with a style that supports the purposes of the intended audience (ACRL, 2000).

All the above skills and abilities build a foundation for higher-level skills that not only reflect those abilities but also go beyond them. These higher-level skills can be summarized as follows:

- transforming information into knowledge and knowledge into judgment and action (AACU, 2002);
- recognizing, understanding, and analyzing the context within which language, information, and knowledge are communicated and presented;
- understanding the relationships among language, knowledge, and power;
- using appropriate technologies to manage information collected or generated for future use;
- critiquing our own and others' works (D'Angelo & Maid, 2004).

There is an organizing heuristic, which views information literacy as a product of its time. It is called *kairos* and demands that we understand

---

[1]http://big6.com/pages/about/big6-skills-overview.php.

all truth claims "as embedded in a context, and all actions as measured responses to that context" (Drabinski, 2014, p. 481).

It is rather self-explanatory that different *declarations* also play an important role in the life of information literacy, the content of some of which are outlined here. While containing significant statements on important issues, to the *Lyon Declaration on Access to Information and Development* (IFLA, 2014) is not concerned with issues, related to research. Nevertheless, it is useful to contemplate one of its statements:

> *Increased access to information and knowledge, underpinned by universal literacy, is an essential pillar of sustainable development. Greater availability of quality information and data and the involvement of communities in its creation will provide a fuller, more transparent allocation of resources.*

This statement points to the fact that—as outlined above—besides information, data has come to the foreground of attention. Nonetheless, the main emphasis of this statement is on the connection between literacy and quality information that is of prime interest for research.

The Declaration also underlines the role of information intermediaries in "connecting stakeholders across regional, cultural, and other barriers to facilitate communication and the exchange of development solutions that could be scaled for greater impact." We can recognize here that this has meaning for scientific research that is global and the major group of stakeholders comprises researchers.

The two information literacy *frameworks* that are the most relevant for our purpose are the *Information Literacy Competency Standards for Higher Education*, conceived by the Association of College and Research Libraries (ACRL, 2000) in the United States of America and the Society of College, National and University Libraries (SCONUL) *Seven Pillars of Information Literacy. Core Model for Higher Education*, devised by SCONUL (2011) in the United Kingdom. Although we do not intend to analyze them in any detail here, they (especially the latter) are referred to several times throughout this book.

There is also a another framework which provides an example to illustrate the distinguished role of information literacy in the researcher's life. It is the *Vitae Research Development Framework*, which defines the knowledge, behaviors, and attributes of the effective and highly skilled researcher. It operates with lenses that focus on knowledge, behaviors, and attributes that are developed or acquired through, or used in, the broader contexts of being a researcher. The information literacy lens is one of a series of lenses that address, among other issues, employability, leadership, public engagement, and mobility.

The framework approaches information literacy in its "knowledge base" domain. IL is described in three phases. It puts the use of information technology into first place, while emphasizing the need to obtain expert advice from information or data managers, archivists, and librarians.

The second phase develops awareness of the creation, organization, validation, sharing, storing, and curation of information and/or data, as well as an understanding of the legal, ethical, and security requirements. Somewhat surprisingly, knowledge on the purpose of metadata appears in this domain. Phase three focuses on advising and educating peers, less experienced researchers, students, and staff in the above requirements. The final phase is about developing new techniques and anticipating trends.

The information literacy lens underlines that IL is necessary not only for finding, analyzing and evaluating data, and searching for literature, but for publishing as well. These qualities are fundamental to the whole process of research.

This lens may be used by the researchers themselves, who can identify:
- how information literacy can contribute to their professional development;
- how the skills and attributes they have developed through research can contribute to their development in information literacy;
- which areas of IL they need to develop to be more effective.

It also provides evidence of the transferability of their information literacy skills in their CV, in job applications, and at interviews.

This lens also may be used to:
- demonstrate how information literacy can contribute toward the overall professional development of researchers;
- enable researchers to recognize how useful and transferable is the learning they have acquired through information literacy related activities;
- explore how the Vitae Researcher Development Framework relates to the SCONUL Seven Pillars of Information Literacy and vice versa (Vitae, 2011).

## THE NEW LITERACIES CONTEXT

Livingstone, van Couvering, and Thumin (2008) identify several purposes of literacies:
- fostering democracy, participation, and active citizenship;
- contributing to knowledge economy and competitiveness in the information economy;
- supporting lifelong learning and personal fulfillment.

They add that information and media literate individuals are not only likely to have more to offer and achieve, but also are more able to make proper choices from the rich array of offers for the consumer.

The concept of *new literacies* comes from New Literacy Studies, a body of work that "has approached the study of literacy not as an issue of measurement or of skills but as social practices that vary from one context to another" (Street, 2008, p. 420).

According to the apparently most widely accepted definition in this vein by Street (1984, p. 1), literacy is conceived as "social practices and conceptions of reading and writing."

This social nature of literacy is expressed by Johnson (2011) as follows:

> Our concept of literacy changes every time there's a major shift in information technology. Being literate used to mean knowing how to sign your name. At one point it meant the ability to read and write Latin. Today, being literate generally means being able to read and understand a newspaper in your own language.

These social practices have been magnified by the growing role of digital technologies (Livingstone, 2004). A number of literacies can be identified within varying social contexts and under varying social conditions.

The nature of these different literacies is changing within the conditions of textual work, that is, reading and writing. They also depend on varying social contexts and equally varying social conditions. Consequently, they change with time, according to the changing purposes and circumstances, as well as the people and tools involved (Lankshear & Knobel, 2004).

For all these changing circumstances, a rapid development of information and communication technologies represents one of the most crucial factors.

The formulation of literacies as social practices led to the appearance of the following requirements:

- Literacies must be foundational capabilities on which particular skills depend. Consequently, literacies and their lack will have a lifelong and life-wide impact.
- Extended literacy practice should be developed continuously, thus they are acquired through continued development and refinement in different contexts.
- Digital practices that emerge in complex situations will involve an interaction between personal capabilities or dispositions and the environment supporting action. Transferring digital capabilities from one environment to another is more problematic than has been acknowledged. Consequently, the transfer from social life to research environments that may happen with the use of social media is problematic.

- Literacies must influence individual identity, specifically on the way a stance toward knowledge in digital forms is adopted.
- Literacies are continually evolving in response to technical, epistemological, and cultural changes (Littlejohn, Beetham, & McGill, 2012).

Information literacy and other (related) literacies are seen as *new* literacies on account of their orientation toward new informational, technological, and societal realities (Buschman, 2009). Leu et al. (2004) provide a review of the roles of literacy that illustrates this. For instance, as agricultural technologies improved thus allowing the Sumerian civilization to expand, it became necessary to record business transactions and tax records. This social necessity prompted the development of the first writing technology.

In medieval Europe, the Christian church used literacy as a vehicle to enforce its religious viewpoint with the help of a literate priesthood, which was able to faithfully copy, read, and interpret common religious texts.

Literacy became much more widespread as Martin Luther argued for the need for individuals to read and directly access religious texts on their own. Reformation went hand in hand with the development of printing technologies.

Street (2008, p. 7) reminds us of the following: "One response to the growing role of technologies of communication in our lives is to overstate their ability to determine our social and cultural activity." He adds that such models were rooted in assumptions about technological determinism, which have later been challenged and discredited.

Nevertheless, Internet technologies and digital forms of communication brought the same thinking back and it is difficult to take sufficient account of the technological dimension of new literacies without such determinism. On the other hand, the pervasive influence of information technology may be regarded to be real and has to be approached taking its complexity into consideration.

This thinking is built on the idea that technological determinism is a pure theoretical position, which tries to understand general patterns of social and cultural change. However, we do not need to choose between different vocabularies and overall frameworks to follow the pervasive nature of the latest information technology solutions (the Internet *per se*, the mobile communication technology, the ubiquitous computer including embedded systems and sensors, nano- and bioinformatics, etc.). We also need to have a broad picture of future technologies to be able to redesign the "old" information literacies and get ready for new ones.

The historical development of literacy clearly shows that there is a difference between being able to appreciate and process an esthetically valuable piece of writing and to cope with present-day socio-technological changes and challenges (Livingstone, van Couvering, & Thumin, 2008). This is one of the reasons why the existence of the World Wide Web and then also the appearance of Web 2.0 have been playing a significant role in forming literacies.

Web 2.0 is generally taken to encompass a variety of sites and tools for shared information creation and updating, and social networking and communication (Bawden & Robinson, 2009). It enables mass participation in social activities. Users and their interests are represented in mediated spaces, which also serve as an environment to activate engagement with others (Jarrett, 2008).

New literacies thus are tied to new technologies, that is, ICTs. While this is true, they also remain related to culture. The fact that being literate also denotes *having erudition* and *being educated* verifies this. However, even this boundary is of a dual nature as the Internet and other forms of information and communication technologies are redefining the nature of reading, writing, and communication. ICTs will continue to change in the years ahead, continuously requiring new literacies to exploit their potential. Information literacy also shows these signs of being Janus-faced.

Beyond recognizing that new literacy skills and practices are required by each new ICT as it emerges and evolves, it is our responsibility to integrate these new literacies into the appropriate curricula (IRA, 2009).

The dimensions of literacy have broadened. The complexities of the current information environment require complicated and broad forms of literacies that are not restricted to any particular technology and that foster understanding, meaning, and context (Bawden, 2001).

Literacies are multiple, multimodal, and multifaceted (Coiro et al., 2008). Contemporary concepts of literacy include visual, electronic, and digital forms of expression and communication. As its scope has broadened, literacy is tied both to technology and culture, and the ability to become and remain literate requires a long-term commitment. Long-term commitment, usually identified as lifelong learning, is the third attribute that also strongly determines information literacy (Cordes, 2009).

According to Leu et al. (2007), our view of literacy, limited to decoding and encoding, reading and writing, or even to producing texts of different genres appropriate to different situations, should be broadened to developing a set of composite skills that will enable learners to decode and negotiate critically the cultural, social, political, and ideological aspects of language use. They also argue for multiple literacies, which include the ability to use reading and writing skills in order to produce, understand, interpret, and critically evaluate multimodal texts.

Taking the concept of *deixis*, used by linguists to define words whose meanings change rapidly as their context changes, we can say that the meaning of literacy has become deictic because we live in an age of rapidly changing information and communication technologies. Having been literate in a world defined primarily by relatively static book technologies does not ensure that we are fully literate today. To be literate tomorrow will be defined by newer technologies that have not yet appeared (Leu et al., 2013).

Literacy education is not about skill development and deep competence, but it is

> *about the institutional shaping of social practices and cultural resources, about inducting successive generations into particular cultural, normative ways of handling texts, and about access to technologies and artefacts (e.g., writing, the Internet) and to the social institutions where these tools and artefacts are used (e.g., workplaces, civic institutions)*
>
> **Luke and Freebody (1999).**

The purposeful social nature of this shaping activity comes to the fore when we underscore that literacy means participating in understanding and composing meaningful written, visual, and spoken texts, as well as using them functionally by negotiating the social relations around them. This includes the understanding that these functions shape the way texts are structured. Such understandings include critically analyzing and transforming texts (Luke & Freebody, 1999).

When arguing for a broad view of information literacy, we can put the accent on knowledge generation and take a knowledge management (KM) perspective, which considers information related to tacit knowledge among other factors in the context of academia (Tirado & Muñoz, 2012).

## THE READING AND WRITING CONTEXT

Information literacy is closely related to *reading literacy*, which, despite its name, involves the integration of listening, speaking, reading, writing, and numeracy. It can be defined as an individual's ability to understand printed text and communicate through print. These also have a close relationship with *functional literacy*, which most commonly denotes the ability to read and use information essential for everyday life (Bawden, 2001).

Peter Morville, a pioneer and one of the best known figures of information architecture, findability, and user experience of research and practice, emphasizes that mastering the skills of written communication—which, by definition, includes reading and writing—is required for efficiently functioning in modern society (Morville, 2005).

In a similar vein, the High Level Group on Literacy, commissioned by the European Union affirms that the digital world is centered on the written word. Even if digitization has added entirely new dimensions to our ways of connecting and communicating, the written word stands at the center of these new dimensions as the common denominator.

This circumstance makes literacy more and more interconnected with our lives in a digital world, where large numbers of people lack the necessary reading and writing skills to make use of it. Literacy competences thus become more central to our work as well as our private and social.

In addition to this, the very nature of literacy is changing, as the digital world requires higher-order problem-solving skills. Reading online demands a greater ability to evaluate information critically, available in unprecedented greater quantity and variety than ever before. There is also a need for the ability to extract and use knowledge from online resources (EU, 2012).

The necessary but not sufficient "roles" for the reader in a postmodern, text-based culture are the following:
- code breaker;
- meaning maker;
- text user;
- text critic.

The role of the code breaker requires competence in coding and decoding. The prerequisite of being a meaning maker is semantic competence. Being a text user in this context presupposes that we have pragmatic competence. Not surprisingly, texts critics have to have critical competence (Luke & Freebody, 1999).

In the latter case, perhaps the plural would be better, i.e., *critical competences*.

These roles do not seem to differ fundamentally from those of reading in a print environment. Coding and decoding enables the use of texts and is overlaid by the search for meaning. In research environments—both print and digital—part of the coding is different as the language of science is a unique hybrid that consists of natural language extended by and embedded in a language of meaningful specialized actions afforded by the technological environments in which science is conducted. The latter part of this hybrid is much more a meaning-making system than a language in the linguistic sense (Lemke, 2004).

Researchers are as much texts users and text producers as they are text critics. While this is also true in the print environment, our focus on information literacy and Research 2.0 dictates emphasizing that these roles should be and indeed are continued in digital environments, even if under different circumstances.

The requirement of being a text critic points toward *critical reading*. However, before discussing it in more detail, let us direct attention toward the fact that, while the actual processes of doing research work differ by discipline and institution, all of them involve a distinctive methodological orientation which values critical reflection, the cumulative aggregation of knowledge and understanding, an emphasis on evidence and reliability, and the ethic of enquiry.

The combination of these characteristics distinguishes the construction of scholarly knowledge from other kinds of knowledge production such as factual knowledge, practical knowledge, common sense, morality, or the wisdom of the crowd (Goodfellow, 2013).

In the case of information literacy, critical reading is required which is based on *critical thinking*. Although critical reading is one of the abilities and activities enumerated above, its special importance requires separate discussion.

In his foundational work on digital literacy, Gilster (1997) underlines the view that critical thinking means distinguishing between content and its presentation. In 2013, the ACRL reinforced the belief that critical thinking has been central to information literacy, and that it continues to be a core value in teaching new literacies (ACRL, 2013).

If we follow the work of Jones (1996), other abilities required for critical thinking can be enumerated as follows:
- differentiating between fact and opinion;
- examining underlying assumptions, including our own;
- looking for explanations, causes, and solutions;
- being aware of fallacious arguments, ambiguity, and manipulative reasoning;
- focusing on the whole picture, while examining the specifics;
- looking for reputable sources.

Taking these into consideration, Beeson (2005) suggests a number of questions we can ask:
- What is the author trying to state (say, write)?
- Why are they stating it?
- Who else is stating similar or different things?
- Why should we believe any of them?

All the above steps lead us toward an evaluation of reliability, validity, accuracy, authority, timeliness, and point of view or bias as well as a recognition of prejudice, deception, or manipulation by examining and comparing information from various sources supplemented by an analysis of the structure and logic of the supporting arguments or methods (ACRL, 2000).

Critical thinking raises complex questions about criticizing our own thinking, either from an egocentric or a socio-centric point of view (Elder, 2011).

In the case of the researcher, it would appear to be self-explanatory that decisions related to the domain of information literacy are governed by socio-centric views defined by professional communities (of knowledge) to which the individual is attached. Obviously, a researcher has a number of personal motivations. Nonetheless, these latter seem to fall outside the sphere of decisions taken from the point of view of IL.

According to Jones (1996), critical reading consists of:

- determining the purpose of the text and assessing how the central claims are developed;
- making judgments about the intended audience of the text;
- distinguishing the different kinds of reasoning in the text;
- examining the evidence and sources of the writing;
  Lynch (1998) adds two more features:
- assessing bias;
- assessing accuracy.

Besides the broader framework of information literacy, critical reading applies to abstracting, which has its own complex relationship with IL. Put simply, abstracting is the activity of writing abstracts that are texts that contain the most important content of existing, another texts in concise, condensed, and abbreviated form (Koltay, 2009). Despite this apparent simplicity, abstracting is one of the higher-level activities of information literacy as maintained by Pinto, Fernández-Ramos, and Doucet (2008).

When we write abstracts, we have to concentrate on deciding what is important in a text. The extraction and summarizing of information play an important role in many forms and phases of communication (Loo & Chung, 2006), and the usefulness of abstracting from the point of view of IL is based on the fact that abstracting employs decoding and encoding as well as critical reading (Guinn, 1979).

Generally, we have to be aware of the fact that knowledge on abstracting pre-dates that on IL. In his book on abstracting, Cremmins (1982), for example, stresses the importance of critical reading, without even mentioning IL. Abstracts serve as important tools in decisions about relevance, thus being information literate supposes an ability to find information and to compare it to the searcher's purpose and interests. In other words, information literacy requires decisions on the relevance of information found in literature searches.

Abstracting, as an activity, fits well into the system of scholarly communication because researchers who publish papers in the scholarly journals of their respective fields of knowledge are usually required to write abstracts of their own articles. The processes related to writing these so-called *author abstracts* does not seem have changed with new developments in scientific communication.

Even though we are focusing on selecting information here, it has to be made clear that, as a result of its complexity, abstracting also means text production with the underlying professional activities of analysis and synthesis (Alonso & Fernández, 2010). It is also closely related to academic literacy (Koltay, 2009; Ondrusek, Thiele, & Yang, 2013) that will be addressed in the next section.

As seen from the definitions and the above discussion, identifying, locating, and evaluating information, in other words information seeking, stands in the very heart of IL. Information seeking, however, is embedded in writing (Attfield, Blandford, & Dowell, 2003).

Besides developing their capacity to understand and evaluate the work of others, information literate people need skills in articulating and explaining their thoughts. They have to able "not only to navigate the Web effectively but also to integrate new information into a personal corpus which is communicable to others" (Beeson, 2005, p. 216). Integrating new information with prior information and knowledge is undoubtedly crucial (Loo & Chung, 2006).

Writing is influenced by a whole range of factors such as the broader situational and pragmatic context in which the text production tasks are embedded and the circumstances of the immediate text production. Scientific texts are firmly embedded in the historically and culturally influenced institution of science. The criteria of acting in a scholarly community are based on this (Jakobs, 2003).

As writing includes organizing, storing, designing, and creating information, as well as communicating and distributing it, information literate people are unavoidably writers as well as readers (Dashkin, 2003). Lynch (1998) adds to this insight that information literacy includes text authoring in a full range of genres including visual and multimedia communication.

From the perspective of writing, information seeking and information behavior in general are embedded processes. Conversely, seen from the perspective of information seeking and information behavior, writing is a common motivating activity (Twidale, Gruzd, & Nichols, 2008). Reflecting on texts includes information seeking as an analytic activity as any writer is devoted to the task of turning ideas into text. They then read the text to form new ideas and to make decisions about what has to be written (i.e., synthesized) and how it should be organized (Attfield, Blandford, & Dowell, 2003).

Researchers' writing activities are closely related to disciplinary (discourse) communities and disciplinary discourse. Holschuh Simmons (2005, p. 297) summarizes what we know about disciplinary discourse, including the ways in which "members of a particular discourse community write, read, speak, and research, as well as the assumptions that they make and the epistemologies with which they craft their arguments."

Academic writing is a pronouncement of membership in a particular discourse community, which is not unchanging as researchers construct, reconstruct, and deconstruct the discourse of the given community with their contributions. Consequently, this discourse is not static but is formed by negotiations between the established and dominant norms of the community and newly introduced perspectives.

A substantial part of the time dedicated to research is dedicated to writing. Successful academic writing, in general, depends on the individual writer's projection of a shared professional context. This is also true for researchers, one of whose principal occupations is writing. Accordingly, there is interest in knowing how researchers fulfill their writing functions (Hyland & Salager-Meyer, 2008).

It would be impossible and perhaps unnecessary to give a full picture of these functions here. Nevertheless, modern approaches to literacy suggest that writers need to embed their writing in a particular social world. This behavior is a mediated interaction that comprises making use of communication channels and technologies by purposeful activities (Scollon, 1998).

According to Hyland and Salager-Meyer (2008), scientific writing has been studied principally from four perspectives. Applied linguists have largely focused on the informational, rhetorical, cross-linguistic, and stylistic organization of written texts for descriptive or pedagogic purposes. Librarians and library and information science (LIS) researchers have focused on the role of texts in the classification, manipulation, retrieval, and dissemination of information. Historians, including several applied linguists, have been interested in the rhetorical evolution of the research article. Sociologists have investigated the interactions between researchers to explore the processes which maintain social order.

The range of written academic genres studied includes article abstracts, scientific letters, acknowledgments, theses, book reviews, conference abstracts, as well as various other genres such as article submission letters, grant proposals, and editors' responses to journal submissions.

As Hjørland (2002) points out, the achievements of composition studies and genre analysis are fruitful for LIS, not only on the concrete but also on the methodological level. The latter is connected with the emphasis on the social and historical dimensions of communication, including the concept of discourse communities (for instance in such foundational works as John Swales' *Genre Analysis* (Swales, 1990)).

Emphasis on discourse communities is one of the reasons why information literacy education shows a number of commonalities with the *Writing Across the Curriculum* (WAC) movement and why both can benefit from collaborating with and learning from the other (Elmborg, 2003). This movement views academic disciplines as discourse communities, each with its own set of assumptions about how knowledge is produced, while keeping in mind that new members of these communities have to do research and write like the specialists who inhabit these communities. WAC does not lose sight of social conventions of research, including the ways of articulating disciplinary knowledge as "content."

Last but not least, WAC stresses the dialogic nature of knowledge, that is, it is negotiated in the discussions, disputes, and disagreements of specialists (Elmborg, 2006).

A different accent is set by linguistic investigations into abstracting (just mentioned above), which show that the success of author abstracts depends not only on subject knowledge but also on linguistic competence and knowledge of the appropriate structure of genres (Busch-Lauer, 1995; Cross & Oppenheim, 2006). This is true for scientific research and its genres in general as well.

Communicating information means not only finding texts but also recombining pre-existing information by selecting, arranging, and filtering, instead of creating original texts (Geisler et al., 2001). This is one of the reasons why the nature of writing related to research is often reproductive in the sense that it requires scholars to possess "a good multi-dimensional synthetic thinking, which helps them create meaningful new combinations from existing information." The framework for this thinking is given by *reproduction literacy* (Eshet-Alkalai, 2004, p. 98).

According to Jakobs (2003), scholarly communication often includes reproductive writing that is characterized by the interaction of receptive, reproductive, and productive processes. It covers all forms of writing which involve the use of other texts. It may convey the contents of other texts, such as the writing of abstracts (mentioned on the previous page) or be part of more complex text production processes.

Recourse to other texts in academic writing is not only a possibility, but it represents a prototypical and indispensable constituent of text production, provided that loans from other texts are clearly identified as such. It is not by chance that academic literacy includes the closely interrelated issues of citing and plagiarism, which is in line with requirements for those who are information literate to use information ethically (Bawden, 2001; Bundy, 2004a, 2004b).

The pursuit of familiar material in a broader sense than reproductive writing is a typical feature of the information behavior of researchers. It occurs when an information seeker has some prior experience of the specific material being sought. This may include the investigation of journals recently published in a given field, sometimes paying special attention to a certain paper. A researcher may find only peripheral relevance in that paper, then—some time later—may rediscover and re-evaluate the paper in line with changes in emphasis in their research. Sometimes, it is only a part of the paper, a single argument or assertion that is important to them. Obviously, researchers also look for new material (Shenton, 2009).

Bronshteyn and Baladad (2006) remind us that joining writing instruction with information literacy education has to go beyond the issues of finding and citing resources. In the particular case of paraphrasing exercises that they present, they stress that understanding and mastering the basic concepts of paraphrasing is key to evaluating and effectively using resources, two key tenets of information literacy.

An interesting perspective on the linguistic study of scientific writing begins with analyzing the strategies that bloggers use to communicate scientific discourse in science blogs. The results of Luzón (2013) show a blending of discursive practices from different discourses. The strategies used involve adjusting information to the readers' knowledge and information needs, while deploying linguistic features typical of personal, informal, and dialogic interaction.

## ADDITIONAL CONTEXTS AND TURNS: CULTURE, LIS, AND OTHERS

First of all, we have to examine the *cultural context* of information literacy. Cultural dynamism and diversity dictate that literacies go beyond the traditional basics of reading and writing, so literacy comprises variables and communication strategies that are in accordance with the cultures and social languages of technologies, functional groups, and types of organization (Cope & Kalantzis, 2009b).

This is the reason why new literacies, such as media literacy, digital literacy, and especially information literacy, form the basis of acquiring culture in a wide sense, since they are broad in scope. They are tied not only to culture but also to technology (Cordes, 2009).

There is also an interrelation between active engagement in the cultural sphere and the uses of information, if we speak about information-as-thing (Buckland, 2012).

In accordance with this, creating a culture of semantic researchers requires that we accompany scientific training with education in data literacy and information literacy in order to establish a new cultural standard, especially because researchers often do not realize that their own scholarly communications constitute a primary source of data (Haendel, Vasilevsky & Wirz, 2012). (Data literacy will be addressed in more detail in the following section of this chapter).

The norms of the disciplinary communities mentioned above go far beyond the pressures of the "publish or perish" culture, which heavily influences the choices involved in communicating research. The culture of disciplinary communities originates in their traditions, customs, practices, beliefs, and morals, as well as the symbolic forms of communication (Elmborg, 2006).

Culture can be interpreted as a complex of codes and meanings on which human communication depends (Buckland, 2012). In other words, we can speak about culture as a "complex whole which includes knowledge, belief, art, morals, law, custom, and any other capabilities and habits acquired by man as a member of society" (Tylor, 1871, p. 1).

As a shared, learned, and symbolic system of values, beliefs and attitudes, culture shapes perception and behavior, and depends on the capacity for symbolic thought and social learning (Wilson et al., 2011).

Accordingly, the ability to understand data-based reasoning, already mentioned in the section on researchers' skills and abilities can be regarded as undoubtedly cultural in its nature. Communities of disciplines define culture in research settings. Big data also has its cultural aspect, as it is a technological and scholarly phenomenon that rests on the interplay of technology, analysis, and mythology.

The evidence of what culture is made of is also expressed in the naming conventions of literacies. The Hungarian term, *információs műveltség* shows that importance can be attached to being educated and erudite, which also shows the influence of thinking in terms of culture. In addition, among the numerous Polish equivalents of information literacy, we find the term *kultura informacyjna* (Koltay et al., 2010). If we translate the latter into English, it becomes *information culture*. However, this understanding is not identical with the concept that bears the same name, but is attributed to effective information management in corporate settings.

As outlined by Oliver (2008), the latter understanding of information culture is tied to the recognition and acceptance of societal and organizational requirements for managing information. It takes attitudes toward sharing information into consideration. It recognizes the importance of utilizing information and communication technologies and underlines trust in written documentation.

Having said this, it is apparent that—despite obvious differences—these latter features of information culture do not sound out of place when applied to information literacy in research settings, which follows basically the same preferences though in a different setting.

The cultural nature of information literacy is reinforced if we accept that literacy is a form of cultural knowledge which enables us to recognize and use language appropriate to different social situations (Campbell, 1990). Therefore, provided that information literacy is a way of functioning within complex communicative situations (Geisler et al., 2001), these situations are also cultural in their character. On the other hand, we may agree that a main constituent of IL is closely related to information seeking, the essence of which is finding texts that answer our information needs.

Yet, the connectedness of information literacy to culture does not end here. The disciplinary culture of researchers and information literacy can also be correlated. Their interface is provided by a *personal information culture* (PIC), defined as a system of knowledge and skills that may be used independently for the optimal satisfaction of information needs through the use of traditional and new information technologies (Gendina, 2008).

There are more—though different—contents in information literacy. The examination of fairly rapid changes of direction are metaphorically called *turns* to focus attention on a new way of thinking (Bawden & Robinson, 2012) in LIS that also provides a helpful context that gives additional insights into the nature of IL. Such moves may be called not only turns, but also new paradigms, new perspectives, or new viewpoints (Nolin, 2007).

There are a number of different classifications of these turns (Cronin, 2008; Nolin & Åström, 2010). However, we will concentrate only on a selection.

The most important turns that have characterized recent decades are the historical turn, the linguistic turn, the cognitive turn, the sociological turn, and the socio-cognitive paradigm.

We can say that the historical turn constitutes a search for the identity of LIS (Nolin, 2007). The linguistic turn can be attributed to discursive approaches, preceded by a turn in philosophy. It was followed by the cognitive turn, which brought with it a shift from a focus on linguistic acts to individual thought processes (Bawden & Robinson, 2012).

In other words, the cognitive turn focused on the cognition of information users and challenged the dominance of traditional approaches toward information retrieval (Cronin, 2008). This turn has been criticized by Nolin (2007) for alienating researchers from a sociological perspective, even though they would view cognitive dimensions as basically social.

As regards the sociological turn, we can say that LIS has long been receptive to sociological thinking, so it is probably misleading to speak of a *sociological* turn but could be named *social* turn instead (Cronin, 2008).

A central point of the socio-cognitive paradigm (also referred to as the domain analytic paradigm) is the claim that tools, concepts, meaning, information structures, information needs, and relevance criteria are shaped in discourse communities (Hjørland, 2002).

It recognizes that there is interplay between domain structures and individual knowledge, as well as an interaction between the individual and the social level (Hjørland & Albrechtsen, 1995).

This paradigm changes the focus of LIS from individuals and computers to the social, cultural, and scientific world. It also implies that the relevant cognitive structures are developed historically, culturally, and socially. One important implication of this paradigm is that the relevant cognitive structures are of a historical rather than of a physiological nature (Hjørland, 2002).

Robinson (2009) underlines the view that the socio-cognitive paradigm avoids the overtly systems approach, common in the early days of LIS, as well as the subjective and personal individual cognition approach. Indeed, Hjørland and Albrechtsen (1995) present this paradigm as an alternative to psychologizing or concentrating on IT issues.

The relationship between IL and these turns is relatively complex and we can approach this question from different directions. This complexity is exemplified by the viewpoint of Johnston and Webber (2005). When proposing information literacy as a soft applied discipline, they use Vannevar Bush's vision of the technologically connected and enabled researcher, giving special attention to specialization.

The four approaches to information literacy, devised by Sundin (2008) and described in more detail in the chapter on shifting approaches to information literacy also illustrate its paradigms. If we recognize the validity of the socio-cognitive paradigm for LIS, the closest approach to IL is the communicative one. This approach is characterized by Sundin (2008, pp. 35–36) as follows:

> It challenges the portrayal of information seeking as an individual process. In contrast to the process approach, information seeking is here understood as social practices embedded in other social practices, which occur in institutional contexts. Among the issues that the communication approach foregrounds are the importance of interaction between users in information seeking, the relation between cognitive authority and source evaluation, and the significance of social navigation.

Last, but not least, we can affirm that if LIS focuses on selecting, organizing, storing, retrieving, disseminating, and using information, then information literacy represents a mixture of LIS and education as it also looks at teaching and learning (Bowler & Large, 2008).

The communication chain in information science is deeply influenced by computing (Bawden & Robinson, 2012), as are information literacy and Research 2.0. The question is whether ubiquitous computing and the increasing social dimension of networked media can bring in something that takes us beyond blogs, twitter feeds, and so forth, and "make possible something truly collaborative – something like the super-critical thinking that is generative of ideas, modes of thought, theories, and new practices" (Berry, 2011, p. 8).

If our previous context was metatheoretical, the next is based on practice, at least in its name and orientation. It is *evidence-based practice* (EBP), which has a number of connections to IL. Adams (2014) shows this by comparing two foundational texts of EBP. He found that the outcomes described in the ACRL *Standards* provide a foundation for EBP and IL skills are highly valued by evidence-based practitioners.

As regards the evaluation of information quality, Adams asserts that EBP de-emphasizes expert opinion and the authority of the researcher, while librarians use the authority of the information creator as a marker of quality. This is true despite the fact that the ACRL *Standards* direct attention to the ability to "analyze the structure and logic of supporting arguments or methods."

On the other hand, EBP works with information already vetted through peer review, so information creators can be judged as "authoritative" by most observers. Some of the information that academic librarians deal with are not amenable to the statistics-based evaluation that is the focus of critical appraisal in EBP.

Moreover, librarians' use of authority as a primary marker of quality "may be an artefact of collection development policies that were created to squeeze the most value from a finite budget, and, for print formats, limited shelf space" (ACRL, 2000, p. 242).

When speaking about the relationship between IL and the researcher, we have to give attention to *information style*. As Johnston and Webber (2003) stress, IL is the adoption of appropriate information behavior. Consequently, it is not by accident that information style can play an important role in it.

According to Steinerová (2010), information style is based on the analysis of an individual's information seeking preferences and perceptions, and the characteristics of their use of electronic resources.

Two main styles can be identified: the pragmatic and the analytic. The former is dominant and is characterized by preferences for simple access to information, simple organization of knowledge, low cost, and fast access to electronic resources. Its representatives would not read extensive texts because they are experiential learners.

Those who represent the analytic style show deeper intellectual information processing. Reliability and verification of information are important for them. They use multidisciplinary terminology and assess information by its relevance, having experience in judging it. They use complex queries in contrast to intuitive, simple ones. Organization of information is integrative, based on expert knowledge and experience. The analytic style requires intellectual processing and the presence of doubts and interpretation is stressed instead of navigation.

In our opinion, the pragmatic style is compatible with amateurism, thus has a place in public library environments, while the analytic style is the ideal for academic users and literacies geared toward their needs should show preferences for this information style. If not, we are taking the risk that the already existing lack of critical thinking within academia will be aggravated (Head & Eisenberg, 2009).

By emphasizing being critical, information literacy and related literacies give attention to *cognitive authority*, which has two levels. At an operational level, cognitive authority is the extent to which users think that they can trust the information.

On a more general level, cognitive authority refers to influences that a user would recognize as proper because the given piece of information is thought to be credible and worthy of belief (Rieh, 2002).

The idea of cognitive authority can be traced back to *Second-Hand Knowledge*, a seminal work of Patrick Wilson who reminds us that a large portion of what individuals know about the world comes from other people. Following the thoughts of Wilson, Rieh (2002, p. 146) defines cognitive authority as "influences that a user would recognize as proper because the information therein is thought to be credible and worthy of belief."

Cognitive authority comes in two forms: a level of trust can be granted in the information communicated by a person or contained in a particular source. Obviously we know that researchers use recorded information, thus they rely on facts that are contained in information sources. On the other hand—as we have already pointed out above—it is known that informal communication plays a significant role in their information acquisition.

In any case, motivation and cognitive ability play a significant role in guiding information assessment and decision-making, and are a main component in building up the skills needed to determine the quality or credibility of information. This is especially true for digital literacy (Metzger, 2007), but the communication approach to information literacy also stresses the relation between cognitive authority and source evaluation (Sundin, 2008). It is also a constituent of information horizons that map information sources (Steinerová, 2010). The nature of digital literacy will be discussed on in the next section, on page 85.

## LITERACIES BEYOND INFORMATION LITERACY

We cannot complain that there are not enough types of literacy.

Snavely and Cooper (1997) provided 34 literacy terms. Their examples include:

- agricultural literacy;
- cinematic literacy;

- dance literacy;
- geographic literacy;
- legal literacy;
- workplace literacy.

In his widely cited review, Bawden (2001) enumerates six extensively used terms related to information literacy which are often used synonymously with each other.

- computer literacy: synonyms—IT literacy, information technology literacy, and electronic literacy;
- electronic information literacy;
- library literacy;
- media literacy;
- network literacy: synonyms—Internet literacy, hyper-literacy;
- digital literacy (with its synonym—digital information literacy).

Meanwhile, the conceptual universe of information literacy is expanding unstoppably and uncontrollably. Visioning the future, Ridley devised *post-literacy*, defining it as "the state in which reading and writing are no longer a dominant means of communication" (Ridley, 2012), while Kress is talking about visual objects instead of letters and screens instead of books (Kress, 2003).

We have also had a colorful *transliteracy* approach since 2005 (which was originally coined to support the cross-sectional approach of communication platforms and later developed into the "3 T"-paradigm: teaching, technology, and transliteracy). As a "unified construct that supports the acquisition, production, and sharing of knowledge in collaborative online communities," *metaliteracy* was born to promote "critical thinking and collaboration in a digital age, providing a comprehensive framework to effectively participate in social media and online communities." [2] (See also the section on overarching literacies.)

It is also very common to identify *new information literacies* in various contexts, such as, for example, writing studies (Shepherd & Goggin, 2012). Nevertheless, the common nature of every activity related to information is invariant: visual representation as information input, processing in the brain, and objectivation (exformation) as information output.

Therefore, the changing nature and complexity of information literacy is not situated within a cognitive or technological framework, but in the field of transformational social practice, embedded into the digitally

[2]Metaliteracy: http://metaliteracy.org/about/.

mediated cultural environment. This also means that the architectures, services, solutions, tools, and gadgets of the universe of future information and communication technologies are important. However, the changing patterns and structure of everyday life are decisive. Putting it the other way around: new literacies are "required for successful participation in an increasingly technologically mediated society" (Forte et al., 2014). This is the reason why the term *transformational literacies* was born in order to prepare users for life, and to help them see connections between working hard as readers and writers (Berger et al., 2014).

Andrea Forte proposed a new framework which highlights the "critical dimensions" of information literacy, while simultaneously indicating the main directions of change on two axes as shown in Table 1.

It is almost impossible to compose a full, overall, perfect classification system of every form of literacy because of the dynamic nature of the field. The emerging literacies become new, the new literacies become old, while the old literacies are continuously augmented with new features and relevancies.

New sets of literacies can be brought into the discourse in order to assist in understanding its disruptive nature. These literacies are *newborn, transforming, hybrid*, and *hyperpeople literacies*. We hope that this enriched conceptual framework will influence not only literacy debates, but also raise the awareness and stimulate the design of new intellectual, educative and work environments, refreshing pedagogy or training practices.

The reason behind the birth of brand new literacy types is not only the cumulative relocation of the basic forms of activity and transaction into the digital ecosystem but also the overflow of closed, professional knowledge

**Table 1    Dynamics of information literacy development**

|  | Social | Technological |
|---|---|---|
| **Consumption** | Educating people to find and use information well | Designing information systems that help people to find and use information well |
| **Approach to** | | *Transforming practice* ➞ |
| **Production** | Educating people to create and contribute information sources | Designing information systems that help people to create and contribute information sources |

*Literacy skills* (vertical axis, downward arrow)

Forte et al. (2014); used by permission.

sets, creating casual, everyday, trivial versions and generating a kind of wave of "literacy emancipation."

The pioneering field of *financial literacy* has evolved into the ability to make informed decisions about how to use and—later—how to manage our money and financial transactions online, including

> saving, banking, budgeting, smart shopping tips, understanding types of loans and credit and how to manage debt, investing and financial planning, choosing suitable mobile phone plans, avoiding scams and rip-offs, and explains the basics about insurance and superannuation
>
> **Healey (2010).**

*Legal literacy* was born as an ordinary digital literacy of lawyers and students of law schools (Margolis & Murray, 2012), while *psycho-literacy* was introduced, especially to students, as the general knowledge of basic terms and concepts within the psychological community (Boneau, 1990).

A few years later, the concept was extended to legally and psychologically literate citizens (Dunn, 2011; Mair, Taylor & Hulme, 2013). Currently, it is more than important for every "netizen" to identify, know, and understand the legally sensitive fields found in typical online activity forms, and the psychologically sensitive found in person-to-person online communication.

The explosion of health information for patients and health practitioners as well as other digital health tools and applications (Behrman, 2012) prompted the change from health awareness to *health literacy*. This marked a step up "from just looking at health information, and moves toward a model that involves behavior changes and digital interaction" with and between patients (Fink, 2014).

The junior concept of *futures literacy* was coined primarily to enhance the skill-set of policy-makers (Miller, 2011). However, the anticipatory systems and models, including the techniques of scenario making, have meant that everyone is able to get better decisions, and are available for civil organizations, local communities, interest groups, and even individuals.

The second cluster of emerging literacies consists of significantly improved versions of earlier literacy forms, following the inherent changes within the given domains, while reflecting the extended playground of activity forms as part of the "gradation" from the receptive to a receptive and productive nature.

*Visual literacy* (or visuacy), as a conceptual approach to graphic problem-solving (Wilde & Wilde, 1991), has been transformed into a more complex form using comic books, graphic novels, anime, cartoons, and more to develop comprehension and thinking skills (Frey & Fisher, 2008). Following the revolution in everyday information architecture and infographics, graphicacy (Aldrich & Sheppard, 2000) is increasingly becoming "infographicacy," and a part of broader design literacy (Heller, 2014).

*Game literacy* entered the vocabulary of academics and teachers to take "seriously the serious play of young people … analysing games and the world of games as text" (Beavis et al., 2012). A few years later, serious games became integral parts of learning environments, while gamification, the use of game thinking, and game mechanics in non-game contexts arose and spread in company and big organizational environments (Deterding et al., 2011). This idea led to the emergence of gamification literacy, that is, *gamificacy*.

Social media stimulate participation in public and semi-public spaces accompanied by a new ability: *participatory (participation) literacy*. Following the shift in emphasis from discussions to real-world interventions and from interaction to decision-making competency and responsible execution, the operative part of social actions established a new literacy set: *operacy*. This includes the abilities needed for agenda setting, strategic planning, managing conflicts, or sharing tasks.

In a wider sense, we can speak about the ability to create public content. This leads to content *creacy*. As this book focuses on research, emphasis has to be put on scientific literacy (on page 89) which will be addressed later. Similarly, there will be a detailed explanation of the nature and importance of data literacy.

Data and game literacies can easily form hybrids with other literacies, since data can be found everywhere and there are almost no limits to gamification in these environments. The combination of health literacy and numeracy is important "to understand, evaluate, and use numbers … to make informed health care choices" (French, 2014). There are many good examples illustrating how gamification could influence clinicians' practice (Miliard, 2014) and patients' behavior (King et al., 2013).

Scientific infographics has also become popular, since data visualizations can assist in the understanding of the conceptual and the practical and communicate scientific results (Jackson, 2014). Furthermore, we also have a long record of combining scientific learning with games (Hilton & Honey, 2011).

Disciplinary differences in information literacy practices also appear. While a substantial part of any IL program that is directed toward researchers must be the same, irrespective of whether they work in the natural sciences, the social sciences, or the humanities, the specificity of a given field has to be taken into consideration. It is enough to mention that work in the humanities is more closely tied to documents than the activities of any other researchers.

Being connected is reflected in the information literacy syllabus for humanities researchers designed by East (2005). This program is divided into two parts: the first addresses general skills, while the second is about specific formats.

The starting point to identify general skills is thinking about how information is disseminated in the given discipline and where this information is located. In other words, those working in the humanities have to understand how information is disseminated in their discipline. Accordingly, researchers should be able to identify the physical or virtual repositories which contain significant collections of relevant materials.

The next element of the syllabus directs attention to the fact that the approach to identifying appropriate print and electronic bibliographic tools has changed in the time that has elapsed since the publication of East's paper.

In fact practically a decade has gone by, which has brought a reliance on search engines, in particular on Google. This primacy also characterizes Google Scholar to an extent, though it can also be regarded as a kind of bibliographic tool (Asher, Duke, & Wilson, 2013).

Not to forget that the literature on the information habits of humanists has traditionally stressed that scholars have made only limited use of major abstracting and indexing journals (East, 2005).

The statements made in 2005 about searching databases effectively are, *mutatis mutandis*, still valid. If there were disparities among researchers in their searching abilities, they did not disappear, even though their nature may have changed. This reminds us of the situation described by Herman and Nicholas (2010), according to whom present-day information seekers consistently demonstrate characteristic patterns of unproductive information behavior. (See the section on disintermediation and re-intermediation).

Last, but not least, we can add that keeping up to date in their field and establishing a network of contacts remains of perpetual value and forms a continuing practice for researchers.

There are a number of other literacies we have to take into consideration. Some have been mentioned in the section, entitled "How many literacies are there?" The literacies that appear below are those that are apparently most closely connected with research activities. These are scientific literacy and academic literacy.

*Scientific literacy* comprises the methods, approaches, attitudes, and skills related to thinking scientifically and doing research. We can also add to this that anyone who has acquired scientific literacy is able to understand articles about research in the popular press and engage in social conversation about the validity of their conclusions (NAS, 1996). This implies that everyone should be scientifically literate, even if only a small number of graduate students become researchers.

*Academic literacy* is more closely associated with formal learning, especially in higher education. Norgaard (2003) characterizes literacy as a culturally situated phenomenon based on the way that communities construct meaning and belonging. This is especially true for academic literacy, which involves the comprehension of the entire system of thinking, values, and information flows of academia. All this is based on a cultural identity among academics in which professional language and literature play a key role. In this system, information has a grammatical dimension that information literate academics must master (Elmborg, 2006).

In higher education, literacy has always included knowledge and skills that go beyond the ability to read and write. It encompasses the skills needed for identifying appropriate materials for study, while presupposing discipline-specific reading and writing skills in order to be critical and articulate.

Having said this, we have to acknowledge that the journey toward today's literacy is complicated and crosses a shifting terrain where technologies and associated practices are constantly changing. Accounts of literacy in online environments have to take into consideration that the acts of communicating and interpreting are not neutral and rely more on socially constructed relationships than on technological affordances.

It is relatively easy to see that both literacies mentioned above are prerequisites of becoming a researcher and fulfilling the researcher's role. It seems to be clear as well that these two literacies complement one another and, at the same time, are strongly dependent on information literacy, at least in research environments.

The essence of academic literacy is the ability to "read, interpret, and produce information valued in academia according to beliefs about how research should be done" (Elmborg, 2006, p. 196).

As mentioned above, these communities are different from the amateur ones on the grounds of the significance of their distinguished credentials and authorship. Friesen (2010) indicates that in commercial social networks, there is a lack of critical comparing and contrasting of different views.

In a broader sense, academic literacy should also include the ability to discern predatory open access journals that seek to exploit the author-pays open access model to gain profit, without living up to the standards of scholarly publishing. To achieve this is much easier for experienced researchers, who usually know the best and most prestigious journals in their fields. Younger researchers who are new to publishing journal papers face a relatively difficult situation as they do not usually have this advantage.

There are some indications to look out for that demonstrate the low quality of these journals. For example, behind them there are no well-established and reliable publishers or publishers associated with universities or learned societies. They apparently have editorial boards, but these often do not play any effective role in the decision to publish particular papers. Fake journals may have no peer review at all, or do not do it properly, as suggested by the suspiciously short deadlines for peer-reviewing manuscripts (Mehrpour & Khajavi, 2014).

*Media literacy* is often mentioned alongside information literacy. Potter (2004) defines media literacy as "the set of perspectives from which we expose ourselves to the media and interpret the meaning of the messages we encounter." Similar to information literacy, media literacy accentuates critical evaluation. It acknowledges both the reception and production of media (EC, 2009) and includes the interpretation of all types of complex, mediated symbolic texts made available by "traditional" or electronic (digital) means (Livingstone, 2004). This demonstrates the relevance of media literacy for a wide array of media, including research data. We can also include the convergence among literacies, which is caused by the convergence of different forms of media and ICT (Livingstone et al., 2008).

Making use of the Web of Science database, Lee and So (2014) have explored the relationship between media literacy and information literacy. They looked for occurrences of the key words "information literacy" and "media literacy" from 1956 to 2012. Their findings show that the two fields have different authors, affiliations, and publication venues.

The authors' academic origin, scope, and social concerns are also different. Information literacy has a closer tie to LIS, but the two fields adopt different analytical approaches. Lee and So state that media literacy cannot be regarded to be a subset of information literacy, even though the two fields share the same goals.

Nonetheless, the arguments of Badke (2009) are valid, as he warned about the danger of living in silos, emphasizing that separation is a hurdle that these literacies must overcome so that they can play a foundational role in today's education. Koltay (2011) also comments that media literacy has to find its essential role in education as one aspect of some kind of multiple or multimodal literacy.

It is not just the quantity of media exposure that justifies the importance of media literacy. All of us have experienced the heavy presence and influence of the different media that more recently has included the Internet. The vital role of information in the development of democracy, cultural participation, and active citizenship also justifies our interest and these features draw media literacy near to information literacy.

In the contemporary media environment, users and their interests are represented in mediated spaces, which also serve as an environment to activate engagement with others (Jarrett, 2008). Media literacy also takes into account that media is constructed and constructs reality. Therefore it consists of the following competencies:

> *A media literate person – and everyone should have the opportunity to become one – can decode, evaluate, analyze and produce both print and electronic media. The fundamental objective of media literacy is critical autonomy relationship to all media. Emphases in media literacy training range widely, including informed citizenship, aesthetic appreciation and expression, social advocacy, self-esteem, and consumer competence*

> **Aufderheide (1992).**

The definition adopted by several organizations in the European Union also stresses the critical aspect as well as acknowledging both the reception and production of media.

> *Media literacy is generally defined as the ability to access the media, to understand and to critically evaluate different aspects of the media and media contents and to create communications in a variety of contexts*

> **EP (2007).**

In accordance with this definition, the various levels of media literacy include:

- feeling comfortable with all existing media from newspapers to virtual communities; actively using media through, *inter alia*, interactive television, use of Internet search engines or participation in virtual communities; and better exploiting the potential of media for entertainment, access to culture, intercultural dialog, learning and daily-life applications (for instance, through libraries, podcasts);
- having a critical approach to media as regards both quality and accuracy of content (e.g., being able to assess information, dealing with advertising on various media, using search engines intelligently);
- using media creatively, as the evolution of media technologies and the increasing presence of the Internet as a distribution channel allow an

ever growing number of Europeans to create and disseminate images, information, and content;

- understanding the economy of media and the difference between pluralism and media ownership;
- being aware of copyright issues, which are essential for a "culture of legality," especially for the younger generations in their double capacity of being consumers and producers of content (EP, 2007).

For IL authors, their main information objects are peer-reviewed and evaluated publications, such as academic books and journals. In contrast, media literacy focuses on mass media such as newspapers and television that are typified by having less source validation because of the rapid production that characterizes them (Lau, 2013).

Let us add that there is *news literacy*, which aims to offer tools for the development of the critical thinking skills necessary to evaluate the veracity of what we receive through 24-h news channels, social media, and other online sources of information (Dowling, 2013).

As said above, media literacy and information literacy partially overlap and complement each other, as both basically aim to foster the same skills (Lau, 2013). Taking this into account, information literacy and media literacy have recently been coupled with each other under the umbrella concept of *media and information literacy*.

For instance, the World Summit on the Information Society advocated the promotion of information and media literacy, regarding them as indispensable individual skills for people in the increasing information flow (WSIS, 2013).

The definition of media and information literacy is basically identical to the definition of information literacy. It "consists of the knowledge, the attitudes, and the sum of the skills needed to know when and what information is needed; where and how to obtain that information; how to evaluate it critically and organise it once it is found; and how to use it in an ethical way" (IFLA, 2011).

The *Moscow Declaration on Media and Information Literacy* adds that media and information literate individuals "can use diverse media, information sources, and channels in their private, professional, and public lives" (IFLA, 2012).

We have to take into consideration the already mentioned convergence among literacies caused by the convergence between different forms of media and ICTs (Livingstone et al., 2008). This move is not surprising, and we may agree with Carbo (2013), who asserts that information literacy and other related literacies are undergoing a transformation which may result in the emergence of a new paradigm of its own. She adds that—instead of looking at the many differences among the various perspectives—this new paradigm, with its broader perspective integrating the many different forms of literacy, should be explored in much more depth.

Referring to the explosion in user-generated media which will be fully felt in the workplace, Davies, Fidler, and Gorbis (2011) speak about *new-media literacy*. They define it as the ability to critically assess and develop content that uses new-media forms, including videos, blogs, and podcasts. New-media literacy also means leveraging these media for persuasive communication.

*Data literacy* pertains to the cluster of emerging literacies mentioned above. We find it at the intersection between scholarly communication and information literacy (ACRL, 2013). Data is no longer limited to quantitative results drawn from experiments or surveys, so humanities and social science researchers represent a new constituency for data literacy education (ACRL, 2013). This expanding view of what we mean by data, coupled with the growing importance of research data mentioned above, has brought with it the growth in the need for data literacy.

The concept of data literacy is not entirely new. However, new and emerging roles have influenced its nature to a substantial extent. The blurring of boundaries between information and data are also having a determining effect. In fact, they never have been rigid, as information literacy has always been interested in the proper understanding and use of data that is converted into information (Schneider, 2013).

Data literacy enables individuals to access, interpret, critically assess, manage, handle, and ethically use data. Managing, as it appears in this definition, comprises preservation and curation (Calzada Prado & Marzal, 2013).

Mandinach and Gummer (2013, p. 30) define data literacy as "the ability to understand and use data effectively to inform decisions." They add that it is a specific skill set and knowledge base that enables us to transform data into information and ultimately into actionable knowledge. Data literacy skills include knowing how to identify, collect, organize, analyze, summarize, and prioritize data. The last two skills are especially worthy of attention as they are the skills that do not appear in other lists. Developing hypotheses, identifying problems, interpreting the data, and determining, planning, implementing, as well as monitoring courses of action are also necessary skills that are among the requirements for tailoring data literacy to its specific uses.

This set of definitions reflects a systemic cultural change in the importance, purposes, language, skills, and processes of data management (Varvel & Shen, 2013). It is also congruent with the opinion of Qin and D'Ignazio, according to whom science data literacy—though named differently—emphasizes the ability to understand, use, and manage science data.

These definitions also subsume the reasoning of the Association of College and Research Libraries (2013), which voted for the term *data literacy*. Their approach focuses on understanding how to find and evaluate data, emphasizes the given version of the data set and the person responsible for it, and does not neglect the questions of citing and ethical use of data. According to the ACRL, data literacy is a literacy conceived for those who will use the data and will need educating about how to understand and interpret them.

This literacy concentrates on ownership and rights issues, and cuts across disciplinary boundaries and the traditional structures of academic library organizations. Such an approach to data literacy shows similarities with media literacy by the use and reuse of content in ways not imagined by its original creator.

There are a number of reasons why we need data literacy. However, perhaps the most important factor is that we are witnessing a widespread belief that the existence and access to research data, in particular to big data, offers a higher form of intelligence and knowledge.

There is an aura of truth, objectivity, and accuracy around it, as well. Big data is seen as a solution to many burning questions, which may raise suspicion. On the other hand, it is often regarded as a tool that threatens privacy and decreases civil freedoms, ushering in increased state and corporate control. The shifts to be expected of big data are probably more subtle than these, even though we cannot see this clearly among our current hopes and fears (Boyd & Crawford, 2012).

This leads to the conclusion that one of the most important goals of data literacy education should be to foster the critical thinking that will keep us away from the pitfalls of being overly optimistic or unduly pessimistic, or behaving in an excessively critical or uncritical way.

Data literacy should take into consideration the framework of future work skills and abilities outlined by Davies et al. (2011). The first, data-based reasoning, we have already mentioned.

The need for being critical is no different from other literacies, so it occupies a special place among the general features of data literacy. It includes placing emphasis on the given version of the data set and identifying the person responsible for it (ACRL, 2013).

On the other hand, there are additional features, such as understanding what data means, including how to read graphs and charts appropriately, drawing correct conclusions from data, and recognizing when data is being used in misleading or inappropriate ways, that are also constituent of data literacy.

The main fields where the core competencies of data literacy can be used are as follows:

- databases and data formats;
- discovery and acquisition of data;
- data management and organization (including the life cycle of data and standard operating procedures for data management and documentation);
- data conversion and interoperability (dealing with the risks and potential loss or corruption of information caused by changing data formats);
- quality assurance;
- metadata;
- data curation and reuse;
- cultures of practice (including disciplinary values and norms and data standards);
- data preservation;
- data analysis;
- data visualization;
- ethics, including citation of data (Carlson et al., 2011).

Data literate people (users, researchers, and librarians) have to know how to select and synthesize data and combine it with other information sources and prior knowledge. They have to recognize source data value, types, and formats; determine when data is needed; and access data sources appropriate to the information needed.

Data literacy seems akin to information literacy as planning, organizing, and assessing ourselves throughout the process are vital and the ability of presenting quantitative information in different and appropriate forms also has to be emphasized (Calzada Prado & Marzal, 2013).

The above sequence of steps is closely associated with the well-known and widely accepted definition of information literacy, according to which information literate people are able to recognize when information is needed. They are also able to identify, locate, evaluate, and use information to solve a particular problem (ALA, 1989).

As said, data management in general and the quality of data in particular for data citation are of significance for data literacy. Tracing back data provenance and its justification (Buckland, 2011) are components of data literacy through data quality. The former includes the tracking of all contexts and transformations which the data has gone through and is of key importance to verifying the authenticity and reliability of data files (Ramírez, 2011).

Data literacy should also include answers to the question of *openness*, primarily open data as advocated by a number of researchers in order to make science more accountable (Stuart, 2011).

From other related fields, where data literacy competencies can be potentially used, the following must be mentioned:

- data analysis;
- data visualization;
- dealing with the risks and potential loss or corruption of information (Carlson et al., 2011).

Calzada Prado and Marzal (2013) emphasize the importance of knowing how to select and synthesize data and combine them with other information sources and prior knowledge. They also enumerate the following abilities:

- to identify the context in which data are produced and reused (data lifecycle);
- to recognize source data value, types, and formats;
- to determine when data are needed;
- to access data sources appropriate to the information needed;
- to critically assess data and their sources;
- to determine and use suitable research methods;
- to handle and analyze data;
- to present quantitative information (specific data, tables, graphs, in reports and similar);
- to apply results to learning, decision-making, or problem-solving;
- to plan, organize, and self-assess throughout the process.

It is not by accident that context is mentioned in the above list in the first place. Context is utterly important. Dissociation of data from its context and the loss of context make reuse difficult, or impossible (Schneider, 2013).

From the content of a series of instructional sessions on socio-economic data described by Wong (2010), we can single out three aspects. The first aspect is exploring data evaluation and use. The second one is guiding students in understanding data-collection methods and dissemination channels. The third aspect is introducing students to different information needs that are fulfilled by data.

As service providers, data librarians should be acquainted with quantitative research methods which enable them to process and analyze research data. To be able to provide support for researchers, they have to possess an extensive understanding of scientific data sources which will enable them to recommend comprehensive and reliable data sources (Si et al., 2013).

As we have already underlined, and as Lee (2013) also emphasizes, many novel and compound literacy concepts have appeared to face the challenges brought about by the changes in the new social and technological environments. These literacies are also often called *overarching literacies* or *twenty-first century competencies*.

All the literacies that have been discussed in the previous sections fit well into the framework of *metaliteracy*, which is undoubtedly an overarching concept as it provides the foundation for media literacy, digital literacy, and other literacies, and fosters both critical thinking and participation via social media. Metaliteracy is a self-referential and comprehensive framework that informs these other literacy types. It provides the foundation for media literacy, digital literacy, and other literacies, and emphasizes content.

According to Mackey and Jacobson (2011, p. 62):

*Metaliteracy promotes critical thinking and collaboration in a digital age, providing a comprehensive framework to effectively participate in social media and online communities. It is a unified construct that supports the acquisition, production, and sharing of knowledge in collaborative online communities.*

They also add the following:

*Metaliteracy expands the scope of information literacy as more than a set of discrete skills, challenging us to rethink information literacy as active knowledge production and distribution in collaborative online communities.*

*(p. 64)*

Witek and Grettano (2014) are of the opinion that metaliteracy has acquired an even greater significance for reframing information literacy in today's information environment. They assume that a fully realized theory of information literacy, the foundation of which is metaliteracy, includes a meta-awareness of what we do with information and why.

The next "overarching" literacy is *transliteracy* that comprises the ability to read, write, and interact across a range of platforms, tools, and media. It intends to be concerned with understanding and explaining the meaning of being literate in the twenty-first century. While it is an overarching concept, it is not meant to replace any of the format-specific literacies. It attempts to understand the relationship among them instead.

Transliteracy maps meaning across different media, in the interaction among different literacies. It is not concerned with developing particular literacies about particular media. It analyzes the social uses of technology by focusing on the relationship between people and technology, most specifically social networking. However, it is not tied to any particular technology.

Due to this holistic nature of transliteracy, it is challenging to define what specific skills are necessary to engage with it. Attention to transliteracy is especially worthwhile as, by exploring the participatory nature of new means of communicating, it intends to break down the barriers between academia and the wider community (Ipri, 2010).

The object of both information literacy and *digital literacy* is invariably the same, that is, information. However, information literacy mobilizes the abilities and skills related to finding, retrieving, analyzing, and using information. In contrast, digital literacy not only accentuates its creation but also emphasizes the use of digital technology (Qin & D'Ignazio, 2010).

The concept of digital literacy in its present understanding was introduced by Gilster (1997). However, he was not the first to use this expression. It had been applied in the 1990s to denote the ability to read and comprehend hypertext (Bawden, 2001).

Gilster explained digital literacy as an ability to understand and to use information from a variety of digital sources without concern for the different "competence lists," often criticized as being restrictive.

The four core competencies of digital literacy are:

- Internet searching;
- hypertext navigation;
- knowledge assembly;
- content evaluation (Bawden, 2008).

Martin's definition of digital literacy emphasizes both its wide meaning and the role of media.

> *Digital Literacy is the awareness, attitude and ability of individuals to appropriately use digital tools and facilities to identify, access, manage, integrate, evaluate, analyze and synthesize digital resources, construct new knowledge, create media expressions, and communicate with others, in the context of specific life situations, in order to enable constructive social action; and to reflect upon this process*
>
> **Martin (2006, p. 19).**

A distinctive feature of digital literacy is expressed by Bawden (2008, p. 26):

> *Digital literacy touches on and includes many things that it does not claim to own. It encompasses the presentation of information, without subsuming creative writing and visualization. It encompasses the evaluation of information, without claiming systematic reviewing and meta-analysis as its own. It includes organization of information but lays no claim to the construction and operation of terminologies, taxonomies and thesauri.*

Digital literacy does not lower the standing of traditional literacies. It is much more inseparable from and fundamental to reading, writing, and arithmetic (Murray & Pérez, 2014). Accordingly, it has to be built both on traditional literacy skills and an orientation to the understanding of twenty-first century socio-technical systems (Meyers, Erickson, & Small, 2013).

In digital literacy, traditional tools (often known from IL) continue to play an important role, while it reflects that ordinary people have become not only receivers but also senders of messages (Bawden, 2001).

In their draft report, the Digital Literacy Task Force of the American Library Association defined digital literacy as, "the ability to use information and communication technologies to find, evaluate, create, and communicate information, requiring both cognitive and technical skills" (ALA, 2012, p. 1). They add that digitally literate persons possess technical and cognitive skills that are needed to find, understand, evaluate, create, and communicate digital information in a wide variety of formats.

These people are able to use diverse technologies appropriately and effectively to retrieve information, interpret results, and judge the quality of that information. As regards researchers, they use their skills and the appropriate technology to communicate and collaborate with peers, colleagues, and occasionally the general public.

Digital literacy includes the ability to read and interpret media and use information in multiple formats from a wide range of sources when presented via computers. It also enables the performance of tasks effectively in a digital environment (Wilson et al., 2011).

We should also mention that data literacy and transliteracy are grouped in a White Paper, *Intersections of scholarly communication and information literacy: Creating strategic collaborations for a changing academic environment* under the rubric of *digital literacies* (ACRL, 2013).

The second perspective on digital literacies, as outlined by Meyers, Erickson, and Small (2013)—emphasizes the application of abstract mental models to activities involving digital content. These models address the processing by individuals of information from a cognitive viewpoint.

The third perspective sees digital literacy as engagement in a set of practices involving digital tools and media that are embedded in socially constructed and situated contexts or activities. Instead of providing a list of discrete skills, this perspective operates within the general capabilities that individuals have for living, learning, and working in a digital society. These capabilities recognize and reflect on the constant changes in technology and the behavior and characteristics of digital citizens.

The notion that digital literacy is an evolving construct is both its strength and weakness: while it privileges a wide range of expertise and a nimble conception of the value of digital literacy in society, it is notoriously difficult to assess, and does not mesh well with the existing formal systems of certification or endorsement. This perspective sees participation as the key to developing digital literacies.

Digital literacy, then, could be seen as the study of written or symbolic representation that is mediated by new technology. Its prime concern would be the production and consumption of the verbal and symbolic aspects of screen-based texts—this would be its initial point of departure from print literacy. Furthermore, the specific affordances of digital literacy could be conceptualized as a product of the technological means of its production and consumption. This is not to deny the complex and often very visual nature of many digital texts (Merchant, 2007).

We classified many of the literacies discussed above as overarching. While in the case of metaliteracy and transliteracy there is less doubt about this quality, it is especially intriguing to examine digital literacy. Martin (2006) stated that digital literacy was an integrating but not overarching concept. Owusu-Ansah (2003) identified the attempts to define information literacy as all-inclusive as the main discernable fault.

Nevertheless, there are a number of literacies that could compete to be named as overarching. Beyond the literacies portrayed in this section, information literacy could be a successful candidate. SCONUL, for example, defines information literacy as "an umbrella term which encompasses concepts such as digital, visual and media literacies, academic literacy, information handling, information skills, data curation, and data management" (SCONUL, 2011).

Let us not forget that it is of little importance what we call the various literacies of the information age and how we define them (Bawden, 2001). As Hunt (2004) explains, there may be no agreement on the precise definition of information literacy. Nonetheless, most people use the term *information literacy* rather than *library instruction* or *information fluency*. However, if we do not use the same language, it will be difficult to convince our stakeholders about the importance of information literacy education. In the case of data literacy, we may experience the same.

## THE RELATIONSHIP OF INFORMATION LITERACY TO INFORMATION OVERLOAD AND PERSONAL INFORMATION MANAGEMENT

It is likely that our previous argument has shown in a convincing manner that it is often difficult to name primary and secondary questions and fields when speaking about issues related to literacies, and especially information literacy. Notwithstanding this, many readers may judge the following problems to be more loosely related to our main argument. On the other hand, these "borderline" fields can easily become mainstream issues within a short period of time. In fact, while they are fundamentally important in their own contexts, they may be perceived to be of secondary importance to a certain (relative) extent in the information literacy context.

Even though we did not do so in the case of information literacy, it seems expedient to conceive of information overload (IO) by looking at what we understand as information. Buckland (1991) differentiates between three principal uses:

- *information-as-process*, that is, the act of informing;
- *information-as-knowledge*, that is, knowledge communicated concerning some particular fact, subject, or event;
- *information-as-thing*, that is, used attributively for objects, such as data and documents, which are regarded as being informative.

IO is related both to information-as-thing, that is recorded information, or—in other words—objective packages of cognitive content in a certain form (Kari, 2007) is important source of IO if it is available in abundance.

IO can also be defined as an impediment to efficiently using information due to the amount of relevant and potentially useful information available (Bawden & Robinson, 2009). The information cycle of personal documents is managed in an individual's own collection, that is, informal, diverse, and expanding memory collections created or acquired and accumulated by individuals in the course of their personal lives, and belonging to them rather than to their institutions or other places of work (Williams, Leighton John, & Rowland, 2009).

We have to add here that IO often remains unrecognized (Badke, 2010) and its very existence is questioned by some authors. For example, Tidline (1999) is of the opinion that the concept functions as a modern-day myth.

However, if we accept that in fact it does exist, it is necessary to differentiate between the macro- and the micro-level of IO. The first is related to the limits of physical storage and processing capacities that present an obstacle to information access. IO at the micro-level is essentially a failure to filter information (Davis, 2011).

Let us add that our information environment is characterized not only by greater amounts of information available in a greater variety of formats and types but also by delivery through a limited number of interfaces (Bawden & Robinson, 2009).

Besides the quantity, a substantial part of the information that we consume and have to manage is becoming more and more volatile (Davis, 2012). These factors contribute to a growing complexity, which materializes in diverse and abundant information choices in almost all fields (Morville, 2005), and is often coupled with people's general inefficiency in performing a given task (Davis, 2012). Presupposing inefficiency is built on the assumption that a person can only digest a certain amount of information in any given time (Ji, Ha, & Sypher, 2014).

Complaints about IO itself are by no means new. A selection of the examples, presented by Bawden and Robinson (2009), shows this in the historical development of IO clearly.

Complaints about the difficulty of keeping up with the amount of information available began early. Nonetheless, information, contained in the printed book, the scholarly journal, and the computer have often been named as the sources of IO.

IO was generally accepted as a problem in the late 1950s and early 1960s. The exponential growth in the number of publications, particularly in science, technology, and medicine, was considered to be the cause. By the 1990s, references to IO began to appear in the business world as well.

IO has been heavily influenced by recent technological and cultural changes (Rapple, 2011). First of all, social media (often called new media) have had a significant effect on it. The fact that most Web 2.0 users express themselves in mediated spaces instead of communicating face to face (Jarrett, 2008) causes IO.

The uncontrolled nature of this communication, the ease of producing information, and the expectation of constant novelty require the rapid updating and posting of new material. This is aggravated by the lack of incentives to remove our production from the net (Brown, 2010).

As said above, the concept of IO involves the notion of excess. However, excess in itself is not a sufficient condition for being overloaded. Overload can be defined in comparison to some norms, which regulate what is an appropriate amount of information and which pieces of information are undesirable (Himma, 2007).

As IO is mainly a social condition propagated by people, it can be combated by offering appropriate education that focuses on critical thinking. The absence of such education and the lack of adequate information filters or the failure to apply them appropriately results in IO (Davis, 2011).

IO can rightly be called pollution. More importantly, however, it is useful to know that we can learn to work around it, instead of treating it as something that must be controlled and regulated (Springer, 2009).

In other words, the wealth of information becomes noise if one cannot make sense of it (Morville, 2005). Indeed, we receive more and more messages that are detached from all contexts, that is, are completely meaningless to us.

In essence, IL is about reconstructing this lost sense and context (Tuominen, 2007). This is why we can affirm that being information literate enables us to recapture "the control lost in the overload situation" (Bawden, Holtham, & Courtney, 1999, p. 253).

IO is the most widely recognized "pathology of information," that is, an example of seemingly strange behaviors that we can observe, when individuals face difficulties in managing information, particularly when large amounts of diverse information are available.

*Information anxiety* is one of these pathologies, and is usually a condition of stress caused by the inability to access, understand, or make use of necessary information. There are *infobesity* and *information withdrawal* as well (Bawden & Robinson, 2009).

When describing another pathology, *information malnutrition*, Herman and Nicholas (2010, p. 246) state:

> Ironically enough, the root of the 'information malnutrition' problem seems to be the very act of switching the information tap on to everyone, which all too often amounts to the removal of the information professional from the information equation.

We find a characterization of the problem a few pages later:

> It is hardly surprising to find, then, that while people do indeed effortlessly acquire vast amounts of information, all too often none, or at most very little of it, aptly meets their needs. In fact, much of it amounts to the information equivalent of fast food: easily obtainable, flattering to the undiscerning palate, but of little actual value at its best, and harmful at its worst. Regrettably, though perhaps not unexpectedly, considering what we know of fast food consumption, people are satisfied enough with their information supply, never realising, or at least comfortably ignoring that they should – indeed could – do much better where their information needs are concerned.

**(pp. 247–248)**

The approach of choosing the most easily accessible information and leaving the rest is not an appropriate behavior, either (Badke, 2010). Such behavior is known as *satisficing*, which means taking just enough information to meet a need, thereby implying that just enough information is good enough. The general background to satisficing is given by convenience, characterizing both academic and everyday information seeking. It is mainly associated with the speed of search engines and the ease of access (Connaway, Dickey, & Radford, 2011).

Neylon (2011, p. 25) clearly expresses how we should approach IO.

> *The problem is not that we have too much information. We are an information-driven society; how could there be too much? The challenge is to make effective use of it. We do not need to block. We don't need to limit. We need to enable. We need the tools for discovery. This is not a problem. It is an opportunity, and we will make much faster progress in solving the problems we face when we see.*

It is information literacy education that is seen by many to be tool to reduce IO among users (Blummer & Kenton, 2014). Information literacy essentially seems to enable us to efficiently process all types of information content (Badke, 2010), thus counterbalancing IO. Apparently, it is at the micro-level where information literacy can be used as an efficient means of managing IO.

Closely allied to IO is *personal information management* (PIM) which is embedded in the PIC mentioned above (See page 80). The PIC model is made up of a pyramid comprising several layers. In this pyramid, information literacy occupies the middle layer, located above the elementary level which relates exclusively to skills, competencies, and abilities. Data literacy, which was mentioned earlier, can be placed on the same level as information literacy, that is, it can occupy the middle layer, located above the elementary level which relates exclusively to individual competencies (Gendina, 2008; Karvalics, 2013).

The re-evaluation of the PIC is a result of simultaneous developments in a number of fields. These fields are technological, such as the sprawl of mobile tools and the design of the network architecture as a *personal area network*. They appear in the economy as personal relationships with the consumers, the personification of the products, and following the online behavior of the users for data mining. An example of the developments in culture is that we are becoming culture producers or *prosumers*. In the field of politics, we witness the process of empowerment and the evolving de-institutionalization. Privacy and transparency laws make the public sphere visible and partly controllable.

Characterizing the novelties of the conceptual innovations, let us review the list of the most featured fields in the PIC:

- *Personal information space* denotes a progressively broadening cloud of discretely composed contents, personalized information services, and information processing tools, including tools that are wearable.
- *Personal learning environments* are more open, student-centered, personal task-focused frameworks than the earlier learning management systems (LMS). Clients can manage the content they produce, write blogs and build personal portfolios. If the goal is integrating or sharing personal files and documents, there are many special tools for structured content management, such as *personal wikis*.[3]
- If we are talking about the mid- and long-term preservation and retrieval of these contents, the number of possibilities are countless to get down and apply the new tools of *personal digital archiving* (Marshall, 2008).
- Second-generation personal assistant platforms, *personal digital secretaries*, are an attempt to simplify the multi-channel interface environments with a striking means of differentiation.
- All the above-mentioned solutions can serve *personal productivity improvement* using software tools, complex applications, and involved experts. The progenitors, called *personal network management (PNM)* tools, could successfully invigorate after the explosion of social media networks and platforms. It was also inevitable that management science would identify separate fields for PIM and *personal knowledge management* (Frand & Hixon, 1999).
- A more comprehensive approach, *personal knowledge governance*, has already appeared, providing a strategic foreground to the digital support of personal development.

In the discourse started with PIM, the practice of and the training in professional skills are needed "to process the information, save time, and work more effectively" (Etzel & Thomas, 1999) in the organizational (business) environment—in other words: how do we manage the constantly and rapidly changing personal information technologies (hardware and software components, methods, services, etc.) at work. Later (Jones, 2007) and more recently (Jones & Marchionini, 2011) William Jones has started to broaden the definition by affirming that PIM is "the practice and study of the activities people perform to acquire, organize, maintain, and retrieve information

[3]http://en.wikipedia.org/wiki/Personal_wiki.

for everyday use." He elevates this onto a more general level by declaring that PIM is about taking charge of the information in our lives.

The organization of information can be interpreted differently, if we examine the recommendations of the American Library Association for information literacy (ALA, 1989). As is well known, IL begins with recognizing the need for information, and then identifying, finding, and evaluating it. The fourth step of the process is organizing information. We may think that this step is identical with the role that the library can play in organizing information (often called classification and indexing). This role, i.e., knowledge organization, is defined by Dahlberg (2006) as "... the science of structuring and systematically arranging knowledge units (concepts) according to their inherent knowledge elements (characteristics) and the application of concepts and classes of concepts ordered by this way for the assignment of the worthwhile contents of referents (objects and subjects) of all kinds." However, organizing information is much more similar to the complex actions and processes that take place in a library. This means that it is not limited to organizing, but encompasses collecting and preserving information, as well as giving access to it, throughout this process. Thus, the principal difference between the library's activities and PIM is that personal collections are in the possession of the users, who "give access" to themselves, being *personal* in the strict sense of the word.

In a PIM framework, the information life cycle of personal documents is managed in an individual's own collection, which is informal, diverse, and expanding, and is created or acquired and accumulated by individuals in the course of their personal lives, and belongs to them, rather than to their institutions or other places of work (Williams, Leighton John, & Rowland, 2009).

Taylor (1968) reminds us that information seeking may also involve the consultation of personal files, which can be understood to refer to a domestic collection of books and other print documents (Shenton, 2009). A subjective but perfectly appropriate remark about his own (personal) library by Manguel (2008) can be generalized as follows. Most people have no catalog in their libraries. They usually know the position of the books by recalling the library's layout as they have placed the books on the shelves themselves. In the digital environment, the situation is different as personal libraries also may be overwhelmed by information, especially in the form of computer files. This may cause problems, though not in regard to storage space, as in the case of print books as mentioned by Manguel (2008). The apparently preferred format for maintaining personal collections is the PDF as new items can be efficiently added to such collections (Newman & Sack, 2013).

PIM refers to the practice and study of the activities performed in order to acquire, organize, maintain, and retrieve information for everyday use, in the right form and quality (Jones & Maier, 2003). PIM allows users to organize information, to store it for future use with the help of their own systems. PIM tools offer solutions that can help to decrease the fragmentation in our information environment caused by the diversity of formats, applications, and tools (Franganillo, 2009). As mentioned earlier, diversity is one of the sources of IO, thus the surge of interest in PIM shows that it is one of the necessary reactions to it. Put differently, PIM is about the handling of information, stored on or available through analogue and digital tools, that is the organization of our personal information environment (Nagy, 2010). According to Bruce, Jones, and Dumais (2004), PIM emerges from the building, managing, and using of a personal information collection, which is a personalized subset of the information world used when we are faced with information needs. It can be defined as the space where we turn to first when we need information to do a task or pursue an interest. It is an organic and dynamic personal construct that consists of information sources and channels, cultivated and organized over time and in response to different stimuli.

The origins of PIM go back to early times. We can see this in an analogue form that is still in use: taking notes on paper in an ordered form, usually on index cards.

Both the definitions and this short historical overview show that PIM is a positively genuine personal occupation which is performed individually, mainly by professionals. Even if it has origins in the past, the interest in PIM has grown as a consequence of IO. This idea is supported by some definitions and approaches to PIM. For example, Franganillo (2009) states that from the set of information that is accessible, individuals create a subset of personal information which can be used when necessary. To achieve this, they apply their own, personal scheme. The fact that PIM can help in retrieving information that has been forgotten underlines its individual nature. We can also speak about personal information space, which is an abstract domain that encompasses all pieces of information that are under the control of an individual (Franganillo, 2009).

Among the variables of PIM identified by Bergman (2013), of prime interest is the organization of information. PIM is one of the answers to the problem of the availability of large quantities of documents in digital form and the technical ability to handle them with relative ease. It is of secondary concern that their preservation depends on the actual needs of the user thus it is far from obligatory for them. Overall, this is why, when we speak about PIM, the word *personal* receives a strong emphasis.

According to Bruce, Jones, and Dumais (2004), PIM materializes in building, managing, and using a personal information collection, which is a personalized subset of the information world that we use when we are faced with information needs. It can be defined as the space which we turn to first when we need information to do a task or pursue an interest. It is an organic and dynamic personal construct that consists of information sources and channels, cultivated and organized over time and in response to different stimuli.

Mioduser, Nachmias, and Forkosh-Baruch (2009) call for seven technology-related literacies for the knowledge society. One is PIM literacy, which is applied by individuals when storing their information items in order to retrieve them later. Whether PIM literacy is a separate literacy is difficult to decide. In any event, it requires skills and abilities which are derived from information literacy.

In addition to this, there is personal knowledge management, qualified by Pauleen and Gorman (2011) as a way of coping with complex environmental changes and developments as well as a form of sophisticated career and life management. It is an emerging concept that focuses not only on the importance of individual growth and learning, but on the technology and management processes which have been traditionally associated with organizational KM.

PKM is not directly connected to IO, at least not to such an extent as PIM. The individual also plays a different role in it, firstly because of PKM's close connection to the corporate world as an extension of KM. If we accept the definition of Brophy, that KM "is the process of creating and managing the conditions for the transfer and the use of knowledge" (Brophy, 2001, p. 36), this becomes clear. Besides KM, cognitive psychology, philosophy, and management science play a role. Its focus is on helping individuals to be more effective in personal, organizational, and social environments (Pauleen, 2009).

While the traditional view of KM is primarily concerned with managing organizational knowledge (including the knowledge that individuals possess), PKM is "personal inquiry"—the quest to find, connect, learn, and explore (Clemente & Pollara, 2005).

In the light of the ACRL Information Literacy Standards, PIM strategies gain especial weight, because they can help researchers to become aware of their information decisions and needs more explicitly. While citation management software products (often provided by libraries) are useful for managing personal collections, libraries play a critical role in supporting the development of related strategies as librarians have the expertise and can provide advice on how information can be organized so as to better organize researchers' personal collections (Exner, 2014).

Nolin (2013) identified areas of potential research support which have not been covered by traditional academic librarians or related professionals. One of these is the problem of overload with regard to both tasks and tools. However, if there is a lack of professional support, researchers may not utilize personalized digital research tools properly, thus they are unable to ease the burden of IO. To optimize researchers' performance, personalized meta-services are required that match individual research practices with appropriate digital tools, based on a regular a dialog between researchers and librarians and thus fine-tuned to researchers' personal preferences. Such services have to be based on using information literacy tools and services.

Usually, researchers, especially in the humanities, aggregate vast quantities of information into their personal research collections. Their information needs dictate that this information must be managed in order to make proper use of it.

Gathering this information is accompanied by decisions to keep or discard a given an item. The decision to keep information has at least two steps. The first is to decide whether the information is useful. If the given piece is judged to be useful, decisions have to be made in what format (print, electronic, or both) to keep it, where to keep it, and how to structure or classify it, taking into consideration its relationship to other items.

Positive decisions about keeping information are followed by creating some sort of personal information space, where recognition and retrieval have to be taken care of. The latter is especially important because most researchers "own" more objects than they can remember.

Personal research information collections differ from other personal information collections by the fact that they come into existence by a conscious effort to control the quantity of incoming information and the way in which it is organized (Bussert, Chiang, & Tancheva, 2011).

# CHAPTER 3

# Transformations of Information Literacy: From Bookshelves to the Web 2.0

As explained in previous chapters, information literacy (IL) is an extensively discussed, researched, and commonly accepted concept, especially in the library and information science (LIS) field. Hardly any information professional would dispute its importance. The same claim can be made for theoretical reflections on IL, in particular when it comes to the interpretation of IL in the context of research processes. Even first characterizations of IL consider the concept as integral to and essential for the research process (Eisenberg & Berkowitz, 1990). Later writings not only highlighted the central position of IL in the context of research (Kuhlthau, 1993) but also described IL as being embedded in the very principles and processes of science (Julien & Barker, 2009).

Nevertheless, before attaining a definitional consensus and wide acceptance of its connectedness to research processes, IL went through a long-lasting process of growth in theoretical and applied understanding characterized by numerous terminological and conceptual contradictions during the 1990s and early 2000s (Arp & Doodard, 2002; Marcum, 2002; Shapiro & Hughes, 1996; Snavely & Cooper, 1997).

Nevertheless, after numerous definitional proposals and re-examinations of the concept, the 2000s led to the consensus that IL is characterized more by convergence than by divergence (Owusu-Ansah, 2003) and was allowed to address common ground and conceptual certainty (Owusu-Ansah, 2005). As expected in the case of multidimensional and context-bound concepts like IL, different definitions have been proposed and different components have been highlighted.

Despite the variety in approaches to defining IL, a thorough analysis reveals that there is a conceptual core which characterizes all IL definitions, regardless of the domain from which they emerged or to which they are applied. This core encapsulates the abilities to access, evaluate, and use

*Research 2.0 and the Future of Information Literacy*

information. Essentially, IL provides individuals with a necessary framework for gathering, interpreting, evaluating, and using information. This basic nucleus is clearly defined and documented in many widely accepted definitions, publications, and statements (e.g., ACRL, 2000; ALA, 1989; ANZIIL, 2004; UNESCO, 2003).

However, quite recently, attempts to re-examine and revisit the concept emerged and led to propositions to abandon or replace it with new and more attractive kinds of "21st century literacies" such as transliteracy, metaliteracy, participatory literacy, etc. (Mackey & Jacobson, 2011). Our earlier argument in the subsection on literacies beyond IL clearly shows this development.

It comes as no surprise that such attempts intensified with the advent of Web 2.0 and social media, since IL, throughout its development, has changed its scope and focus in parallel with changes in the information environment. This causal relationship was acknowledged by many authors, either explicitly or implicitly (Farkas, 2011; Markless, 2009; Shapiro & Hughes, 1996; Špiranec & Banek Zorica, 2010; Sundin, 2008; Tuominen, 2007). This development can be traced by analyzing writings that deal with the history of IL.

Firstly, historical reviews have pointed out that IL is an abstract and conceptually vague term, which stems from the fact that historical meanings of both literacy and information diffuse by themselves (Behrens, 1994). In the same vein, Tyner (1998, p. 97) wrote:

*Information literacy is an abstract concept. As a metaphor, it is a neatly packaged, imaginative and descriptive phrase that is not literally applicable or interpretable, employing something more qualitative and diffuse than is evident in the historical meaning of both literacy and information.*

Nevertheless, despite the obvious conceptual vagueness, the first uses of the term were already based on straightforward pragmatic descriptions of who may be called information literate, which were first articulated (as mentioned before) by Zurkowski (1974) and 2 years later by Burchinal (1976). Both IL pioneers have stressed the aspect of using information for problem solving and decision-making. In addition, both statements clearly link IL to information, information tools, and sources. More precisely, what could be perceived as the main trigger for introducing IL was the rising complexity of information handling, which was a result of the exponential growth in the amount of information available. For instance, Zurkowski (1974) explicitly referred to the emergence of "information banks, electronic databases and machine-readable files, and the need to prepare for imminent changes in the informational environment."

The trend of commenting on IL developments through the lens of technological changes in the information environment continued in the 1980s (Behrens, 1994). Thus, the first IL statements have a strong technological stance, in which the development of and need for IL is brought into connection with technological transformations of information tools and sources.

Although later writings about IL continued to pinpoint technological changes as a major impulse in its development, using a solely technological lens would offer a very limited interpretational framework. In the process of conceptual formulation, we can see how IL interpretations have been differentiated more and more from technological literacy.

Representative in this regard are the writings of Shapiro and Hughes, who define the IL spectrum in the range from knowing how to use a computer and access information, to a critical reflection on the nature of information itself, its technical, social, and cultural infrastructure, and the impact it has on the environment (Shapiro & Hughes, 1996).

Thus, the development of IL is conditioned not only by changes in technology, but generally, by changes in the information environment, which certainly offers a more holistic perspective for interpreting the development of and transformations in IL. It was the information environment, and not technology *per se*, that was singled out by Talja and Lloyd (2010, p. X) as a key driver of IL development:

> As literacy originated from text-based information environments, so too did information literacy as a teaching project, stimulated especially by the availability of reference databases and other finding aids in libraries. Information literacy was first understood as 'systematic research skills' and, more specifically, 'library-based research'; the term was used initially used in connection with bibliographic instruction.

Bawden (2014, pp. 14–15) argued in the same vein that technology-focused IL conceptualizations are rather narrow, and proposed to regard IL as "a conceptual understanding of, and ability to adapt to, changing information environments/ecologies/contexts," a definition that has the promise of remaining stable and sensible over time.

That IL was never conceived as a wholly technical project was stressed by Whitworth (2014, p. 56), who cited IL pioneers like Zurkowski, Burchinal, and Hamelink, who, to varying degrees, differentiated IL from IS (information systems) by introducing a human element, which does not lend itself to systematization, that is

> seeing people not as akin to components in a machine or information system, but as manifesting essential aspects of knowledge formation which cannot be systematised.

The augmentation of the meaning of IL, compared with earlier conceptualizations, began in the late 1980s (Behrens, 1994). The definitions of the 1970s had emphasized the fact that IL required a new set of skills for the utilization of information and its access tools, and that the use or application of the information located was intended for problem solving.

This initial construct was enriched during the 1980s in several ways. Among others, the definitions widened their focus from the procedural and skills-oriented towards affective dimensions (e.g., awareness of information need, willingness to use information, appreciation of the value of information). Furthermore, they stressed the importance of higher-order critical skills. Libraries were recognized as important but not exclusive access points to information, and various concepts such as independent learning, lifelong learning, citizenship, etc. came into play.

The trend of augmentation in the meaning of IL certainly continued in the 1990s and after 2000, with the result that other different literacy types have entered the discourse in order to cover genuinely complex and changing sets of information-related issues and problems to be mapped.

The conceptual enrichment described can be interpreted as a form of development, but it can also be seen as a transformation and widening of core IL attributes. From a bird's eye view, the variety of different factors that have contributed to the transformations of IL may be analyzed on theoretical and practical levels.

At the level of practice, transformations in the IL domain can be interpreted in the light of an evolution from bibliographic instruction (BI) and traditional conceptualizations of user education and library instruction to IL, and subsequent shifts in IL which have brought about new themes and concepts to be covered in IL instruction.

On the theoretical level, the variety of factors that have contributed to transformations in IL can be derived from the changing perspectives and frameworks in education and information and library science. Both levels will be discussed in the remainder of this chapter.

## THE PRACTICAL LEVEL: FROM BIBLIOGRAPHIC INSTRUCTION TO IL

IL is rooted in library user education, that is—to use the concept that dominates the literature of US provenance—it is rooted in BI. Such forms of library instruction were focused on teaching students the tools, resources, and strategies for using a specific library's information resources. IL differs from this kind of library-focused instruction in a range of its attributes, principally in the shift of its focus on tools and the methods of using them toward concepts and problems, and moving from isolated instruction toward teacher–librarian partnerships.

In general, the concept of IL is seen as advancing from the practice of teaching tool-based skills toward teaching competencies that are applicable in various diverse environments. In other words, BI, as a predecessor of IL, was clearly oriented at print-based environments, the book and bookshelf paradigm. Gibson (2008) commented on such an orientation by stressing that the BI movement achieved considerable success in responding to library assignments. Such commentaries highlight the book-oriented paradigm and also critique BI for being reactive, limited, place-bound, and constrained in terms of wider impact.

IL transcends this book- and library-oriented paradigm, as pointed out by Owusu-Ansah (2004, p. 5), who declares that "IL goes beyond teaching mainly retrieval skills, to addressing a more total research environment in the confuse of finding and using information." This means that—whereas BI provided a limited experience with the information universe—IL seeks to traverse its full length and breadth.

Saunders (2011, p. 5) has linked the transformations in IL with changes in the curriculum:

> Historically, BI seems to have focussed largely on skills-based instruction. As instruction shifts to dealing with online resources, students need to learn how to find and access a more expansive variety of information and to develop the transferable and critical thinking skills of evaluation and synthesis of information.

The transition from BI to IL was also described by Talja and Lloyd (2010, p. X):

> The term was initially used in connection with bibliographic instruction… In the 1990s, information literacy became more widely understood as a concept. The information literacy concept was first, therefore tightly intertwined with library tools and resources, reflecting the skills that librarians possessed in these areas. Later this link loosened and information literacy became synonymous with searching skills, especially systematic keyword searching and the application of Boolean operators. When information literacy became linked with information society discourses, it came to mean the abilities needed for lifelong learning and the skills of learning to learn.

When referring to the differences between and shifts from BI to IL, Gilton (2011) states that IL completes and fulfills the potential and work of BI. It has more of a theoretical base, it promotes lifelong learning, it deals with information wherever it is, and it emphasizes determining information needs and evaluating and using information as well as finding it. While traditional BI was somewhat book- and library-based, IL is tied more to electronic information and computers.

Brevik (1989) and Rader (1990) suggested that BI was a forerunner to IL and that most BI programs evolved into IL programs. However, Rader and Coons (1992, p. 118) stress the differences between them when they state:

> Information literacy is not a synonym for bibliographic instruction ... Information literacy adds another dimension by representing a broader approach and offering the opportunity to produce students who understand the importance of information and who have the competence to locate, evaluate and manage it.

The initial conceptions and early transformations of IL, described above, show that shifts in IL are closely related to changes in the information environment, which traverse a purely library-focused, analogue, and ordered information world and the more fuzzy world of digital information. This process started within end-user education, that is, bibliographic or library instruction programs which in their early stages focused on teaching users how to make the most effective use of the library, the library system, or the resources available within the library.

The list of potential objects of instruction was largely uniform. Apart from the resources and systems that were accessible within the library (OPACs, card catalogs, the library shelves, classification schemes, reference books, etc.), this list gradually started to include information structures that were not exclusively accessible within library institutions and did not strictly belong to the domain of libraries (academic databases, the Web).

This broadening marked the movement toward IL, which widened its focus by breaking out of the library walls and attempting to include as many places that make up our information universe as possible.

Without a doubt, the process of transformation did not stop with the Web. New information environments brought about new facets of IL and enriched and widened the concept further. Farkas (2011) has recognized three phases in the evolution of the concept:

- library-focused user education;
- Internet-focused IL education;
- IL in the Web 2.0 era.

The first phase was the result of the predominantly print-based environment. The ultimate aim of IL in this phase was to educate the user in finding information in print resources. Therefore, educational practices concentrated on tools available in the library to augment the processes of locating, accessing, and finding information (i.e., how to use the library catalog, how to use bibliographies, etc.).

The advent of the Internet shifted the focus of IL in terms of practice and research. Therefore, this phase can be considered the second in the evolution of the concept. Farkas (2011) describes this phase as skills-oriented, in recognition of the focus on procedural skills that can be applied in closed and highly structured systems like academic databases (the distinction between basic and advanced search, what options to use in a particular case, how to use the thesaurus, etc.).

With the emergence of Web 2.0, there has again been a shift in how information flows online that is characterized by less predictability, more complex information structures, socially produced information, and the need for a stronger focus on evaluation that is more nuanced and sophisticated.

Thus, contemporary information environments are characterized by the third, Web 2.0 and social media-oriented, phase. Therefore, it makes sense to shift the focus of IL again, this time toward evaluation that is much more complex and layered than it was before, as well as toward socially and community-oriented dimensions of IL.

Within such an environment, IL needs to recognize that information and knowledge are socially produced and distributed. In the words of Gibson (2008), the landscape with which students must now contend has multiple dimensions: of surface (the surface Web), of depth (the deep Web), of temporality (with accelerated information cycles, changing paradigms of publishing such as the open access models, and other phenomena), and of mode of representation (graphical representations, data sets, simulations, tutorials, etc.). This landscape presents many vexations (but also opportunities) that IL should reflect upon.

## THEORETICAL PERSPECTIVES INFLUENCING SHIFTS IN IL

As described in the previous section, from the initial definitions in the 1970s, IL was conceived more broadly. It also became more distinct from bibliographic instruction. This process was accompanied by the provision of stronger theoretical frameworks and the anchoring of IL within these theoretical frameworks.

A vital factor that reinforced a stronger theoretical anchor for IL was education. This comes as no surprise, since education is fundamentally information-based. According to Eisenberg (2008), every aspect of learning and teaching requires the gathering, processing, and communication of information.

A strong correlation between education and IL is well expressed through often cited statements, such as "information literacy as a catalyst for educational change" (Bruce, 2004) or "information literacy as a prerequisite for lifelong learning," which are commonly used in explaining and promoting the concept.

The frequently cited final report that was issued by the ALA Presidential Committee on IL in 1989 (ALA, 1989) explicitly highlights the link between IL and learning.

Milestones during the 1970s and 1980s in the earlier bibliographical instruction movement advanced the emerging IL agenda by incorporating theoretical shifts in education and learning, in particular, shifts from behavior- and skills-based approaches to cognitive ones.

According to Saunders (2011, p. 3), a changing pedagogy was the starting point for the development of IL and changes in higher education in general. A closer look reveals that the rationale behind those curriculum changes may be interpreted in the light of transformations in the learning environment, in particular in relation to learning resources. For example, early American colleges and universities generally applied a fixed classical curriculum, relying almost exclusively on assigned reading from textbooks.

With the expansions of curricula, collections became more complicated, which created the need to educate patrons in how to use them (Lorenzen, 2001; Saunders, 2011). Therefore, IL can be perceived as a corollary of resource-based learning and a requisite for lifelong learning.

Similar assertions can be found in Wilkinson (2000), who saw an increasing need for resource-based education which multiplies the required resources and complicates access and evaluation, thus intensifying the need for IL. Eisenberg (2008) also draws the attention to the changes and transformations in learning resources which require the widening and intensifying of IL approaches. He explains that in the past there was a reliance on one primary information resource: the textbook, which is rapidly changing to a substantial extent due to the explosion in information technology and networked information. Hence, changes in education, new learning environments, and new learning theories have contributed to the crystallization of concepts in the IL discourse.

The core idea behind the IL–education feedback loop that has been described is that education is not a transfer of information and knowledge but a process that involves creation, reflection, and critical awareness. Hence, the ability to interact meaningfully with a wealth of information is deemed important for successful learning.

This interrelation became even more evident when the basic building blocks of learning process, that is, educational resources and technologies, started to change substantially. With the introduction and extensive use of digital information in classrooms, which is characterized by pluralism, controversy, autonomy, fluidity, replicability, and accessibility as opposed to uniqueness, reliability, authenticity, and control commonly associated with the traditional paper-based resources, the need for IL in the learning process became more than apparent (Špiranec & Banek Zorica, 2010).

One of the first authors to expand the discussion of resource-based learning to include questions of ideology and transformative learning was Kapitzke (2003). She claimed that the linear and hierarchical approaches to thinking and learning are inadequate for the webbed cyberspace of information, and that users in the context of an information glut do not spend their time so much with searching but with interpreting, filtering, and value-adding by creating relationships among ideas.

She proposes a shift from conventional IL approaches which view knowledge as facts, propositions, or skills that are located in the heads of individual learners. It is more appropriate and useful to consider knowledge and learning as socially distributed across people and technology, far beyond individual minds and bodies. Kapitzke challenges older process-based models that are limited by their orientation to a print culture and its language of cognitive science. As explained by Riddle (2010, p. 136):

*traditional information literacy as a pedagogy is objective and externalized, its core values (information, facts, knowledge) reified into book collections and databases, and its methodology instrumental. A transformative literacy practice, on the other hand, posits what we call knowledge and information as always culturally mediated, socially constructed, and especially now through digital technology, decidedly fragmented and non-linear.*

This turn, which fosters understanding about issues regarding ideology or authority, might be perceived as a new evolutionary stage for IL. These arguments generally illustrate how IL gained a foothold in education by the very transformation of information sources and learning environments. Nonetheless, authors like Markless (2009) or Špiranec and Banek Zorica (2010) are more specific in this regard, claiming that it was not until the emergence of Web 2.0 and social media that more profound transformations and changes in the conceptualization of IL actually took place.

According to Markless (2009, p. 32), with the advent of the World Wide Web as a vehicle for storing and delivering information, "students began to work with larger amounts of information, much of it of questionable quality, but this did not result in fundamental changes in the way they learned.

Existing models of information literacy seemed as relevant to electronic as to print-based resources." Although information behavior models changed, being less linear in their nature, IL approaches were more or less the same, focusing on an ordered sequence of skills to be transmitted to students.

Web 2.0 brings the usefulness of such approaches into question. Transformations are needed since the ordered, systematic, and sequential approaches implicit in many IL frameworks are a reflection of the book-oriented, print-based culture, which cannot be transferred to the Web 2.0 environment since the learner is less likely to involve systematic information seeking.

As Markless has pointed out, Web 2.0's disregard for authority, hierarchy, and order and its focus on the voice of the individual and on ever-changing constructed groups, supports nonlinear information behavior, clicking, zapping, etc. Finding information is less likely to involve systematic information seeking than, for example, interest groups, peer Web pages, or social bookmarking, and any contemporary approach to IL must consider how to accommodate and reflect these changes.

The shifts in IL analyzed above are conceptualized by using an educational lens, but also involve theoretical strands from the larger LIS field, namely, information seeking and information behavior. Williamson et al. (2007) have addressed this connection by stressing that due to the rapid uptake of information and communication technology, understanding the ways in which information seeking has changed over the past decade is crucial to gaining a picture of how IL may also be changing in the electronic age.

There is clearly a strong linkage between information-seeking behavior and IL, and tracing different perspectives in information seeking reveals shifting perspectives in IL as well. Transformations in IL brought about changing perspectives in information-seeking point to the movement between different epistemological camps, such as the behaviorist, cognitive, constructionist, relational, etc.

According to Julien and Williamson (2011), the work of authors such as Tuominen et al. (2005), Elmborg (2006), and Lloyd (2006, 2007) promoted constructionist approaches to IL research as superior to those associated with constructivist or cognitive perspectives. Collectively, such writings inspired by constructionist approaches suggest that IL is influenced by complex contextual, social, and cultural factors.

Constructionist approaches represent a clear turn from the neutral and linear view of skills deployment that has been questioned by other authors in information science and IL as well (Bawden & Robinson, 2009; Marcum, 2002; Markless, 2009; Webber & Johnston, 2000).

Authors such as Kuhlthau or Bruce view IL as a continuous activity rather than a series of on–off information searches, while Bruce specifically sees IL as something that is nonlinear, multifaceted, and rooted in the general process of learning rather than the library specifically (Whitworth, 2014).

Linear and neutral approaches may be to some extent suitable for analyzing and conceptualizing IL in print and analog environments, but the Web environment and even more contemporary participatory environments challenge any linear premises of information behavior. From the many models reflecting an altered approach to information seeking and behavior, we will present a few that mark the departure from defining information behavior in a linear manner consisting of stages and interactive activities, foremost in the light of changes in the information environment.

One such model reflecting changes in the information environment is Bates' berry-picking model (Bates, 1989), which is deemed to be much closer to the way that people actually seek information. In this model, an individual is not assumed to understand the full nature of the problem or question for which he or she is seeking information, but is instead imagined to have only a piece of it: a term, a relevant detail, a vague concept.

The individual uses this piece of information to find another piece of information, plucking it from the Web or the library shelf as if it were a berry on a branch. It is then this piece of information, which could be anything from a peer-reviewed journal article to a Wikipedia entry, which provides enough additional illumination of the question to lead the individual further. The individual's quest for information is thus described as taking place a bit at a time, the nature of their search constantly evolving as their personal information store grows like a collection of berries in a bucket (Williams, 2007).

Another author who argues for abandoning linear approaches is Foster (2004). His nonlinear or nonsequential model takes advantage of technological developments that allow individuals to make choices and navigate between options. The framework is designed for students to construct their own problem-solving approaches to finding and using information.

The impact of context on learning should lead students to make different choices depending on the nature of the task they are addressing. The basic assumption of this model is to encourage students to stop seeing research and related assignments as a process of collecting information and instead to see it in terms of forming their own perspectives. In this way, Foster contrasted his own model with earlier models of information-seeking behavior and offered a potential guide for a reinterpretation of information-seeking behavior as a dynamic flowing holistic process.

Both Bates and Foster were obviously inspired by the Web, whose entire structure of documents linking to one another lends itself to a nonlinear interpretation of information behavior. These two models illustrate conceptual shifts of information (seeking) behavior and complementary shifts in IL.

Both models also represent an alternative to the dominant standard-based or process-driven models like the ACRL IL competency standards for higher education (2000), or the Big Six (Eisenberg & Berkowitz, 1990) which consists of a list of skills and attributes and a series of steps and stages that the individual progresses through in a linear manner. (Both have been mentioned previously.)

A detailed overview of different shifting approaches to IL, inspired by transformations in information environments and changing perspectives in information behavior as described above, has been provided by Sundin (2008). He identified four main approaches to IL and named them the source approach, the behavioral approach, the process approach, and the communication approach.

The source approach to IL focuses on information sources and bibliographical tools. This approach corresponds to what has often been described as system orientation, which takes the information system and not the user as its point of departure.

While the main teaching interests in the behavioral approach are still bibliographical tools and information sources, this approach provides a generalized structure for information seeking which users can apply in various situations, practices, and contexts.

In the process approach, the different aspects of information seeking are presented from the perspective of the user, focusing on how users experience information seeking and create meaning. This approach corresponds to user-oriented research. It is based on the constructivist view of information seeking.

Finally, the communication approach emphasizes the social and communicative aspects of information processes, which are context-sensitive. Hence, various kinds of information-seeking practices are understood within the context in which they are carried out.

The communication approach stresses the relation between cognitive authority and source evaluation as well as the significance of social navigation. (More details on cognitive authority can be found in the subsection on digital literacy.) The focus of this approach largely consists of an awareness of the importance of understanding the socio-cultural conditions for the production, mediation, and consumption of information. Sundin's research and his construction of an empirical framework have resulted in the drawing of an outline of the developmental stages of IL, the beginnings of which are closely related to user education with a marked resource orientation.

The last phase identified by Sundin is the communication phase, which has emerged from new multimodal and socially mediated information landscapes. The features of the communication phase are compatible with the attributes of information environments that emerged from the Web 2.0 environment and indicate shifts in IL conceptions.

When discussing shifting theoretical perspectives in IL, it is important to reflect upon the different conceptual lenses that have framed IL discourses:

- generic skills (behavioral) lens;
- situative and social practice (socio-cultural) lens;
- the transformative (critical) lens (Lupton & Bruce, 2010, p. 4).

Although these different conceptual lenses cannot be perceived in a sequential manner where one theoretical perspective has transformed into the next, they imply a shifting view of what literacy is, and also reflect upon transformations in the information environment. Lupton and Bruce (2010, p. 5) have pointed out that in the first generic perspective, literacy is regarded as a discrete set of skills to be learned by individuals; it is neutral, objective, text-based, apolitical, reproductive, standardized, and universal. In the second, situated and social perspective, literacy is contextual, authentic, collaborative, and participatory, while the third transformative perspective goes beyond socio-cultural practices by being concerned with emancipatory processes that challenge the status quo to effect social change. Here, literacy can be considered as critical, consciousness-raising, empowering, political, etc.

The first, behavioral and generic skills perspective obviously reflects an ordered, centrally managed and document-centric information universe, while the situational, social, and critical perspective takes into account user-centered and participatory approaches with new frontiers of information creation, organization, dissemination, services, and provision.

Generic and behavioral approaches, manifested in IL standards and models (e.g., ACRL, 2000), have generally neglected the social and collective dimensions of IL by predominantly considering and dealing with documents.

The center of information activities and processes within such IL approaches are documents, document-like objects, or collections that have to be searched, accessed, evaluated, used, etc. The user is perceived as an individual working with documents or information sources which, at least on a theoretical level, create straightforward relationships in the form 1–to–1 (one user—one document) or 1-to-many (one user—many documents or information sources).

However, contemporary information environments function quite differently. Users are discovering, evaluating, using, and producing information within networks and communities. Other humans, peers, and communities—in collaborative and participative Web 2.0 environments more than ever—function as information sources, filters, digesters, and co-creators of information.

Therefore, instead of being conceptualized as an individual competence, IL in contemporary environments is intrinsically social and participative, as conceived in the situational, social practice paradigm.

The critical turn in IL entails moving IL from the confines of the library to the arenas of language use, social dimensions, and multimodal information. This kind of critical information curriculum and pedagogy reframes conventional notions of text, knowledge, and authority (Kapitzke, 2001). Related issues were mentioned previously in the subsection on the reading and writing context of IL.

Swanson (2004) has contributed to the discussion on critical IL by foregrounding the argument that IL is moving away from the print-based model, and that this move starts by giving students an understanding of information. Understanding entails the ability to make judgments about the information they find as they search. As Swanson (2004, p. 264) puts it, "Critical literacy pushes students toward self-reflection, interpretation, understanding, and ultimately action." Thus, the critical IL model is based on recognizing and choosing from the various types of information to meet information needs best, regardless of format.

That said, it becomes clear that in information environments based on participatory technologies and services, critical IL is of the utmost importance. Specifically, some features of contemporary environments, like the blurring of authority, which result from what Tuominen (2007) calls "the erosion of information context" require critical IL. In the era of print culture, the information context was based on textual permanence, unity, and identifiable authorship, and was therefore stable.

The appearance of the Web has already undermined that stability by the very nature of digital information, which may be easily modified, copied, and duplicated. Web 2.0 with its collaborative model of knowledge production and mash-up philosophy finally brought an end to the stability of information context by creating flat and fluid information spaces.

All this brings us to the conclusion that IL should have its focus on the critical understanding of the social origins of information and their importance in different practices. Of course, critical thinking and questioning was always at the core of the critical literacy agenda, even in the pre-web textual era, but the intricacies of contemporary information and knowledge production models have emphasized the need for critical perspectives. Evaluation of information or decision-making related to information should incorporate a wider critical perspective on any social, political, and economic ideology acting as the background behind that information and take into account the values and perspectives that are always present in the context of the generation of information and knowledge.

Shifting theoretical perspectives in IL imply that one potential subsequent shift should be mentioned. This shift from IL standards toward conceptually based frameworks is currently the subject of lively discussion, especially in the US-based literature and by professional associations. Such a shift can be seen if we follow the efforts to replace the Information Literacy Competency Standards in Higher Education (ACRL, 2000) by the emergent Framework for Information Literacy in Higher Education (ACRL, 2014b), which is currently under construction.

In the context of the theoretical perceptions (generic vs. situational vs. critical) described above, authors such as Lupton and Bruce (2010, p. 8) interpret standards as being more weighted to the generic perspective, with some elements of the situated perspective. Jacobs (2014, p. 194) argues that critical information literacy emerged, "in part, as a response to the limited and limiting approaches to competency-based information literacy and its emphasis on 'how-to' questions."

Kuhlthau (2013, p. 94) has stressed a number of different flaws associated with the Standards in that they are too "simplistic, positivist, one-right-answer for all" in their approach. Although standards are necessary in the course of the integration of IL into formal education, their major downside is a limited perception of IL as a neutral process which is entirely unaffected by any kind of social, political, or historical background (Špiranec & Banek Zorica, 2010, pp. 141–142).

Furthermore, the use of a set of standards as a framework significantly reduces the complex structure of competencies and knowledge to limited and isolated units (Webber & Johnston, 2000), and inevitably leads to over-systematization, the predominance of a certain form of generic rubric, and a decontextualized form of administrative paperwork which entirely disconnects IL from pedagogical theories (Jacobs, 2008). In criticizing the

Standards, Martin (2013, p. 116) takes technologies and the subsequent impact on information processes as a point of departure for understanding IL:

> *Many information literacy models were published before the creation of social media and open access platforms to create and disseminate information. Models, such as the ACRL standards, imply information is static and found in distinct units; however, today's information interactions are more fluid and collaborative. Furthermore new information containers (e-books, mobile apps and browsers) outdate some guidelines in the models. Even scholarly publishing changed with the advent of digital repositories, open source journals, and e-books. The emerging technologies not only changed how individuals interact with information, these technologies also empower individuals to become creators and disseminators of information.*

In a similar vein, Jacobs (2014, p. 194) argues that the Standards, on the whole, tend to position students as information consumers: they select, access, evaluate, incorporate, use, and understand information:

> *Beyond mentions of 'using' information, these standards rarely position students as information creators or as citizens with power and potential to shape, share, develop, preserve, and provide access to information today or in the future.*

This assertion suggests a move away from the standards and other formulaic approaches not only because of changes in the information ecosystem initiated by participative technologies but also because of the empowerment of users to change and transform realities, as implied in critical IL.

In the section, entitled *Literacies beyond information literacy* (that begins on page 84) we have already pointed out how important it is to produce texts that are valued in academia. While we put it into the context of academic literacy, nonetheless research has always gone beyond consuming information, and it is self-explanatory that one of researchers' main activities is publishing, that is, producing information.

## THE INFORMATION ENVIRONMENT AS A PRINCIPAL DRIVER OF IL TRANSFORMATIONS

The preceding discussion has portrayed the transformative nature of IL and illustrated that these transformations are multidimensional and can be interpreted on several levels. Transformations in IL were analyzed and characterized on a practical level, portraying the transformation from BI to IL. In discussing the theoretical levels, we depicted the transformations of learning environments and the transformations in information seeking and behavior models, as well as the transforming of theoretical perspectives in IL.

Still, when comparing both theoretical and practical aspects that have influenced IL transformations, it is possible to identify one driver that lies in the heart of both theoretical and practical aspects: the shifts in the information environment.

The central features of IL have always been influenced and determined by the current information environment. The concept itself appeared partly as the result of a growing heterogeneity and complexity of information, information resources, and information structures, as indicated by the shift from BI to IL.

IL reflects the characteristics and features of the information environment within which IL is conceived, researched, and put into action. For instance, when IL began to evolve as a concept, the information environment was predominantly print-based. This condition determined IL practices, programs, and research topics. When information began to flow online, IL practice and research underwent a transformation and changed its focus.

Several authors have commented on the evolution of IL in the context of changes in information environments (Farkas, 2012; Špiranec & Banek Zorica, 2010; Markless & Streatfield, 2009; Tuominen, 2007).

These writings testify that, with the growth in the complexity of the various information resources, the need for emphasizing evaluation, critical awareness, and selection became more evident and thus enabled the rise of IL.

The advent of the World Wide Web highlighted the need for evaluation and significantly widened the number of information genres and resources that needed to be taken into account, although the user was still a customer and a passive recipient of information (Špiranec & Banek Zorica, 2010), which is why the "rules of the game" were still the same. In such an environment, IL functions within the traditional model of knowledge conception, production, and use, and after a linear interpretation, one is able to arrive at the unified truth.

Epistemologically, it is considered that each phenomenon stems from a single "correct" assumption, and proper information paths and strategies have to be applied and preferred sources used in order to find the "right" and "best" information (Dede, 2008).

In the context of research and scholarly communication, the traditional model of knowledge conception is reflected in a central model where the scholar undergoes the process of peer review in the creation of new knowledge, following a set of methods and values in knowledge creation, use, and dissemination, which rely on predefined channels that define the research enterprise.

It was not until Web 2.0 and social media that this epistemology-wise ordered, linear, and controlled universe began to change. The traditional model is largely implicit in IL practices of demonstrating what is scholarly and what is not instead of being structured so as to acknowledge the existence of different and often conflicting versions of reality.

The exclusive focus on such a traditional model is problematic, since it relies on a linear and over-simplified trajectory of knowledge, which does not reflect the more varied, fuzzy, and decentralized features of contemporary research landscapes. According to Shanbhag (2006), the traditional model fails to convey the process of knowledge production as a continuous negotiation between different stakeholders in time and space.

On the other hand, by informing complexities of various knowledge domains, alternative models facilitate critical inquiry into multiple ways of thinking, learning, reasoning, and arriving at "the truth."

As opposed to traditional epistemological presumptions, IL, owing to its current environment, can no longer be conceived of as a black-and-white or strictly rules-driven process. Current information-solving or decision-making processes show that it is hardly possible to determine *a priori* the best information and resources that we want to use. A similar difficulty emerges in deciding the strategy to apply for solving a problem.

We cannot say either that formal communication channels are always better than informal ones. Thus, IL conceptualizations should move forward by abandoning the limited approaches of the present, manifest in the traditional knowledge model according to which there is only one right answer or path to a given answer. Instead, we have to offer an insight into the variety of complex layers of which our current information universe consists.

In summary, the theoretical and practical shifts discussed above illustrate that IL has undergone changes throughout its history in order to accommodate new realities within which IL is conceptualized, researched, and put into action.

The transformations first reflected the features prevailing in the analogue, print- and book-oriented environment, and shifted first in order to cope with the digital and networked, and then the socially coconstructed information environment.

In other words, IL within print-based environments has different functions and manifestations, and addresses different issues than in, for example, digital or collectively constructed environments. Print-based environments are much more stable, structured, and linear, whereas in digitized and Web

2.0 environments, information is decoupled not only from its material carrier, but equally from authority and sometimes trust.

In respect to this, issues such as credibility and authority, intellectual property, coping with information overload, problems in privacy, understanding publishing mechanisms, and gaining deeper understandings of contemporary information environments should become part of IL activities. When writing about new forms of scholarship in the context of social networks, Veletsianos and Kimmons (2012, p. 770) argue that these new forms:

> break away from norms of 20th century university scholarship with regard to fundamental epistemological questions regarding what knowledge is, how it is gained, how it is verified, how it is shared, and how it should be valued. These epistemological reframings of learning take form in scholarly practice in a variety of ways, but they are perhaps most noticeable in how scholars are increasingly beginning to question many heretofore non-negotiable artefacts of the 20th century scholarly world.

Besides particular artifacts such as peer review or online education, when thinking about social, participatory research and its challenges, the list of potential issues to be included in IL is far more extensive.

A central tenet in this context is to create meta-awareness of why a researcher sees what he sees when searching and finding scholarly knowledge, that is, to understand how new tools filter what a researcher is likely to find and access and how these tools establish new ways for knowledge to be organized and accessed. This includes a critical perspective of phenomena such as search engines, bibliometrics, altmetrics, open access, the organization of research data, copyright, digital publishing, etc. The list of potential issues may well be longer—and certainly will be longer as information environments, reinforced by media and technology developments, continue to change.

The comprehensive nature of IL, with its potential to reflect attributes of contemporary information environments continually, allows researchers to understand this changing nature, and not only adapt to it or act and react in it but also change and transform it.

# CHAPTER 4

# Conclusion: Shaping Forces, Future Challenges

In this book, we have examined the relationship between Research 2.0 and information literacy (IL) in a number of contexts. First of all, Research 2.0 itself was scrutinized. This was followed by an investigation of the nature of information literacy. It became clear that a number of issues addressed in this book have been identified as key trends that represent both opportunities and challenges to different stakeholders directly or indirectly involved in research processes.

In this chapter, we will concentrate on academic libraries as the primary and most stratified locus of IL in the context of research, although we think that the institutionalization of IL, its standardization, and prevailing library-centric perceptions, as epitomized by Johnston and Webber (2003), Lloyd and Williamson (2008), Lloyd (2011), Markless (2009), and Whitworth (2014), constrain the concept in many ways. This seems especially true in the light of contemporary transformations in information environments, where questions such as who has access to information, who controls it, how authority is distributed, how to participate in creating information and whether it is public or private, frame the concept, and obviously transcend a library-centric view.

Thus, although we will be focusing on academic libraries, we will not be discussing the relationship between IL and Research 2.0 from a purely functional, competency-based standpoint, but rather be interpreting it in the light of core values intrinsic to both concepts.

As discussed in the previous chapters, issues that determine future directions in academic libraries are as follows:
* increased migration to digital environments;
* new forms of scholarly communication;
* changes in accessing information, storing, retrieving, and using information;
* open access;
* new metrics of scholarly communication (Delaney & Bates, 2014).

*Research 2.0 and the Future of Information Literacy*
Copyright © 2016 Elsevier Ltd. All rights reserved.

However, we know that we have paid less attention to the work that needs to be done in academic libraries. We make up for this in the following pages by discussing some questions that require further explanation, even though they are not exclusively directed toward academic libraries. Accordingly, we will look at the roles and functions of the academic library that have to be fulfilled if librarians want to be of efficient help and support to researchers, working among changing circumstances. In doing this, we will give special attention to the effect that a data–intensive paradigm has on academic libraries. However, other issues, which are linked to the questions that have been discussed throughout this book, are also valid for this analysis.

The central idea behind Research 2.0 is to enable access to information, which is also a key tenet of IL initiatives. Open research, Research 2.0, and open access together are driven by the idea to facilitate the sharing of knowledge as a public good. Open access in particular is aimed at taking the control of knowledge resources away from commercial publishers and giving it back to researchers. A guiding principle of Research 2.0 is also increasing the efficiency of research that may then lead to higher returns on public investment (Neylon, 2011; Veletsianos & Kimmons, 2012). Without knowledge transfer, inequalities are quickly created, and political and economic power rapidly becomes concentrated in the hands of only a few at the expense of the public. Smart democracies can only progress when information is open and available to everyone and the OA movement is on its way to achieving this (Kelly & Autry, 2013). Such objectives very much fall into the spectrum of core IL values.

The last decade has brought changes in the way in which researchers discover and access information resources relevant to their research, create and manage information, and communicate their findings. These reconfigurations within the domains of research culture and scholarly communication have a direct impact on IL. The reason for this is quite obvious: research activities are based on basic competencies associated with finding, evaluating, and using information. However, the relationship also works the other way round in the sense that research practices may change as a result of their being affected by IL.

In our book, we have analyzed these correlative dimensions and argued that research is changing as a result of Web 2.0 developments and that IL for researchers in turn should also affect this interrelation. Although the conceptual core of IL is focused on finding, evaluating, and using (communicating) information, it rises to meet the challenges brought by the new information environments in which researchers act. This involves reconsidering the main themes and priorities of IL research acknowledging current social media and

Web 2.0 environments, with their problematic aspects of credibility, trust, seriousness, recognition, information overload, and so on. Therefore, it comes as no surprise that current studies indicate a slow uptake of Web 2.0 services in the domain of scientific research and observations about a marginal influence of Web 2.0 on the "scholarly ivory tower" are not unknown.

Let us confirm that information literacy designed for researchers is to a substantial extent identical with information literacy defined for the general public. On the other hand, a literacy perspective on scholarship focuses on the highly contextualized social meanings created by the producers, consumers, and communicators of the digital texts that are recognized as scholarship (Goodfellow, 2013). These producers, consumers, and communicators are the researchers whose needs are very close to those of faculty members and different categories of students, laid down in different frameworks of information literacy in higher education, named in the subsection that deals with definitions, declarations, and frameworks that are related to IL.

If we examine an operational definition of information literacy, originally designed for citizens of developing countries, that is, a different target group than that of researchers, we find elements which are relevant to the latter. This definition includes the different abilities of individuals and groups as follows:

- to be aware of why, how, and by whom information is created, communicated, and controlled, and how it contributes to the construction of knowledge;
- to understand when information can be used to improve their daily living or to contribute to the resolution of needs related to specific situations, such as at work or school;
- to know how to locate information and to critique its relevance and appropriateness to their context;
- to understand how to integrate relevant and appropriate information with what they already know to construct new knowledge that increases their capacity to improve their daily living or to resolve needs related to specific situations that have arisen (Dorner & Gorman, 2006).

In the pre-Internet era, it was natural to suppose that a researcher would be able to decide all the questions related to the provenance of information. Even more, in this regard, the degree of awareness among the general public seemed to be higher than today.

As to the second assertion in this definition, it is obvious that information literacy for researchers is not primarily meant to solve issues in their

daily lives, but a specific goal, that is, research. This also applies to construct-
ing knowledge by understanding how to integrate relevant and appropriate
information with previous knowledge.

Without wanting to repeat what we have said in this book, it is necessary
to affirm that a critical approach towards information has gained weight in
modern times. We hope that our argument has convincingly demonstrated
that a number of specific values and features pertaining to information literacy have been designed and offered to researchers.

In the progression from general approaches to those that are tailor-made,
we find the already mentioned *Seven Faces of Information Literacy in Higher
Education*, in which we want to highlight categories two, three, and four.
Category two focuses on the concept of information sources that seems to
be similar to the source approach described by Sundin (2008), as discussed
above. From this obvious approach, we make it clear that sources of information may also be people, and doing so is in accordance with the notable
role of informal communication for researchers that has been touched on
several times in this book. All three different orientations to the problem of
information retrieval appear to be present when researchers are involved in
the processes. In an ideal case, they know the information sources and their
structure. They use them flexibly, either independently or with the help of
an intermediary. Obviously, information literacy education is the potential
means to achieve this ideal.

In category three, information literacy is seen to be the execution of a
process. As Bruce puts it:

> *Essentially, information literacy is seen as the ability to confront novel situations,
> and to deal with those situations on the basis of being equipped with a process for
> finding and using the necessary information.*

> *Bruce (1997)*

A researcher' life is full of encounters with novel situations, thus information literacy should emphasize this aspect.

The substance of category four lies in the concept of information control that is closely connected to personal information management, irrespective of whether the control of information is established using filing
cabinets, computers, or someone's own brain. Information organization, in
this context, is about storing information and ensuring its easy retrieval as
well as bringing resources under the controlling influence of the user.[1]

[1] http://www.christinebruce.com.au/informed-learning/seven-faces-of-information-
literacy-in-higher-education/

Clearly, there is more to say about information literacy tailored to the needs of the researcher. The revised version of the *SCONUL Seven Pillars of Information Literacy Core Model for Higher Education*, in particular its *Research Lens* (SCONUL, 2011), enumerates several understandings and abilities, many of which are also needed by an information literate researcher. However, we will not characterize selected pillars and outcomes from this document.

Many of the abilities specified in the first pillar are simply attributes of a good researcher. However, in our opinion, the ability to use new tools as they become available has to be emphasized.

The third pillar describes strategies that can be used for locating information and data, including understandings of complex search strategies that can make a difference to the breadth and depth of information found and the need for not always relying on the most familiar resources, that is, using new tools for each new question. Among the abilities listed under this pillar, we find selecting the most appropriate search tools, which include—in accordance with the *Seven Faces* by Bruce—people, as well.

The fourth pillar underlines locating and accessing data among other matters by understanding how digital technologies are providing collaborative tools to create and share information, the relevance of open access resources, or the risks involved in operating in virtual environments.

Reviewing the research process and comparing and evaluating information and data as contained in the fifth pillar directs attention to the information and data landscape of the researchers' respective discipline, as well as to issues of quality, accuracy, relevance, bias, reputation, and credibility in relation to information and data sources. It is declared that a researcher is required to be able to assess these.

Organizing information professionally and ethically as laid out in the sixth pillar presupposes using appropriate data handling and curation methods and sharing research data ethically. Understanding the importance of metadata also pertains to this pillar. The ability to use appropriate bibliographical software to manage information and make appropriate information available is also relevant.

A researcher can apply the knowledge gained by presenting the results of their research, synthesizing new and old information and data and disseminating it in a variety of ways. This statement from the seventh pillar encompasses knowing the difference between summarizing and synthesizing, and the responsibilities related to disseminating information and knowledge.

IL for researchers also should include awareness of the (not always evident) limitations of Google that we do not need and will not discuss here. Some of the constraints of Google have been detected apparently by its producer, as well. This discovery led to the launch of Google Scholar[2]. Even though there is also a lack of clarity regarding what it indexes, it allows us to broadly search for scholarly literature (Asher et al., 2013).

There is reasonable concern that algorithms determined by nonhuman software and intended to tailor search results to search needs characterizes Google as a general search engine and is directing users to misleading results or—at least—restricting their ability to obtain correct results. The proprietary (bibliographic) databases for academic literature offered by EBSCO, ProQuest, etc. are exempt from this bias.

Clearly, searching the Web is not the same as searching a well-defined set of scholarly literature. However, awareness of this difference is crucial for the researcher. It is not by accident that the *Research Lens* of the *Seven Pillars* directs our attention to an understanding of the differences between search tools (e.g., bibliographic databases, subject gateways, search engines) and the need to be familiar with a range of different retrieval tools and recognize their advantages and limitations (SCONUL, 2011). As Badke (2012, p. 48) points out, "search engines are not doing much to work with what they do have to enable searchers to find what they ask for." It is well known that most search engine users tend to look only at the first page of results, thus the first four or five results seem to be the limit that many searchers want to consider. Badke (2012, pp. 48–9) goes on to explain that

> personalization is based on the assumption that what I was is what I will be. For the researcher, however, the past is of little significance to today's search requirements. Most new research projects are ventures into fresh territory that the machinations of personalization can't address.

It is also Badke, who points out that the assumption, according to which practice makes perfect, is wrong. Users can pick up the search skills they need by trial and error only to a limited extent, if at all. The key to developing their skills is information literacy education.

Certainly, it would be utterly naive to presume that researchers easily (and readily) accept the need for acquiring IL skills. There is substantial evidence that people in general hold themselves competent and skillful in dealing with information. This is especially true with regard to their use of technology. People's aptitude for using computers is often mistaken for

---

[2]https://scholar.google.com/

evidence of a high level of information literacy. In this way, it disguises the unsatisfactory level of information literacy among the general population (Herman & Nicholas, 2010). The same has been observed among researchers by Nicholas et al. (2008).

Satisficing, as mentioned in the subsection that explains some features of information overload, is not entirely new. A decade ago, Lynch (1994) indicated that

> the natural tendency of library patrons is to use the best of what is available and to ignore even very high quality materials that are available only in printed form.

Kroll and Forsman (2010, p. 5) also found that US researchers "use and prefer easy solutions that are adequate, not optimal."

An important task is raising awareness of the simple fact that people do not become information literate by osmosis. Practice in itself without proper education does not automatically lead to the acquisition of skills. However, giving academia the false impression that information literacy is a short-term, remedial issue would be a serious mistake (Badke, 2010). The reason for this is that information literacy involves an effort that is closer to learning a new language than to learning to read a spreadsheet as it is about understanding information and how it works (Badke, 2011).

The words of Duncan et al. (2013, p. 269) can also be adapted to our case. They state the following:

> University faculty members rarely like to hear what they are doing is wrong, let alone illegal. So woe to the librarian who presumes to bear the bad news that, in fact, these selfsame faculty members are flagrantly violating copyright law; this messenger should probably expect to receive an earful about the way things should be as opposed to how they are.

Exner (2014) also confirms that it is not easy to teach information literacy to researchers, either. The situation is not much different in the case of most types of researchers, even if doctoral students and the numbers of graduate students involved in research activities seem to be more approachable in this regard.

The roots of the above phenomena may be found in a variety of different issues. First, there seems to be a lack of understanding of faculty lives and needs among librarians, which complicates the problem. Second, the socialization of researchers also may contribute to the difficulties.

As Leckie (1996) describes this process, almost all of them learned their research methods by trial and error on their own with minimal guidance. Learning to do research by doing research is the only training method they have gone through. However, this does not mean that they learnt it well

(Leckie & Fullerton, 1999). It is much more that their experience suggests that they do not need outside assistance.

We do not argue for the absolute necessity of intermediaries, even though we have pointed out some of the advantages of mediation. Nonetheless, it is worth directing our attention to the case of abstracting (addressed in the subsection on reading and writing). Learning to write a good abstract may be just as important as learning to write a good article (Staiger, 1965). However, the skills, necessary for authors to write abstracts, which are part of their scholarly articles, do not automatically come with their diplomas or simply by being professionals and/or researchers.

Ethical values, critical thinking, and understanding are intrinsic to IL, thus they forbid its reduction to elements that only count for tenure and promotion. The reason for this is the following. If we do this, we would deny the entire raison d'être of IL, which presupposes the adoption of the broadest possible perspective on information and research landscapes and is closely related to critical insights into the prevailing mechanisms in scholarly publishing.

Moreover, the core values of IL are related to social justice, democratization, public good, political empowerment, social responsibility, and so on. This is, at least, what many proclamations and declarations on information literacy and related issues are suggesting. To name just a few, this is part of the message of the following documents:

- the *Prague Declaration: Towards an Information Literate Society* in 2003;
- the *Alexandria Proclamation on Information Literacy and Lifelong Learning*, adopted in 2005;
- the *Moscow Declaration on Media and Information Literacy* from 2012; and
- the (already mentioned) *Lyon Declaration on Access to Information and Development* (IFLA, 2005, 2012, 2014; UNESCO, 2003).

What exactly is understood by these core values and "virtues" in the context of research and information literacy may be discerned from the words of Kranich (2004) who has dealt with the concept of information (knowledge) commons. He asserted that the commons-based production of knowledge fundamentally alters the current system in which commercial producers and passive consumers are the primary players. While not challenging individual authorship, peer production allows everyone to be a creator, thereby privileging more idiosyncratic, unpredictable, and democratic genres of expression (Bollier, 2003).

Thus, new forms of scientific inquiry and knowledge production are promoting democratic participation and interactive discourse. They also serve wider social purposes that are identical with those that are encouraged by IL.

A shared value-based core, as explained above, underlies both Research 2.0 and information literacy. Thus, aligning, reorienting, and shifting IL principles and practices towards Research 2.0 will help to overcome at least some of the points of criticism raised in IL discussions mentioned earlier (e.g., Jacobs, Whitworth, Webber & Johnston, etc.).

Information literacy comprises—but is not limited to—instrumental and functional dimensions (i.e., how to pursue an aim, how to fulfill a specific task, etc.). Nor should it be limited to its programmatic dimension.

The potential harm of existing IL practices was stressed by Cowan (2014), who points out that clinging to the programmatic success of information literacy as a program run by libraries and librarians may cause potential loss to libraries and the mission itself. To the contrary, the alignment of IL and Research 2.0 principles would help libraries to evolve into "institutions of collective action" (Kranitch, 2007, p. 103), which foster not just access to, but also the creation and exchange of ideas among diffuse communities of scholars. For IL, this means a turn from a dedication to techniques of searching and organizing information to a commitment to the critical and socially responsible production and distribution of information. In contemporary research environments, this commitment implies the advocacy of new directions in scholarly information access, new information production and dissemination practices, and critical thinking about research environments, especially the monologic nature of its traditional outputs (e.g., article journals) and its new deregulated, de-hierarchized, and decentralized counterparts as instantiated in diverse Web 2.0-based services.

The traditions and resistance that may be experienced among researchers dictate that even among the conditions of Research 2.0 we have to offer literacies that reflect on the differences between amateurs and professionals already discussed earlier (on page 54). If we consider that professional contents are different, literacies also have to be different in a way that is similar to the traditional distribution of work between libraries, which involves serving their stakeholders with the awareness that different user groups need diverse kinds of information.

To achieve this, distinct types of libraries are designed to cater for differentiated user needs. Vice versa, varied categories of users tend to seek the information they need in different types of libraries.

Amateur content that dominates social media is useful mainly for public library users; thus, it could be offered, among others, to students in their role of consumers. Public libraries have always been offering amateur content in the sense that it was not geared toward the needs of professionals. This is obviously not a question of quality, but shows a different orientation toward providing value.

It is well known that public libraries may offer valuable services that are designed for professional users, even though these users are typically served by special and academic libraries. In many cases, public libraries cannot aim to fulfill the functions of these types of library and usually there is no intention to do so.

All these features are in accordance with the mission of library services to facilitate convenient access to documents and to support the mission of the institution or the interests of the population served (Buckland, 1992). In our understanding, the academic library is designed to serve both, as the university is roughly identical with its students, teaching staff, and researchers. Similarly, a research institute's interests are basically the same as those of the researchers working there. The mission of the public library, however, is to support the interests of the population served, but not the institution itself, at least not primarily.

The notions of the *public library* and the *academic library* can be taken literally, as well as in a more general sense, to denote "public" and "expert" online spaces. The separation of professional content from amateur may be based on classic criteria of evaluation (Smith, 1997). As pointed out throughout this book, in the case of scholarly contents, the presence of content peer review is still the most reliable means of filtering, while quality control by editors and editorial boards can be acceptable. Literacies based on these principles represent very much the presence of or education toward awareness of these differences.

Making use of social media could mean fulfilling in particular the goals, set forth in points three and five of the IFLA/UNESCO Public Library Manifesto (IFLA/UNESCO, 1994). Key mission three stresses the need to provide opportunities for personal creative development, while key mission five is about promoting awareness of cultural heritage, appreciation of the arts, scientific achievements, and innovations.

Personal development is in many regards, although not exclusively, self-development that corresponds to the needs of amateurs of Web 2.0. The orientation toward culture and the arts hardly needs explanation in this regard. Awareness of scientific achievements is highly valuable. Nonetheless, it usually does not include scholarship in a strict sense, the basics of which are acquired in higher education and which is performed by researchers and university teaching staff members as a professional practice.

A possible "Public Library 2.0" idea depicts an institution which provides a platform for the storage and dissemination of local community knowledge using digital technologies as well as Library 2.0 principles (Chowdhury, Poulter & McMenemy, 2006). This does not contradict the principle of differentiating between amateur and professional content. Information related to local communities and especially to local history represents a mix in this regard (Reid & Macafee, 2007). It has been one of the vital components of public libraries and has the potential to reach wider audiences, especially as it has involved local nonprofessional and professional researchers.

Digitization and harnessing the active participation of users with Library 2.0 tools undoubtedly add a new dimension to this important segment of public library activities. On the whole, however, it does not change it substantially. The question arises whether responsibility for information literacy education in the Web 2.0 era is solely up to public librarians or should all librarians take note (Godwin, 2008). The answer seems to be obvious. It is an integral part of all librarians' roles, though we should not forget the differences outlined above.

Scholarly communication and information literacy will continue to be essential growth areas for academic libraries. Sutton (2013) underpins this statement by explaining that the *Intersections* White Paper (already mentioned in this book) advocates for the integration of scholarly communication and information literacy to strengthen the educational roles of academic libraries. Merging these areas represents something of a new frontier that will require many libraries to shift models that presently support scholarly communication and information literacy as separate endeavors. The paper effectively makes the case for this shift, based on the premise that scholarly communication knowledge is vital to information literacy skills and the ability to navigate the world of digital information.

The authors of *Common Ground*, Davis-Kahl et al. (2014), have repeatedly declared that information literacy and scholarly communication are two major outreach activities in academic libraries. They have enumerated several strategies and opportunities for integrating scholarly communication concepts into students' academic lives. The examples are formal instruction, exhibits, symposia, and including student work in institutional repositories.

As in today's information world we have to concentrate on content. An important lesson to be learnt here is that information literacy in academic settings can be valid only within the context of a subject discipline, the discourse of which is decisive, even if its rules are often unwritten (Badke, 2008). This principle often appears in writing about information literacy as a requirement of collaboration between librarians and faculty members (e.g., Anderson & May, 2010; Fruin, 2013; Malefant, 2010). We do not find much difference in research settings.

The Research 2.0 paradigm has brought with it serious challenges for academic libraries. In 1994, Lynch had already indicated that the transition from print sources will involve systemic and often subtle changes which could call the historical role of libraries in collecting, preserving, and providing access to information into doubt. He sees the reason for this in the fact that digital information is not usually sold but licensed. This substantially reduces access to this body of information, among other material, by precluding the sharing of it through the interlibrary loan system in the way that printed works historically have been shared (Lynch, 1994).

The situation of the e-book substantiates these claims, as in the majority of the cases we do not buy e-books; we license them under typically very complex terms that constrain what we are allowed to do with them (Lynch, 2013).

Nolin (2013) is of the opinion that academic librarians have shifted their attention away from researchers in several ways. They focus their services more on students and give more attention to online resources which results in them distancing themselves from issues related to print documents located at the library and the actual building itself. This implies that a substantial part of the attention given to students and resources has to be refocused on the researcher.

The library community has recognized an ever-more pressing need to take issues and developments related to scientific research into account and has begun to deal with them by publishing the *Intersections* White Paper (ACRL, 2013). The document explores and articulates different intersections between scholarly communication (related to research activities) and information literacy, arguing that these intersections should be carefully considered by librarians in order that libraries become "resilient" with regard to the tremendous changes occurring in the research information environment.

Still, the congruence between the core values of IL and Research 2.0 principles (e.g., openness, critical thinking, democratization, public good, empowerment, social responsibility, justice, etc.) provides a fruitful interpretative ground for identifying and highlighting an interconnectedness existing between transformations in both concepts.

Today more than ever, IL should deal less with finding information and focus more on the evaluation, use, and communication of research information, considering the many paths opened up as a result of Web 2.0 developments. Primarily, a holistic approach to IL in social media environments implies a shift toward social dimensions and practices that would affect and remodel the processes of discovering, evaluating, using, and producing (communicating) information.

Making IL more "2.0-ish" would result in more critical perspectives on current research landscapes and facilitate the realization of all the positive aspects of Research 2.0 such as openness, fair accessibility, visibility, informal communication, collaboration, etc.

We should not forget that making researchers familiar with appropriate literacies is an important educational activity that might reinstitute the profession of information specialist as significant, at least to some extent.

On the other hand, librarians have to be familiar with the processes and requirements of scholarly communication. The Association of College and Research Libraries, for instance, recommends integrating scholarly communication into educational programs for librarians to achieve the ideal of information fluency. This recommendation also includes developing new model curricula for information literacy, incorporating the evolution in scholarly communication issues. Library leaders should seek out and share organizational models that break down barriers between information literacy and scholarly communication programs (ACRL, 2013).

By contemplating the interrelationship between IL and Research 2.0, we found that there are points of congruence between them in their core ideas and guiding principles. Apart from this, the need to take a wider perspective on IL arises from practical considerations. For example, as OA initiatives have shown, the openness of research can improve its visibility as evidenced by citation analyses often showing high impact factors for open access materials (Ginsparg, 2007).

Such a high (and desirable) impact can be complemented by Research 2.0 when it comes to informal modes of scholarly communication. Whereas formal modes of communication are concerned with academic reward, informal modes are central to academic practice and it is difficult to imagine research functioning without informal communication practices.

One of the main messages of this book is that academic libraries and librarians need to be increasingly comfortable with areas of scholarly communication (Palmer & Gelfand, 2013). Assessing what researchers need and how the library can collaborate with them is crucial in doing this. However, this task goes beyond the simple questioning of individual researchers to include exploring the diversity and complexity of researchers' information behavior and needs. This is especially true, as researchers usually cannot envisage library potential (Maceviciute, 2014).

In addition, if we understand how much Research 2.0 influences the thinking and working of today's researchers, we will know what they will require in the library and what kind of information literacy has to be offered to them to achieve the maximum effect to the satisfaction of all stakeholders. A possible shift in the library's role may mean that libraries will be able to serve as research consultants and project managers. In particular, four roles stand out:

1. providing active support in order to help increase researcher productivity;
2. acquiring (buying) resources;
3. preserving these resources;
4. providing gateways (starting points) for locating information.

Many of these are a continuation of the traditional roles that libraries have fulfilled. These roles materialize in different functions, from which the following seem to have especial relevance to the researcher:

- helping to keep current in their field;
- providing databases with an alert capability;
- keeping informed of new publications;
- selecting research materials;
- offering reference and research assistance (Brown & Tucker, 2013).

Academic libraries often introduce posts that redefine librarians' roles in the new academic environment, including Research 2.0. One of the labels put on these functions is *scholarly communications librarian*. It is obviously not the only one. Nonetheless, it shows a number of essential features that can fulfill the needs generated by this new environment.

What we outline below, following the thoughts of Bonn (2014), is based on a broad understanding of information literacy as it mirrors a wide range of skills and abilities. The list begins with a detailed understanding of copyright law and its implications. Issues of intellectual property and copyright have been affecting library work in and outside of academic libraries.

Advising researchers is obviously a new branch of this activity. Bonn's list (based on an analysis of job advertisements) is followed with a rather down-to-earth requirement for knowing how to read an author contract and understand its ramifications. This is extremely helpful and is not intended to underestimate researchers' capabilities. On the contrary, it is much more a recognition that they need help with "technical" issues in a broad sense.

Being familiar with standard and emerging modes of scholarly communication is a much more advanced and truly professional situation. There are many examples of librarians who are knowledgeable in both print and digital publishing, be it formal or based on social media.

It is not by accident that experience in or familiarity with formal publishing appears as the next item on this list, to an extent duplicating the preceding item.

Understanding the economics of scholarly communication is also a salient aspect, and includes not only the costs of publishing but also the question of reputation. This leads us back to alternative ways of measuring impact and prominence.

These issues are closely connected to the role of digital technology and networked communication across the disciplines, familiarity with which seems to be a self-explanatory requirement for librarians supporting scholarly communication activities.

Another range of responsibilities arises under the name of *embedded librarian*. The model of embedded librarianship takes librarians out of the traditional library and places them in a setting that enables close coordination and collaboration with researchers. This empowers librarians to demonstrate their expertise as information specialists and to apply this expertise in ways that will have a direct and deep impact on the research being done.

Embedded librarianship raises librarians from a supporting role to a partnership that allows them to develop stronger connections and relationships with those they serve. In the research context, embedded librarians could work with information resources that are generated over the course of the research. This includes data which could be prepared for reuse by others or for long-term preservation. Embedded librarians may also design workflows and systems to organize, manage, and deliver project documentation or other needed materials (Carlson & Kneale, 2011).

Reflecting on the possible future of academic libraries, Neil (2014) has pointed out several new research paths and program opportunities. These include migrating from product to service, and focusing on the role of the library in teaching and learning, as well as research and scholarship. Providing a service-oriented approach and giving more attention to research and researchers is no longer an experiment but a working example.

Identified by the NMC Horizon Report (NMC, 2014) as a long-range trend, forecasted to be adopted by academic and research libraries in five or more years, is the support for new, evolving forms of multidisciplinary research. While the contemporary workforce is inherently multidisciplinary in that a diverse range of skills is needed for a person to be successful in their position, digital humanities and computational social science research approaches fulfill a pioneering role here.

We are facing a new generation of challenges that are evolving simultaneously with other issues. From a technological point of view, it seems we cannot escape the constant integration and assimilation of the latest software solutions, social media platforms, and popular applications into library work. At the same time, the inevitable loss of library jobs would appear to be imminent following the latest round of automation.

However, information technology innovation brings with it a growing need for a multiskilled workforce, and the loss of low-level jobs should imply the growth of high-level jobs along the value chain. It is not the hardware and the algorithms, but the brains that are in the strategic focus of knowledge production: the future of library work is a turn to rediscover human technology.

We have examined the growing role of research data which confirms that literacy should be seen in the context of library and information science which has begun to take nontextual resources into consideration. In other words, librarians as well as library users need to be literate not only in terms of text but also in terms of data. As Seadle puts it:

> The fact that libraries have text has not traditionally involved librarians in teaching people to read, but reading data requires skills that librarians may need to teach to users to help them get meaning from information in the collection.

**Seadle (2012, p. 207)**

Librarians have expertise that can help researchers create better research output in the form of more useful data, thus they can participate in the phase of research that precedes publication (Federer, 2013). However, the academic library can become a key agent involved in the stewarding of research data if librarians "skill up" for new roles in supporting complex scientific systems (Ramírez, 2011). As Tenopir et al. (2012, p. 41) put it:

> The convergence of data-intensive science, technological advances, and library information expertise provides academic libraries with the opportunity to create a new profile on campus as a partner in knowledge creation, helping it expand beyond the traditional roles of libraries. This new environment allows libraries to take a more active and visible role in the knowledge creation process by placing librarians at all stages in the research planning process and by providing expertise to develop data management plans, identify appropriate data description, and create preservation strategies

While there is a lack of standardization and consistency in organizing data (Carlson et al., 2011), there are opportunities not only for librarians but also for institutional repository managers and library data curation specialists to encourage positive change. Information professionals can operate in close collaboration with researchers and they can promote the use of data citation standards, especially those that use the publishing convention of the DOI (digital object identifier) (Mooney & Newton, 2012).

The ways in which we can label the roles that information specialists are involved in are still evolving. Among the roles we find *data consultant, data librarian, data manager, data management consultant, data curator, data officer, data scientist, and research informationist* (Loukides, 2012).

Traditional library services have generally focused on the finished product of the research process, that is, the peer-reviewed literature, but there is still a demand for new professional roles, which may go beyond the information professions. Despite the forecasts, we will need *waste data handlers* before 2030. Defending our privacy and eliminating our trails safely in the virtual world will become more important than sorting and digitally incinerating corporate and scientific data waste. Undoubtedly, it is important to avoid situations where data has to be restored or deletions undone, so we will need *data archeologists*—who have been around since 1993—specialized in saving data from obsolete storage facilities.

The roles of *data steward* and *data custodian* are decoupling. The former is sensitive to the business and usability aspects, while the latter provides the technological background. The emerging new field of *data journalism* (Orr, 2011) can play a pivotal role in critical and civic monitoring.

These are not simply targets for headhunting: these jobs are accumulative by nature. Whatever the scientific domain (genetics, astronomy, geography), business field (social media, automobile industry, air transport), or government division (health, cartography, national security), we can find many subcategories of data experts. This flexibility is reasonable. We should remember the old Internet saying, *data never sleeps*.

Whatever names we use and responsibilities we identify, the Association of Research Libraries declared in 2012 that academic libraries are in a favorable position to help researchers meet the challenges of the data–intensive research paradigm for a number of reasons:

- Libraries are increasingly providing data consultation services and have experience and skills in fostering cross-departmental, cross-campus, etc., communication and collaboration, needed for effective research data management.

- Librarians are familiar with the research data needs of researchers and have been among the supporters of innovative publishing models, including open access publishing. They are already involved in acquiring the necessary abilities to manage data (Hswe and Holt, 2012).

In other words, libraries are in the knowledge business and thus foster conversation (Lankes, 2011), while librarians' information retrieval skills allow them to facilitate the conversations involved (Wanser, 2014).

The involvement of academic and research libraries lies in the provision of research data services that cover the full data life cycle, including planning, curation, and metadata creation and conversion (Tenopir et al., 2013). They may also play a critical role as data quality hubs on campus with the provision of data quality auditing and verification services for the research communities (Giarlo, 2013).

An empirical investigation by Tenopir et al. (2013) examined the opinions of librarians employed by the Association of Research Libraries. The majority of the respondents did not have research data services (RDS) as an integral part of their job responsibilities. Nonetheless, many ARL librarians believe that they have the knowledge, skills, and opportunities to provide RDS in the future.

An online survey of 140 libraries in Australia, New Zealand, Ireland, and the United Kingdom identified the need for guidance in the handling and management of unpublished research data, including data literacy education (Corral et al., 2013).

As Mooney and Silver (2010, p. 480) state, librarians "will not only need to learn how to apply traditional techniques of reference, instruction, and collection management to the unique format of data, but also how to raise awareness of this new service to the wider academic community."

The Association of European Research Libraries (LIBER) published 10 recommendations for libraries to get started with research data management. There is no need to repeat these here, but many of the recommendations characterize and define the roles that librarians who serve researchers can fulfill in the data-intensive environment. These include:

- offering research data management support, including data management plans for grant applications, intellectual property rights advice and information materials, and integration of data management into the curriculum;
- developing metadata and data standards and providing metadata services for research data;
- participating in institutional research data policy development;

- liaising with researchers, research groups, data archives, and data centers to foster an interoperable infrastructure for data access, data discovery, and data sharing;
- promoting data citation.

To fulfill the above roles, the reskilling of librarians is of crucial importance as only a few libraries are able to hire new, specialized staff (Christensen-Dalsgaard et al., 2012).

What do these recommendations have to do with data literacy and information literacy? If academic libraries begin to put some of these recommendations into practice and continually provide reliable and successful service to researchers under these novel circumstances, the chances that they can educate users will grow enormously.

The rules for using and caring for data suggested by Goodman et al. (2014) can guide researchers in how to ensure that their data and analyses continue to be of value. These rules can also offer guidance to librarians engaged in data-related issues, notably assisting researchers in their data management. The bottom line is that they can have the same effect as the guidelines noted above and may raise the researcher's trust in the expertise of the librarian.

The complex issue of instruction on research-focused information literacy needs to be framed in terms of the research process. Its target audience is faculty, doctoral students, and other research-based graduate students, postdoctoral researchers, and other researchers.

Researchers' information needs are complex and rarely linear. This means that information literacy education has to give attention to the everyday working processes used by researchers. For instance, they often use gap analysis, that is, examining the existing research and literature to identify gaps in the existing knowledge (Exner, 2014).

It is well known that a literature review is an obligatory part of any scholarly article as it maps out the research already conducted and published. One of the main goals of such a review is to identify a gap (or gaps) in the knowledge that may serve as the justification for a scientific study. This gap then needs to be filled by the actual research (Connor & Mauranen, 1999). Thus by identifying the gaps in the literature review, niches in the existing research can be identified which provide the necessary information to justify the need for a given researcher's activities.

Consequently, gap analysis must be included in information literacy sessions for (future) researchers at an advanced level. However, this must be preceded by the production of mind maps that break up pieces of a given topic to enable a multipart search strategy outlining the context and background around the question, as well as reviewing the literature for methods and designs at the fundamental level.

These steps can be followed by brainstorming activities to identify potential methodological approaches, as well as searching to find articles in the topic area that apply specific methods or discuss methodology. After this intermediate level activity, a search of databases relevant to the researcher's discipline can follow in order to identify current trends in cutting-edge research (Exner, 2014).

For example, a Web site-based investigation of job advertisements for scientific data specialists, combined with an analysis of courses, degrees, and programs relating to scientific data curation provided by schools of library and information science, resulted in two ranked lists. The first list sets out responsibilities as follows:

- offering consultation and reference services for scientific research and data curation;
- inquiring into data curation requirements of researchers and collecting users' feedback;
- providing instruction and training on scientific data curation;
- creating metadata standards and adding metadata for scientific data;
- helping users with the collection and analysis of research data;
- helping users with the storage of research data;
- developing policies and procedures to support scientific data curation;
- participating in different levels of programs and initiatives concerning data curation;
- participating in different levels of related organizations.
  The second list sets out the required qualifications as follows:
- the ability to collaborate and work in teams;
- oral and written communication skills;
- interpersonal skills;
- knowledge of data curation tools and technologies;
- a graduate degree in library science, information science, or archival science;
- knowledge of general metadata standards;
- an awareness of trends and developments in data curation and a willingness to pay attention to them;
- familiarity with quantitative research methods;
- familiarity with scientific data sources;
- relevant working experience (Si et al., 2013).

As Weber (2013) puts it, research data are experiencing a cultural moment, and this should also be a cultural moment for library and information science. Repeating our earlier argument, we must add that managing big data in a broad sense might be an opportunity for the library and for the information professional.

On the one hand, this space is already crowded with sociologists, economists, computer scientists, and statisticians. While this is true, librarians could apply the knowledge they have traditionally possessed. Knowledge about citation behavior, document retrieval, and information seeking matches well the data-intensive paradigm (Weber, 2013).

If libraries want to ensure that they remain relevant, services related to research data offer an opportunity to put the expertise of information professionals to good use (Christensen-Dalsgaard et al., 2012). In the same way as the library has traditionally facilitated access to documents, it can facilitate access to data, even though data do not necessarily fit into the same document formats that libraries used to offer (Stuart, 2011). However, the lack of tools, infrastructure, standardized processes, and properly skilled personnel may impede this (Carlson et al., 2011).

According to Calzada Prado and Marzal (2013), academic libraries can have different responses to Research 2.0 and the growing need to use research data. They can hire specialized staff (data librarians or data specialists) or set up data management and analysis training for (generally reference) librarians. Intensifying the collection of data sources and providing access to them, including participation in the development of institutional data repositories, is another option. Last but not least, they can incorporate data literacy into their instructional programs and services.

Data literacy also appears in the predictions that were made about the future directions of academic libraries in the Library 2.0 world (Merrill, 2011).

A noteworthy idea is to see the library in the life of the user rather than the user in the life of the library (Wiegand, 2005). Such thinking may also define the future of information literacy. As indicated in Figure 1, one of our main messages is that future directions in information literacy should be inspired by Research 2.0, but not from a purely functional perspective. Functional and instrumental aspects are not insignificant since new research environments require new abilities, which, on a pragmatic level, may influence the IL offered to researchers. But even more important are mutual relations based on core values shared by both concepts, such as openness, social dynamics, conversation, sharing, societal impact, epistemological shifts, dialogic forms of knowledge production, etc. These relationships reinforce each other.

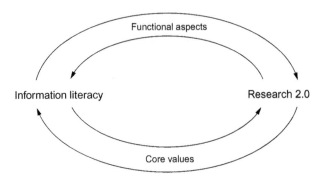

**Figure 1** Mutual relationship between IL and Research 2.0.

We believe that the reciprocity centered on both functional dimensions and core values will help to bring us closer to the promises of Research 2.0, since researchers who deeply understand the information environment they act in and who have developed awareness of the critical issues framing research processes are more open to accept Research 2.0 principles and values. On the other hand, focusing on Research 2.0 principles will help IL to overcome many of its problematic dimensions discussed earlier, such as library-centeredness, linearity, and generic approaches. Moreover, such an orientation will also help to achieve some of the transformations described in the previous chapter, such as the transformation from linear and sequential toward constructionist approaches, from print- and resource-focused approaches toward communicative approaches, or from generic and standard-based toward critical and transformative approaches.

Let us round up this chapter with the intriguing prospect of putting researchers into the context of Ranganathan's laws as reordered and actualized. Two earlier attempts were successful in setting new accents on all five laws, taking the changed environment into consideration (McMenemy, 2007; Noruzi, 2004). The requirement of Ranganathan's Fourth Law was to save the time of the reader (Ranganathan, 1931). Most authors are of the opinion that this law gains particular importance as the vast array of content being offered through a multitude of information service providers, the scarcity of time, and shortness of attention are among the most pressing issues facing people today.

Silipigni Connaway and Faniel (2014, p. 8) provide new conceptions of the laws in the current environment, and change the Fourth Law to "Save the time of the researcher." The efforts to improve the user's experience in the physical library environment dictate that we minimize the amount of time that is required for using services. However, while saving time is still important, convenience also has become important to today's information seekers. People are not making choices about how to satisfy their information needs in a vacuum. Researchers do not wake up one morning and decide, "I'm going to stop reading so many paper journals and start spending some of that time watching YouTube videos of live conference presentations." Nor do students decide, "This is the year that I'll begin using a citation generator for my bibliographies." They make these decisions in an increasingly complex and rich environment. They may make a new choice because of a need to decrease spending or because they have acquired a new device. Consequently, it is not by accident that conceptualizations of information literacy have always been influenced by the information environment in which they are situated (Špiranec & Banek Zorica, 2010).

We have listed and analyzed a number of literacies in order to give an approximation of the rich variety of skills and abilities that characterize the researcher, and we have illustrated the wealth of approaches to those literacies. In doing this, we have tried not to lose sight of the following: "No single name or descriptive term for contemporary literacy has gained common currency nor is there complete agreement about what the terms currently in circulation mean" (Ingraham et al., 2007).

We should also take note of the assertion of Bawden (2008) that there is no single literacy that would be appropriate for all people or for one person over all their lifetime, without constantly updating concepts and competences in accordance with the changing circumstances of the information environment.

The perpetual development of information literacy brings in new points of view. Let us but mention one: in his LILAC 2014 (Librarians' Information Literacy Annual Conference) video presentation,[3] Paul Zurkowski proposed *action Literacy*, which attempts to bridge the gap between information literacy and the general public (NFIL, 2015).

Let us now summarize the main message of this book. Research 2.0 has changed researchers' behavior. We have outlined that this change may not have influenced all researchers and its impact is varied across disciplines, communities, and generations (to list just a few of the players in this field, not to mention the numerous stakeholders).

The evidence presented throughout this book indicates that Research 2.0 may only marginally be associated with the realm instead of being a mainstream of the researcher, in particular when it comes to using new

[3]https://www.youtube.com/watch?v=8DXnUvseNTs#t=24

and alternative ways of publishing research. Thus, our attention is drawn to the fact that there are burning questions to be answered with regard to the interrelationship between IL and Research 2.0. The outcomes of Research 2.0 activities may not be recognized or accepted by the academic community. If this is the case and the issues of trustworthiness and credibility—which represent the pillars of research—are currently not even near to being resolved within Web 2.0 environments, then it seems futile to seriously consider the possibility of changing IL in the interests of integrating it into the principles of research in social media environments. However, in order to determine the potential effects and influences of Research 2.0 on IL, we need different grounds for interpretation. These effects and influences are rooted in the core values of IL, which are congruent with Research 2.0 principles in many respects.

We believe that information literacy should move from being an add-on to being regarded as a foundation because it has the power to train people, in every aspect of their education, how to process content (Badke, 2010). Let us add that IL should be integral part of the researcher's life.

Nevertheless, Research 2.0 is with us and librarians have begun to understand that in the wide scope of information literacy, which they offer to their stakeholders, there is a place for IL that serves the needs of researchers. If we take this mission seriously and count on the weight of Research 2.0, we can say that without doubt Research 2.0 is the future of information literacy.

# REFERENCES

AACU. (2002). *Greater expectations: A new vision for learning as a nation goes to college.* Washington, DC: Association of American Colleges and Universities.

Aalbersberg, I. J., Atzeni, S., Koers, H., Specker, B., & Zudilova-Seinstram, E. (2013). Bringing digital science deep inside the scientific article: The Elsevier article of the future project. *LIBER Quarterly*, 23(4), 274–299. http://liber.library.uu.nl/index.php/lq/article/view/8446/9920.

Acord, S. K., & Harley, D. (2013). Credit, time, and personality: The human challenges to sharing scholarly work using Web 2.0. *New Media & Society*, 5(3), 379–397.

ACRL. (2000). *Information literacy competency standards for higher education.* Chicago, IL: Association of College and Research Libraries.

ACRL. (2003). *Principles and strategies for the reform of scholarly communication.* Chicago, IL: Association of College and Research Libraries. http://www.ala.org/acrl/publications/whitepapers/principlesstrategies.

ACRL. (2013). *Intersections of scholarly communication and information literacy: Creating strategic collaborations for a changing academic environment.* Chicago, IL: Association of College and Research Libraries. http://acrl.ala.org/intersections/.

ACRL. (2014a). *Framework for information literacy for higher education draft 3.* Chicago, IL: Association of College and Research Libraries. http://acrl.ala.org/ilstandards/wp-content/uploads/2014/11/Framework-for-IL-for-HE-draft-3.pdf.

ACRL. (2014b). ACRL Research Planning and Review Committee. Top ten trends in academic libraries. A review of the trends and issues affecting academic libraries in higher education. *College & Research Libraries News*, 75(6), 294–302.

Adams, N. E. (2014). A comparison of evidence-based practice and the ACRL information literacy standards: Implications for information literacy practice. *College & Research Libraries*, 75(2), 232–248.

ALA. (1989). *Final report, American library association presidential commission on information literacy.* Chicago, IL: American Library Association. http://www.ala.org/ala/mgrps/divs/acrl/publications/whitepapers/presidential.cfm.

Aldrich, F., & Sheppard, L. (2000). Graphicacy: the fourth R? *Primary Science Review*, 64, 8–11.

Alonso, M. I., & Fernández, L. M. M. (2010). Perspectives of studies on document abstracting: Towards an integrated view of models and theoretical approaches. *Journal of Documentation*, 66(4), 563–584.

Alvarado, R. (2012). The digital humanities situation. In M. K. Gold (Ed.), *Debates in the digital humanities.* Minneapolis, MN: The University of Minnesota Press. http://dhdebates.gc.cuny.edu/debates/text/50A.

American Library Association (ALA) Office for Information Technology Policy Digital Literacy Task Force. (2012). *Draft: Digital literacy, libraries, and public policy.* Washington, DC: American Library Association. http://connect.ala.org/files/94226/digilitreport2012_COMMENT%20DRAFT_9%2018%2012.pdf.

Anderson, K., & May, F. A. (2010). Does the method of instruction matter? An experimental examination of information literacy instruction in the online, blended, and face-to-face classrooms. *Journal of Academic Librarianship*, 36(6), 495–500.

ANZIIL. (2004). *Australian and New Zealand Information Literacy Framework* (2nd ed.) (A. Bundy, Ed.). *Adelaide: Australian and New Zealand Institute for Information Literacy.* http://www.caul.edu.au/content/upload/files/info-literacy/InfoLiteracyFramework.pdf.

Arms, W. Y. (2002). What are the alternatives to peer review? Quality control in scholarly publishing on the web. *Journal of Electronic Publishing*, 8(1). http://www.press.umich.edu/jep/08-01/arms.html.

Arms, W., & Larsen, R. (2007). *The future of scholarly communication: Building the infrastructure for cyberscholarship*. Phoenix, AZ: National Science Foundation & British Joint Information Systems Committee. http://www.sis.pitt.edu/~repwkshop/NSF-JISC-report.pdf.

Arp, L., & Doodard, B. S. (2002). Recent trends in information literacy and instruction. *Reference and User Services Quarterly*, 42(2), 124–132.

Asher, A. D., Duke, L. M., & Wilson, S. (2013). Paths of discovery: Comparing the search effectiveness of EBSCO discovery service, summon, Google scholar, and conventional library resources. *College & Research Libraries*, 74(5), 464–488.

Atkinson, R. (1996). Library functions, scholarly communication, and the foundations of the digital library: Laying claim to the control zone. *Library Quarterly*, 66(3), 239–264.

Attfield, S., Blandford, A., & Dowell, J. (2003). Information seeking in the context of writing: A design psychology interpretation of the "problematic situation". *Journal of Documentation*, 59(4), 430–453.

Auckland, M. (2012). *Re-skilling for research*. RLUK Research Libraries UK. http://www.rluk.ac.uk/wp-content/uploads/2014/02/RLUK-Re-skilling.pdf.

Aufderheide, P. (1992). *Media literacy. A report of the national leadership conference on media literacy*. Washington, DC: Aspen Institute. http://www.medialit.org/reading_room/article356.html.

Badke, W. (2004). *Research strategies: Finding your way through the information fog* (2nd ed.). Lincoln, NE: iUniverse.

Badke, W. (2008). A rationale for information literacy as a credit-bearing discipline. *Journal of information Literacy*, 2(1). http://jil.lboro.ac.uk/ojs/index.php/JIL/article/view/RA-V2-I1-2008-1.

Badke, W. (2009). Media, ICT, and information literacy. *Online*, 33(5), 47–49.

Badke, W. (2010). Information overload? Maybe not. *Online*, 34(5), 52–54.

Badke, W. (2011). Why information literacy is invisible. *Communications in Information Literacy*, 4(2), 129–141.

Badke, W. (2012). Personalization and information literacy. *Online*, 36(1), 47–49.

Bardi, A., & Manghi, P. (2014). Enhanced publications: Data models and information systems. *Liber Quarterly*, 23(4), 242–273.

Bates, M. J. (1989). The design of browsing and berrypicking techniques for the online search interface. *Online Review*, 13(5), 407–424.

Bawden, D. (2001). Information and digital literacies: A review of concepts. *Journal of Documentation*, 57(2), 218–259.

Bawden, D. (2008). Origins and concepts of digital literacy. In C. Lankshear & M. Knobel (Eds.), *Digital literacies: Concepts, policies and practices* (pp. 17–32). New York, NY: Peter Lang.

Bawden, D. (2013). The declining impact of the impact factor? *Journal of Documentation*, 69(2), 153.

Bawden, D. (2014). Being fluent and keeping looking. In S. Kurbanoglu, et al. (Eds.), *Information literacy: Lifelong learning and digital citizenship in the 21st century* (pp. 13–18). Cham: Springer International.

Bawden, D., Holtham, C., & Courtney, N. (1999). Perspectives on information overload. *Aslib Proceedings*, 51(8), 249–255.

Bawden, D., & Robinson, L. (2009). The dark side of information: overload, anxiety and other paradoxes and pathologies. *Journal of Information Science*, 35(2), 180–191.

Bawden, D., & Robinson, L. (2012). *Introduction to information science*. London: Facet.

Beall, J. (2014). Predatory publishing is just one of the consequences of gold open access. *Learned Publishing*, 26(2), 79–84.

Beavis, C., OMara, J., & McNeice, L. (Eds.), (2012). *Digital games: Literacy in action*. Cambridge, MA: Wakefield Press.

Becher, T., & Trowler, P. (2001). *Academic tribes and territories: Intellectual enquiry and the culture of disciplines*. Columbus, OH: McGraw-Hill International.

Beeson, I. (2005). Judging relevance: A problem for e-literacy. *ITALICS*, 4(2). http://www.ics.heacademy.ac.uk/italics/vol5iss4/beeson.pdf.

Behrens, S. J. (1994). A conceptual analysis and historical overview of Information literacy. *College & Research Libraries*, 55(4), 309–322.

Behrman, D. (2012). A health expert at your fingertips—The latest medical apps. *The Telegraph*. 22 October, http://www.telegraph.co.uk/health/9621612/A-health-expert-at-your-fingertips-the-latest-medical-apps.html.

Beniger, J. R. (1986). *The control revolution. Technological and economic origins of the information society*. Cambridge, MA: Harvard University Press.

Beniger, J. R. (1988). Information society and global science. *The Annals of the American Academy of Political and Social Science*, 495(1), 14–28.

Berger, R., Woodfin, L., Plaut, S. N., & Dobbertin, C. B. (2014). *Transformational literacy: Making the common core shift with work that matters*. Hoboken, NJ: Wiley.

Bergman, O. (2013). Variables for personal information management research. *ASLIB Proceedings*, 65(5), 464–483.

Berners-Lee, T., Bizer, Ch., & Heath, T. (2009). Linked data—The story so far. *International Journal on Semantic Web and Information Systems*, 5(3), 1–22.

Berry, D. (2011). The computational turn: Thinking about the digital humanities. *Culture Machine*, 12. http://www.culturemachine.net/index.php/cm/article/viewArticle/440.

Björk, B.-Ch. (2004). Open access to scientific publications—An analysis of the barriers to change? *Information Research*, 9(2). http://InformationR.net/ir/9-2/paper170.html.

Björk, B.-C., & Paetau, P. (2012). Open access to the scientific journal literature—Status and challenges for the information systems community. *Bulletin of the American Society for Information Science and Technology*, 38(5), 39–44.

Bladek, M. (2014). DORA San Francisco declaration on research assessment. *College & Research Libraries News*, 75(4), 191–196.

Blummer, B., & Kenton, J. M. (2014). Reducing patron information overload in academic libraries. *College & Undergraduate Libraries*, 21(2), 115–135.

BOAI. (2002). *Budapest open access initiative*. http://www.budapestopenaccessinitiative.org/.

Boekhorst, A. (2003). Becoming information literate in the Netherlands. *Library Review*, 52(7), 298–309.

Bollier, D. (2003). *Artists, technology and the ownership of creative content*. Los Angeles, CA: Norman Lear Center at the USC Annenberg School for Communication.

Boneau, C. A. (1990). Psychological literacy: A first approximation. *American Psychologist*, 45(7), 891.

Bonn, M. (2014). Tooling up. Scholarly communication education and training. *College & Research Libraries News*, 75(3), 132–135.

Borgman, Ch. (2007). *Scholarship in the digital age: Information, infrastructure, and the Internet*. Cambridge, MA: MIT Press.

Borgman, Ch. (2010). *Research data: Who will share what, with whom, when, and why?* In China-North America library conference, Beijing. http://works.bepress.com/borgman/238.

Borgman, Ch. (2012). The conundrum of sharing research data. *Journal of the American Society for Information Science and Technology*, 63(6), 1059–1078.

Borgman, Ch., Abelson, H., Dirks, L., Johnson, R., Koedinger, K. R., Linn, M. C., & Szalay, A. (2011). *Fostering learning in the networked world: The cyberlearning opportunity and challenge*. DIANE Publishing.

Bowler, L., & Large, A. (2008). Design-based research for LIS. *Library & Information Science Research*, 30(1), 39–46.

Boyd, D., & Crawford, K. (2012). Critical questions for big data: Provocations for a cultural, technological, and scholarly phenomenon. *Information, Communication & Society*, 15(5), 662–679.

Boyer, E. L. (1990). *Scholarship reconsidered: Priorities of the professoriate*. Princeton, NJ: Carnegie Foundation for the Advancement of Teaching.

Bradford, P., & Wurman, R. S. (1996). *Information architects*. Zürich: Graphis.

Brevik, P. S. (1989). Information literacy: Revolution in education. In G. E. Mensching & T. B. Mensching (Eds.), *Coping with information illiteracy: Bibliographic instruction for the information age*. Papers presented at the seventeenth national LOEX library instruction conference (pp. 1–6). Ann Arbor, MI: Pierian Press.

Bronshteyn, K., & Baladad, R. (2006). Perspectives on… librarians as writing instructors: Using paraphrasing exercises to teach beginning information literacy students. *Journal of Academic Librarianship, 32*(5), 533–536.

Brophy, P. (2001). *The Library in the Twenty-first Century: New services for the information age*. London: Library Association Publishing.

Brown, D. (2010). Eight principles of information architecture. *Bulletin of the American Society for Information Science and Technology, 36*(6), 30–34. http://www.asis.org/Bulletin/Aug-10/AugSep10_Brown.pdf.

Brown, J. M., & Tucker, C. (2013). Expanding library support of faculty research: Exploring readiness. *Portal: Libraries and the Academy, 13*(3), 257–271.

Bruce, C. S. (1997). *The seven faces of information literacy*. Adelaide: Auslib Press.

Bruce, C. (2004). Information literacy as a catalyst for educational change. In C. Macpherson, F. Nouwens, & D. Orr (Eds.), *Lifelong learning: Whose responsibility and what is your contribution?* (pp. 8–19). Rockhampton: Central Queensland University Press.

Bruce, H., Jones, W., & Dumais, S. (2004). Information behaviour that keeps found things found. *Information Research, 10*(1). http://www.informationr.net/ir/10-1/paper207.html.

Buckland, M. (1991). Information as thing. *Journal of the American Society for Information Science, 42*(5), 351–360.

Buckland, M. (1992). *Redesigning library services: a manifesto*. Chicago, IL: American library Association.

Buckland, M. (2011). Data management as bibliography. *Bulletin of the American Society for Information Science and Technology, 37*(6), 34–37.

Buckland, M. (2012). What kind of science can information science be? *Journal of the American Society for Information Science and Technology, 63*(1), 1–7.

Bundy, A. (Ed.), (2004a). *Australian and New Zealand information literacy framework* (2nd ed.). Adelaide: Australian and New Zealand Institute for Information Literacy. http://www.caul.edu.au/content/upload/files/info-literacy/InfoLiteracyFramework.pdf.

Bundy, A. (2004b). One essential direction: Information literacy, information technology fluency. *Journal of eLiteracy, 1*, 7–22. http://www.jelit.org/6/.

Burchinal, L. G. (1976). The communications revolution: America's third century challenge. In *The future of organizing knowledge* Papers presented at the Texas A&M university library's centennial academic assembly. College Station, TX: Texas A&M University Library. http://personalpages.manchester.ac.uk/staff/drew.whitworth/burchinal_the_communications_revolution.pdf.

Burdick, A., Drucker, J., Lunenfeld, P., Presner, T., & Schnapp, J. (2012). *Digital humanities*. Cambridge, MA: MIT Press.

Busa, R. (2004). Foreword: Perspectives on the digital humanities. In R. Schreibman, R. Siemens, & J. Unsworth (Eds.), *A companion to digital humanities* (pp. XVI–XXI). Oxford: Blackwell.

Busch-Lauer, I. A. (1995). Abstracts in German medical journals: A linguistic analysis. *Information Processing and Management, 31*(5), 769–776.

Buschman, J. (2009). Information literacy, "new" literacies, and literacy. *Library Quarterly, 79*(1), 95–118.

Buschman, M., & Michalek, A. (2013). Are alternative metrics still alternative? *Bulletin of the American Society for Information Science and Technology, 39*(4), 35–39.

Bussert, K., Chiang, K., & Tancheva, K. (2011). Personal management of scholarly information. In N. F. Foster (Ed.), *Scholarly practice, participatory design and the extensible catalog* (pp. 123–150). Chicago, IL: Association of College and Research Libraries.

Calvi, L., & Cassella, M. (2013). Scholarship 2.0: Analyzing scholars' use of Web 2.0 tools in research and teaching activity. *Liber Quarterly*, 23(2), 110–133.

Calzada Prado, J., & Marzal, M.Á. (2013). Incorporating data literacy into information literacy programs: Core competencies and contents. *Libri*, 63(2), 123–134.

Campbell, B. (1990). What is literacy? Acquiring and using literacy skills. *Australasian Public Libraries and Information Services*, 3(3), 149–152.

Carbo, T. (2013). *Conceptual relationship of information literacy and media literacy: Consideration within the broader mediacy and metaliteracy.* In *Conceptual relationship of information literacy and media literacy in knowledge societies* (pp. 92–101). Paris: UNESCO.

Carlson, J., & Kneale, R. (2011). Embedded librarianship in the research context navigating new waters. *College & Research Libraries News*, 72(3), 167–170.

Carlson, J., Fosmire, M., Miller, C.C., & Nelson, M. S. (2011). Determining data information literacy needs: A study of students and research faculty. *Portal: Libraries and the Academy*, 11(2), 629–657.

Carpenter, J., Wetheridge, L., Smith, N., Goodman, M., & Struijvé, O. (2010). *Researchers of tomorrow: A three year (BL/JISC). Study tracking the research behaviour of generation Y doctoral students: Annual report 2009-2010.* London: Education for Change.

Chan, S. K., & Foo, R. (2004). Interdisciplinary perspectives on abstracts for information retrieval. *IBERICA*, 8, 100–124. http://www.aelfe.org/documents/07-RA-8-Chan-Foo.pdf.

Chowdhury, G., Poulter, A., & McMenemy, D. (2006). Public Library 2.0. Towards a new mission for public libraries as a network of community knowledge. *Online Information Review*, 30(4), 454–460.

Christensen-Dalsgaard, B. (2012). *Ten recommendations for libraries to get started with research data management.* LIBER, http://www.libereurope.eu/news/ten-recommendations-for-libraries-to-get-started-with-research-data-management.

Clemente, B. E., & Pollara, V. J. (2005). Mapping the course, marking the trail. *IT Professional*, 7(5), 10–15.

Coiro, M., Knobel, C., Lankshear, C., & Leu, D. (2008). Central issues in new literacies and new literacies research. In J. Coiro, M. Knobel, C. Lankshear, & D. Leu (Eds.), *The handbook of research on new literacies* (pp. 25–32). Mahwah, NJ: Erlbaum.

Collins, E. (2013). Social media and scholarly communications: The more they change, the more they stay the same? In D. Shorley & M. Jubb (Eds.), *The future of scholarly communication* (pp. 89–102). London: Facet.

Collins, E., & Jubb, M. (2012). How do researchers in the humanities use information resources? *Liber Quarterly*, 21(2), 176–187. http://liber.library.uu.nl/index.php/lq/article/view/8017/8365.

Connaway, L. S., Radford, M. L., & Dickey, T. J. (2008). Virtual reference services: On the trail of the elusive non-user: What research in virtual reference environments reveals. *Bulletin of the American Society for Information Science and Technology*, 34(2), 25–28.

Connor, U., & Mauranen, A. (1999). Linguistic analysis of grant proposals: European Union Research Grants. *English for Specific Purposes*, 18(1), 47–62.

Cope, B., & Kalantzis, M. (2009a). Signs of epistemic disruption: Transformations in the knowledge system of the academic journal. *First Monday*, 14(4–6). http://www.uic.edu/htbin/cgiwrap/bin/ojs/index.php/fm/article/viewArticle/2309/2163.

Cope, B., & Kalantzis, M. (2009b). Multiliteracies: New literacies, new learning. *Pedagogies: an international journal*, 4(3), 164–195.

Cordes, S. (2009). *Broad horizons: The role of multimodal literacy in 21st century library instruction.* http://www.ifla.org/files/hq/papers/ifla75/94-cordes-en.pdf.

Corrall, S., Kennan, M. A., & Afzal, W. (2013). Bibliometrics and research data management services: Emerging trends in library support for research. *Library Trends*, 61(3), 636–674.

Cowan, S. M. (2014). Information literacy: The battle we won that we lost? *Portal: Libraries and the Academy*, 14(1), 23–32.

Cox, A. M. (2008). Flickr: A case study of Web 2.0. *Aslib Proceedings*, 60(5), 493–516.

Cremmins, E. T. (1982). *The art of abstracting*. Philadelphia, PA: ISI Press.

Cronin, B. (2008). The sociological turn in information science. *Journal of Information Science*, 34(4), 465–475.

Cross, C., & Oppenheim, C. (2006). A genre analysis of scientific abstracts. *Journal of Documentation*, 62(4), 428–446.

D'Angelo, B. J., & Maid, B. M. (2004). Moving beyond definitions: Implementing information literacy across the curriculum. *Journal of Academic Librarianship*, 30(3), 212–217.

Dahlberg, I. (2006). *Definitionen aus dem Begriffsfeld Wissensorganisation*. http://www.isko-de.org/index.php?id=dahlbergdefinitionen.

Dalbello, M. (2011). A genealogy of digital humanities. *Journal of Documentation*, 67(3), 480–506.

Dashkin, M. (2003). Electronic writing: defining the core competency. *Information Outlook*, 7(9), 34–37.

David, P. A. (2000). *The digital technology boomerang: New intellectual property rights threaten global 'open science'*. In: World Bank ABCDE (Europe) conference (Paris). http://cmap-tools.cicei.com:8002/rid=1203015448477_487251007_1227/The%20digital%20Technology%20boomerang-copyright-contra-openscience.pdf.

Davies, A., Fidler, D., & Gorbis, M. (2011). *Future work skills 2020*. Palo Alto, CA: Institute for the Future. http://www.iftf.org/our-work/global-landscape/work/future-work-skills-2020/.

Davis, N. (2011). Information overload, reloaded. *Bulletin of the American Society for Information Science and Technology*, 37(5), 45–49. http://www.asis.org/Bulletin/Jun-11/JunJul11_Davis.html.

Davis, N. (2012). *IA strategy: Addressing the signatures of information overload*. UXmatters, February 2012. http://www.uxmatters.com/mt/archives/2012/02/ia-strategy-addressing-the-signatures-of-information-overload.php.

Davis-Kahl, S., & Hensley, M. K. (Eds.), (2013). *Common ground at the nexus of information literacy and scholarly communication*. Chicago, IL: Association of College and Research Libraries.

De Sompel, H. V., Payette, S., Erickson, J., Lagoze, C., & Warner, S. (2004). Rethinking scholarly communication—Building the system that scholars deserve. *D-Lib Magazine*, 10(9). http://www.dlib.org/dlib/september04/vandesompel/09vande-sompel.html.

Dede, C. (2008). A seismic shift in epistemology. *EDUCAUSE Review*, 43(3), 80–81.

Delaney, G., & Bates, J. (2014). Envisioning the academic library: A reflection on roles, relevancy and relationships. *New Review of Academic Librarianship*, 21(1), 30–51.

Dervin, B. (1998). Sense-making theory and practice: An overview of user interests in knowledge seeking and use. *Journal of Knowledge Management*, 2(2), 36–46.

Deterding, S., Dixon, D., Khaled, R., & Nacke, L. (2011). *From game design elements to gamefulness: Defining gamification*. In *Proceedings of the 15th international academic MindTrek conference: Envisioning future media environments* (pp. 9–15). New York, NY: ACM.

Dinescu, A. (2010). The coming "république des lettres" the academic world and the Web 2.0. Risks and challenges. In M. Anandarajan & A. Anandarajan (Eds.), *e-Research collaboration* (pp. 263–275). Berlin, Heidelberg: Springer.

Donovan, M. (2011). Networking and the changing environment for academic research. In N. Fried Foster (Ed.), *Scholarly practice, participatory design and the extensible catalog* (pp. 51–74). Chicago, IL: Association of College and Research Libraries.

Dorner, D. G., & Gorman, G. E. (2006). Information literacy education in Asian developing countries: Cultural factors affecting curriculum development and programme delivery. *IFLA Journal*, 32(4), 281–293.

Dowling, B. (2013). Libraries and news literacy. *Public Libraries*, 52(1), 13–14.

Drabinski, E. (2014). Toward a Kairos of library instruction. *Journal of Academic Librarianship*, 40(5), 480–485.

Duckett, K., & Warren, S. (2013). Exploring the intersections of information literacy and scholarly communication: Two frames of reference for undergraduate instruction. In S. Davis-Kahl & M. K. Hensley (Eds.), *Common ground at the nexus of information literacy and scholarly communication* (pp. 22–45). Chicago, IL: Association of College and Research Libraries.

Duncan, J., Clement, S. K., & Rozum, B. (2013). Teaching our faculty. Developing copyright and scholarly communication outreach programs. In S. Davis-Kahl & M. K. Hensley (Eds.), *Common ground at the nexus of information literacy and scholarly communication* (pp. 269–286). Chicago, IL: Association of College and Research Libraries.

Dunn, D. (2011). *The psychologically literate citizen: Foundations and global perspectives.* Oxford: Oxford University Press.

East, J. W. (2005). Information literacy for the humanities researcher: A syllabus based on information habits research. *Journal of Academic Librarianship*, 31(2), 134–142.

EC. (2009). *Mapping foresight. Revealing how Europe and other world regions navigate into the future.* Brussels: European Commission, Directorate-General for Research, Communication Unit. ftp://ftp.cordis.europa.eu/pub/fp7/ssh/docs/efmn-mapping-foresight.pdf.

Eisenberg, M. (2008). Information literacy: Essential skills for the information age. *DESIDOC Journal of Library & Information Technology*, 28(2), 39–47.

Eisenberg, M., & Berkowitz, R. E. (1990). *Information problem solving: The big six approach to library and information skills instruction.* Norwood, NJ: Alex.

Elder, L. (2011). Becoming a critic of your own thinking. *HR Matters Magazine*, 15. http://www.hr-matters.info/feat2011/2011.jul.BecomingACriticOfYourOwnThinking.htm.

Elmborg, J. (2003). Information literacy and writing across the curriculum: Sharing the vision. *Reference Services Review*, 31(1), 68–80.

Elmborg, J. (2006). Critical information literacy: Implications for instructional practice. *Journal of Academic Librarianship*, 32(2), 192–199.

EP. (2007). *A European approach to media literacy in the digital environment.* The European Parliament, the Council, the European Economic and Social Committee and the Committee of the Regions.

Erway, R. (2013). Starting the conversation: University-wide research data management policy. *Educause Review Online.* 6 December, http://www.educause.edu/ero/article/starting-conversation-university-wide-research-data-management-policy.

Eshet-Alkalai, Y. (2004). Digital literacy: A conceptual framework for survival skills in the digital era. *Journal of Educational Multimedia and Hypermedia*, 13(1), 93–107.

Etzel, B., & Thomas, P. (1999). *Personal information management: Tools and techniques for achieving professional effectiveness.* New York, NY: NYU Press.

EU. (2012). *For 1 in 5 young Europeans, the world is hard to read.* High Level Group on Literacy, http://ec.europa.eu/education/library/reports/literacy_en.pdf.

Evens, A. (2012). Web 2.0 and the ontology of the digital. *DHQ: Digital Humanities Quarterly*, 6(2). http://www.digitalhumanities.org/dhq/vol/6/2/000120/000120.html.

Exner, N. (2014). Research information literacy: Addressing original researchers needs. *Journal of Academic Librarianship*, 40(5), 460–466.

Eysenbach, G. (2008). Credibility of health information and digital media: New perspectives and implications for youth. In *Digital media, youth, and credibility* (pp. 123–154). Cambridge, MA: MIT Press. http://www.mitpressjournals.org/doi/pdf/10.1162/dmal.9780262562324.123.

Farkas, M. (2011). Technology in practice: Information literacy 2.0. *American Libraries.* 1 November, http://americanlibrariesmagazine.org/columns/practice/information-literacy-20.

Farkas, M. (2012). Participatory technologies, pedagogy 2.0 and information literacy. *Library Hi Tech*, 30(1), 82–94.

Federer, L. (2013). The librarian as research informationist: a case study. *Journal of the Medical Library Association*, 101(4), 298–302.

Fenner, M., & Lin, J. (2014). Novel research impact indicators. *Liber Quarterly*, 23(4), 300–309.

Fink, S. (2014). Can doctors prescribe apps instead of medicine? *Policy Exchange.* 19 June, http://www.policyexchange.org.uk/media-centre/blogs/category/item/can-doctors-prescribe-apps-instead-of-medicine.

Flanders, J. (2009). The productive unease of 21st-century digital scholarship. *DHQ: Digital Humanities Quarterly*, 3(3). http://www.digitalhumanities.org/dhq/vol/3/3/000055/000055.html.

Forte, A., Andalibi, N., Park, T., & Willever-Farr, H. (2014). *Designing information savvy societies: An introduction to assessability.* In Proceedings of ACM SIGCHI conference on human factors in computing systems (CHI14), Toronto, Canada. http://www.andreaforte.net/ForteCHI14Assessability.pdf.

Foster, A. E. (2004). A non-linear model of information seeking behaviour. *Journal of the American Society for Information Science and Technology*, 55(3), 228–237.

Frabetti, F. (2011). Rethinking the digital humanities in the context of originary technicity. *Culture Machine*, 12, 1–22. http://www.culturemachine.net/index.php/cm/article/viewDownloadInterstitial/431/461.

Franganillo, J. (2009). Gestión de información personal: elementos, actividades e integración. *El Profesional de la Información*, 18(4). http://franganillo.es/gip.pdf.

Frand, J., & Hixon, C. (1999). *Personal knowledge management: Who, what, why, when, where, how?.* http://www.anderson.ucla.edu/faculty/jason.frand/researcher/speeches/PKM.htm.

French, M. G. (Ed.), (2014). *Health literacy and numeracy: Workshop summary.* Washington, DC: National Academies Press.

Frey, N., & Fisher, D. (Eds.), (2008). *Teaching visual literacy: using comic books, graphic novels, anime, cartoons, and more to develop comprehension and thinking skills.* Thousand Oaks, CA: Corwin Press.

Friesen, N., (2010). Education and the social Web: Connective learning and the commercial imperative. *First Monday*, 15(12). http://journals.uic.edu/ojs/index.php/fm/article/view/3149/2718.

Frischer, B. (2011). Art and science in the age of digital reproduction: From mimetic representation to interactive virtual reality. *Virtual Archaeology Review*, 2(4), 19–32. http://varjournal.es/doc/varj02_004_06.pdf.

Fruin, C. (2013). Scholarly communication in the field. In S. Davis-Kah & M. K. Hensley (Eds.), *Common ground at the nexus of information literacy and scholarly communication* (pp. 249–267). Chicago, IL: Association of College and Research Libraries.

Fruin, C., & Rascoe, F. (2014). Funding open access journal publishing article processing charges. *College & Research Libraries News*, 75(5), 240–243.

Fuchs, C. (2009). Information and communication technologies and society. A contribution to the critique of the political economy of the internet. *European Journal of Communication*, 24(1), 69–87.

Geisler, Ch., Bazerman, Ch., Doheny-Farina, S., Gurak, L., Haas, Ch. Johnson-Eilola, J., et al. (2001). ITex. Future directions for research on the relationship between information technology and writing. *Journal of Business and Technical Communication*, 15(32), 269–308.

Gendina, N. (2008). *The concept of a persons information culture: View from Russia.* http://archivesic.ccsd.cnrs.fr/docs/00/35/94/75/PDF/TexteGendinaColloqueErte2008.pdf.

Giarlo, M. (2013). Academic libraries as quality hubs. *Journal of Librarianship and Scholarly Communication*, 1(3), 1–10.

Gibson, C. (2008). The history of information literacy. In Ch. N. Cox & E. Blakesley Lindsay (Eds.), *Information literacy instruction handbook* (pp. 10–26). Chicago, IL: American Library Association.

Gilster, P. (1997). *Digital literacy.* New York: Wiley.

Gilton, D. L. (2011). *History of information literacy instruction: A history in context.* http://www.uri.edu/artsci/lsc/Faculty/gilton/InformationLiteracyInstruction-AHistoryinContext.htm.

Ginsparg, P. (2007). Next-generation implications of open access. *CTWatch Quarterly*, 3(3). http://www.ctwatch.org/quarterly/articles/2007/08/next-generationimplications-of-open-access/.

Godwin, P. (2008). Introduction: Making the connections. In P. Godwin & J. Parker (Eds.), *Information literacy meets Library 2.0* (pp. 3–18). London: Facet.

Godwin, P. (2012). Library 2.0: A retrospective. In P. Godwin & J. Parker (Eds.), *Information literacy beyond Library 2.0* (pp. 3–18). London: Facet.

Golumbia, D. (2013). Communication, "Critical". *Communication and Critical/Cultural Studies*, 10(2–3), 248–252.

Goodfellow, R. (2013). The literacies of digital scholarship-truth and use values. In R. Goodfellow & M. R. Lea (Eds.), *Literacy in the digital university: Learning as social practice in a digital world—Critical perspectives on learning, scholarship and technology* (pp. 67–78). New York, NY: Routledge.

Goodman, A., Pepe, A., Blocker, A. W., Borgman, Ch. L., Cranmer, K., Crosas, M., et al. (2014). Ten simple rules for the care and feeding of scientific data. *PLoS Computational Biology*, 10(4), e1003542.

Gordon-Murnane, L. (2012). Big data: A big opportunity for librarians. *Online*, 36(5), 30–34. September-October.

Grand, A., Wilkinson, C., Bultitude, K., & Winfield, A. F. (2012). Open science a new "Technology"? *Science Communication*, 34(5), 679–689.

Granville, S., & Dison, L. (2005). Thinking about thinking: Integrating self-reflection into an academic literacy course. *Journal of English for Academic Purposes*, 4(2), 99–118.

Grier, D. A. (2005). *When computers were human*. Princeton, NJ: Princeton University Press.

Gu, F., & Widén-Wulff, G. (2011). Scholarly communication and possible changes in the context of social media: A Finnish case study. *The Electronic Library*, 29(6), 762–776.

Guinn, D. M. (1979). Composing an abstract: A practical heuristic. *College Composition and Communication*, 30(4), 380–383.

Haendel, M. A., Vasilevsky, N. A., & Wirz, J. A. (2012). Dealing with data: A case study on information and data management literacy. *PLoS Biology*, 10(5), e1001339.

Harley, D., Acord, S. K., Earl-Novell, S., Lawrence, Sh. & King, C. J. (2010). *Assessing the future landscape of scholarly communication: An exploration of faculty values and needs in seven disciplines*. In Berkeley, CA: Center for Studies in Higher Education, UC Berkeley. http://escholarship.org/uc/cshe_fsc.

Harnad, S. (1991). Post-Gutenberg galaxy: The fourth revolution in the means of production of knowledge. *Public-Access Computer Systems Review*, 2(1), 39–53.

Harnad, S. (1995). Electronic scholarly publication: Quo vadis. *Serials Review*, 21(1), 70–72.

Harnad, S. (1999). Free at last: The future of peer-reviewed journals. *D-Lib Magazine*, 5(12). http://www.dlib.org/dlib/december99/12harnad.html.

Head, A. J., & Eisenberg, M. B. (2009). *Lessons learned: How college students seek information in the digital age. Project information literacy progress report*. Seattle, WA: Project Information Literacy, University of Washington iSchool. http://projectinfolit.org/publications/.

Healey, J. (2010). *Financial literacy*. Thirroul, NSW: The Spinney Press.

Heath, T., & Bizer, C. (2011). Linked data: Evolving the web into a global data space. *Synthesis Lectures on the Semantic Web: Theory and Technology*, 1(1), 1–136.

Heller, S. (2014). *Design literacy: Understanding graphic design* (3rd ed.). New York, NY: Allworth Press.

Herman, E., & Nicholas, D. (2010). The information enfranchisement of the digital consumer. *Aslib Proceedings*, 62(3), 245–260.

Hey, T., & Hey, J. (2006). E-science and its implications for the library community. *Library Hi Tech*, 24(4), 515–528.

Hilton, M., & Honey, M. A. (Eds.), (2011). *Learning science through computer games and simulations*. Washington, DC: National Academies Press.

Himma, K. E. (2007). The concept of information overload: A preliminary step in understanding the nature of a harmful information-related condition. *Ethics and Information Technology*, 9(4), 259–272.

Hjørland, B. (2002). Domain analysis in information science: Eleven approaches-traditional as well as innovative. *Journal of Documentation*, 58(4), 422–462.

Hjørland, B., & Albrechtsen, H. (1995). Toward a new horizon in information science: Domain-analysis. *Journal of the American Society for Information Science*, 46(6), 400–425.

Holschuh Simmons, M. (2005). Librarians as disciplinary discourse mediators: Using genre theory to move toward critical information literacy. *Portal: Libraries and the Academy*, 5(3), 297–311.

Hswe, P., & Holt, A. (2012). *A new leadership role for libraries*. Association of Research Libraries. http://old.arl.org/rtl/eresearch/escien/nsf/leadershiproles.shtml.

Hunt, K. (2004). The challenges of integrating data literacy into the curriculum in an undergraduate institution. *IASSIST Quarterly*, 28(2), 12–15. http://www.iassistdata.org/downloads/iqvol282_3hunt.pdf.

Hyland, K., & Salager-Meyer, F. (2008). Scientific writing. *Annual Review of Information Science and Technology*, 42(1), 297–338.

IFLA. (2005). *Alexandria proclamation on information literacy and lifelong learning*. Den Haag: International Federation of Library Associations and Institutions. http://www.ifla.org/publications/beacons-of-the-information-society-the-alexandria-proclamation-on-information-literacy.

IFLA. (2011). *IFLA media and information literacy recommendations*. Den Haag: International Federation of Library Associations and Institutions. http://www.ifla.org/publications/ifla-media-and-information-literacy-recommendations.

IFLA. (2012). *Moscow declaration on media and information literacy*. Den Haag: International Federation of Library Associations and Institutions. http://www.ifla.org/publications/moscow-declaration-on-media-and-information-literacy.

IFLA. (2014). *Lyon declaration on access to information and development*. Den Haag: International Federation of Library Associations and Institutions. http://www.lyon-declaration.org/.

IFLA/UNESCO. (1994). *IFLA/UNESCO public library manifesto 1994*. Den Haag: International Federation of Library Associations and Institutions. http://www.ifla.org/publications/iflaunesco-public-library-manifesto-1994.

Ingraham, B., Levy, P., McKenna, C., & Roberts, G. (2007). Academic literacy in the 21st century. In G. Conole & M. Oliver (Eds.), *Contemporary perspectives in e-learning research: Themes, methods and impact on practice* (pp. 160–173). New York, NY: Routledge.

Ipri, T. (2010). Introducing transliteracy: What does it mean to academic libraries? *College & Research Libraries News*, 71(10), 532–567.

IRA. (2009). *New literacies and 21st-century technologies. Position statement*. Newark, DE: International Reading Association.

Jackson, A. (2014). The power of using infographics to communicate science. *Nature Blog*. 20 January, http://blogs.nature.com/ofschemesandmemes/2014/01/20/the-power-of-using-infographics-to-communicate-science.

Jacobs, H. (2008). Information literacy and reflective pedagogical praxis. *Journal of Academic Librarianship*, 34(3), 256–262.

Jacobs, H. (2014). Pedagogies of possibility within the disciplines: Critical information literacy and literatures in English. *Communications in Information Literacy*, 8(2), 192–207.

Jakobs, E. M. (2003). Reproductive writing-writing from sources. *Journal of Pragmatics*, 35(5), 893–906.

Jamali, H. R., Nicholas, D., Watkinson, A., Herman, E., Tenopir, C., Levine, K., et al. (2014a). How scholars implement trust in their reading, citing and publishing activities: Geographical differences. *Library & Information Science Research*, 36(3–4), 192–202.

Jamali, H. R., Russell, B., Nicholas, D., & Watkinson, A. (2014b). Do online communities support research collaboration? *Aslib Journal of Information Management*, 66(6), 603–622.

James, L., Norman, J., De Baets, A. S., Burchell-Hughes, I., Burchmore, H., Philips, A., ... & Wolffe, J. (2009). *The lives and technologies of early career researchers*. Cambridge: CARET, University of Cambridge/Open University/JISC.

Jarrett, K. (2008). Interactivity is evil! A critical investigation of Web 2.0. *First Monday*, 13(3). http://firstmonday.org/htbin/cgiwrap/bin/ojs/index.php/fm/article/viewArticle/2140/1947.

Ji, Q., Ha, L., & Sypher, U. (2014). The role of news media use and demographic characteristics in the possibility of information overload prediction. *International Journal of Communication*, 8(16), 699–714.

Johnson, C. A. (2011). *The information diet: A case for conscious consumption*. Sebastopol, CA: O'Reilly.

Johnson, A. M., Sproles, C., Detmering, R., & English, J. (2012). Library instruction and information literacy 2011. *Reference Services Review*, 40(4), 601–703.

Johnston, B., & Webber, S. (2003). Information literacy in higher education: A review and case study. *Studies in Higher Education*, 28(3), 335–352.

Johnston, B., & Webber, S. (2005). As we may think: Information literacy as a discipline for the information age. *Research Strategies*, 20(3), 108–121.

Jones, D. (1996). *Critical thinking in an online world*. Santa Barbara, CA: University of California, Santa Barbara Library. http://misc.library.ucsb.edu/untangle/jones.html.

Jones, W. (2007). *Keeping found things found: The study and practice of personal information management (interactive technologies)*. Burlington, MA: Morgan Kaufmann.

Jones, W., & Maier, D. (2003). Report from the session on personal information management. In *Workshop of the information and data management program*. Seattle, WA: National Science Foundation Information.

Jones, W., & Marchionini, G. (2011). *Personal information management (synthesis lectures on information concepts, retrieval, and services)*. San Rafael, CA: Morgan Claypool.

Jubb, M. (2014). Communication or competition: What motivates researchers to write articles for journals? *Learned Publishing*, 27(4), 251–252.

Julien, H., & Barker, S. (2009). How high-school students find and evaluate scientific information: A basis for information literacy skills development. *Library and Information Science Research*, 31(1), 12–17.

Julien, H., & Williamson, C. (2011). Discourse and practice in information literacy and information seeking: gaps and opportunities. *Information Research*, 16(1), 1–10.

Južnič, P., Vilar, P., & Bartol, T. (2014). What do researchers think about altmetrics and are they familiar with their abilities? *Libraries in the Digital Age (LIDA) Proceedings:* Vol. 13. http://ozk.unizd.hr/proceedings/index.php/lida/article/view/128.

Kapitzke, C. (2001). Information literacy: The changing library. *Journal of Adolescent and Adult Literacy*, 44(5), 450–456.

Kapitzke, C. (2003). Information literacy: A positivist epistemology and a politics of outformation. *Educational Theory*, 53(1), 37–53.

Kaplan, A. M., & Haenlein, M. (2010). Users of the world, unite! The challenges and opportunities of social media. *Business Horizons*, 53(1), 59–68.

Kari, J. (2007). Conceptualizing the personal outcomes of information. *Information Research*, 12(2), 292. http://InformationR.net/ir/12-2/paper292.html.

Karvalics, L. Z. (2013). From scientific literacy to lifelong research: A social innovation approach. In S. Kurbaglu, et al. (Eds.), *Worldwide commonalities and challenges in information literacy research and practice* (pp. 126–133). Cham: Springer International.

Keen, A. (2007). *The cult of the amateur*. London: Nicholas Brealey Publishing.

Kelly, A. R., & Autry, M. K. (2013). Access, accommodation, and science: Knowledge in an "open" world. *First Monday*, 18(6). http://firstmonday.org/ojs/index.php/fm/article/view/4341/3684.

Khodiyar,V. K., Rowlett, K. A., & Lawrence, R. N. (2014). Altmetrics as a means of assessing scholarly output. *Learned Publishing*, 27(5), 25–32.

King, D., Greaves, F., Exeter, C., & Darzi, A. (2013). Gamification: Influencing health behaviours with games. *Journal of the Royal Society of Medicine*, 106(3), 76–78.

Knoth, P., & Herrmannova, D. (2014). Towards semantometrics: A new semantic similarity based measure for assessing a research publication's contribution. *D-Lib Magazine*, 20(11–12). http://www.dlib.org/dlib/november14/knoth/11knoth.html.

Koltay, T. (2009). Abstracting: Information literacy on a professional level. *Journal of Documentation*, 65(5), 841–855.

Koltay, T. (2011). The media and the literacies: Media literacy, information literacy, digital literacy. *Media, Culture & Society*, 33(2), 211–221.

Koltay, T., Krakowska, M., Landova, H., & Prókai, M. (2010). Information literacy in the Visegrad group countries: Literature and initiatives. *Education for Information*, 28(1), 57–76.

Kowalczyk, S., & Shankar, K. (2011). Data sharing in the sciences. *Annual Review of Information Science and Technology*, 45(1), 247–294.

Kranich, N. (2004). *The Information Commons: A Public Policy Report*. New York, NY: Free Expression Policy Project. http://www.brennancenter.org/publication/information-commons.

Kranitch, N. (2007). Countering enclosure: Reclaiming the knowledge commons. In C. Hess & E. Ostrom (Eds.), *Understanding knowledge as a commons: From theory to practice* (pp. 85–123). Cambridge, MA: MIT Press.

Kress, G. (2003). *Literacy in the new media age*. London, New York: Routledge.

Kroll, S., & Forsman, R. (2010). *A slice of research life: Information support for research in the United States*. Dublin, OH: OCLC. www.oclc.org/research/publications/library/2010/2010-15.pdf.

Kuhlthau, C. C. (1993). *Seeking meaning: a process approach to library and information services*. Norwood, NJ: Ablex.

Kuhlthau, C. (2013). Rethinking the 2000 ACRL standards. *Communications in Information Literacy*, 7(20), 92–97.

Kwanya, T., Stilwell, Ch., & Underwood, P. (2012). Intelligent libraries and apomediators: Distinguishing between Library 3.0 and Library 2.0. *Journal of Librarianship and Information Science*, 45(3), 187–197.

Ladley, J. (2012). *Data governance: How to design, deploy and sustain an effective data governance program*. Burlington, MA: Morgan Kaufmann.

Lankes, R. D. (2011). *The atlas of new librarianship*. Cambridge, MA: MIT Press.

Lankshear, C., & Knobel, M. (2004). *New literacies: Research and social practice*. http://www.geocities.com/c.lankshear/nrc.html.

Lau, J. (2013). Conceptual relationship of information literacy and media literacy. In *Conceptual relationship of information literacy and media literacy in knowledge societies* (pp. 76–91). Paris: UNESCO.

Lavoie, B., Childress, E., Erway, R., Faniel, I., Malpas, C., Schaffner, J., et al. (2014). *The evolving scholarly record*. Dublin, OH: OCLC.

Leadbeater, C., & Miller, P. (2004). *The Pro-Am revolution: How enthusiasts are changing our economy and society*. London: Demos.

Leckie, G. J. (1996). Desperately seeking citations: Uncovering faculty assumptions about the undergraduate research process. *Journal of Academic Librarianship*, 22(3), 201–208.

Leckie, G. J., & Fullerton, A. (1999). Information literacy in science and engineering undergraduate education: Faculty attitudes and pedagogical practices. *College & Research Libraries*, 60(1), 9–29.

Lee, A. Y. (2013). Literacy and competencies required to participate in knowledge societies. In *Conceptual relationship of information literacy and media literacy in knowledge societies*. Paris: UNESCO.

Lee, A. Y., & So, C. Y. K. (2014). Media literacy and information literacy: Similarities and differences. *Comunicar*, 21(42), 137–145.

Lemke, J. (2004). The literacies of science. In E. W. Saul (Ed.), *Crossing borders in literacy and science instruction: Perspectives on theory and practice* (pp. 33–47). Newark, DE: International Reading Association.

Leu, D. J., Kinzer, C. K., Coiro, J., & Cammack, D. (2004). Toward a theory of new literacies emerging from the Internet and other information and communication technologies. In R. B. Ruddell & N. Unrau (Eds.), *Theoretical models and processes of reading* (5th ed.)(pp. 1568–1611). Newark, DE: International Reading Association.

Leu, D. J., Zawilinski, J., Castek, J., Banerjee, M., Housand, B.C., Liu, Y., et al. (2007). What is new about the new literacies of online reading comprehension. In L. Rush, et al. (Eds.), *Secondary school literacy: What research reveals for classroom practice* (pp. 37–68). Urbana, IL: National Council of Teachers of English.

Leu, D. J., Kinzer, C. K., Coiro, J., Castek, J., & Henry, L. A. (2013). New literacies: A dual level theory of the changing nature of literacy, instruction, and assessment. In D. E. Alvermann, N. J. Unrau, & R. B. Ruddell (Eds.), *Theoretical models and processes of reading* (6th ed.)(pp. 1151–1180). Newark, DE: International Reading Association. http://www.reading.org/Libraries/books/IRA-710-chapter42.pdf.

Lewis, D. W. (2013). From stacks to the Web: The transformation of academic library collecting. *College & Research Libraries*, 74(2), 159–177.

Lievrouw, L. A. (2011). Social media and the production of knowledge: A return to little science? *Social Epistemology*, 24(3), 219–237.

Littlejohn, A., Beetham, H., & McGill, L. (2012). Learning at the digital frontier: A review of digital literacies in theory and practice. *Journal of Computer Assisted Learning*, 28(6), 547–556.

Livingstone, S. (2004). Media literacy and the challenge of new information and communication technologies. *Communication Review*, 7(1), 3–14.

Livingstone, S., van Couvering, E. J., & Thumin, N. (2008). Converging traditions of research on media and information literacies: Disciplinary and methodological issues. In D. J. Leu, et al. (Eds.), *Handbook of research on new literacies* (pp. 103–132). Hillsdale, NJ: Lawrence Erlbaum Associates.

Lloyd, A. (2006). Information literacy landscapes: An emerging picture. *Journal of Documentation*, 62(5), 570–583.

Lloyd, A. (2007). Learning to put out the red stuff: Becoming information literate through discursive practice. *The Library Quarterly*, 77(2), 181–198.

Lloyd, A. (2011). Trapped between a rock and hard place: What counts as in the workplace and how is it conceptualized. *Library Trends*, 60(2), 277–296.

Lloyd, A., & Williamson, K. (2008). Towards an understanding of information literacy in context: Implications for research. *Journal of Librarianship and Information Science*, 40(1), 3–12.

Lohnes, S., & Kinzer, C. (2007). Questioning assumptions about students' expectations for technology in college classrooms. *Innovate*, 3(5). http://www.editlib.org/p/104341/.

Loo, A., & Chung, C. W. (2006). A model for information literacy course development: A liberal arts university perspective. *Library Review*, 55(4), 249–258.

Lorenzen, M. (2001). A brief history of library information in the United States of America. *Illinois Libraries*, 83(2), 8–18.

Loukides, M. (2012). *What is data science?* Sebastopol, CA: O'Reilly.

Lozano, G. A., Larivière, V., & Gingras, Y. (2012). The weakening relationship between the impact factor and papers citations in the digital age. *Journal of the American Society for Information Science and Technology*, 63(11), 2140–2145.

Luke, A., & Freebody, P. (1999). Further notes on the four resources model. *Reading Online*, 3. http://www.readingonline.org/research/lukefreebody.html.

Luke, A., & Kapitzke, C. (1999). Literacies and libraries: Archives and cybraries. *Curriculum Studies*, 7(3), 467–491.

Lupton, M., & Bruce, C. S. (2010). Windows on information literacy worlds: Generic, situated and transformative perspectives. In A. Lloyd & S. Talja (Eds.), *Practising information literacy: Bringing theories of learning, practice and information literacy together* (pp. 4–27).Wagga Wagga, NSW: Centre for Information Studies, Charles Sturt University.

Luzón, M. J. (2009). Scholarly hyperwriting: The function of links in academic weblogs. *Journal of the American Society for Information Science and Technology*, 60(1), 75–89.

Luzón, M. J. (2013). Public communication of science in blogs: Recontextualizing scientific discourse for a diversified audience. *Written Communication*, 30(4), 428–445.

Lynch, C. (1994). Rethinking the integrity of the scholarly record in the networked information age. *Educom Review*, 29(2), 38–40.

Lynch, C. (1998). *Information literacy and information technology literacy: New components in the curriculum for a digital culture.* http://www.cni.org/wp-content/uploads/2011/08/info-and-IT-literacy.pdf.

Lynch, C. (2009). Jim Grays fourth paradigm and the construction of the scientific record. In T. Hey, S. Tansley, & K. M. Tolle (Eds.), *The fourth paradigm: Data-intensive scientific discovery* (pp. 177–183). Redmond, WA: Microsoft Research.

Lynch, C. (2013). Ebooks in 2013: Promises broken, promises kept, and Faustian bargains. *American Libraries*, E-Content Supplement, 12-16. http://americanlibrariesmagazine.org/2013/06/24/ebooks-in-2013/.

Lynch, C., Greifeneder, E., & Seadle, M. (2012). Interactions between libraries and technology over the past 30 years: An interview with Clifford Lynch 23.06.2012. *Library Hi Tech*, 30(4), 565–578.

Mabe, M. (2010). Scholarly communication: A long view. *New Review of Academic Librarianship*, 16(S1), 132–144.

Maceviciute, E. (2014). Research libraries in a modern environment. *Journal of Documentation*, 70(2), 282–302.

Mackey, T., & Jacobson, T. (2011). Reframing information literacy as a metaliteracy. *College & Research Libraries*, 72(1), 62–78.

MacMillan, D. (2014). Data sharing and discovery: What librarians need to know. *Journal of Academic Librarianship*, 40(5), 541–549.

Madrid, M. M. (2013). A study of digital curator competences: A survey of experts. *The International Information & Library Review*, 45(3–4), 149–156.

Mair, C., Taylor, J., & Hulme, J. (2013). *An introductory guide to psychological literacy and psychologically literate citizenship.* Heslington: The Higher Education Academy.

Malefant, K. J. (2010). Leading change in the system of scholarly communication: A case study of engaging liaison librarians for outreach to faculty. *College & Research Libraries*, 71(1), 63–76.

Mandinach, E. B., & Gummer, E. S. (2013). A systemic view of implementing data literacy in educator preparation. *Educational Researcher*, 42(1), 30–37.

Manguel, A. (2008). *The library at night.* New Haven, CT: Yale University Press.

Marcum, J. W. (2002). Rethinking information literacy. *Library Quarterly*, 72(1), 1–26.

Margolis, E., & Murray, K. E. (2012). Say goodbye to the books: Information literacy as the new legal research paradigm. *University of Dayton Law Review*, 38(1), 117.

Markless, S. (2009). A new conception of information literacy for the digital learning environment in higher education. *Nordic Journal of Information Literacy in Higher Education*, 1(1), 25–40.

Markless, S., & Streatfield, D. R. (2007). Three decades of information literacy: Redefining the parameters. In S. Andretta (Ed.), *Change and challenge: Information literacy for the 21st century* (pp. 15–36). Adelaide: Auslib Press.

Markless, S., & Streatfield, D. R. (2009). Reconceptualising information literacy for the Web 2.0 environment? In S. Hatzipanagos & S. Warburton (Eds.), *Social software and developing community ontologies* (pp. 316–334). Hershey, PA: IGI Global.

Marshall, C. C. (2008). Rethinking personal digital archiving, Part 1: Four challenges from the field. *D-Lib Magazine*, 14(3), 2. http://www.dlib.org/dlib/march08/marshall/03marshall-pt1.html.

Martin, A. (2006). Literacies for the digital age. In A. Martin & D. Madigan (Eds.), *Digital literacies for learning* (pp. 3–25). London: Facet.

Martin, J. (2013). Refreshing information literacy: Learning from recent British information literacy models. *Communications in Information Literacy*, 7(2), 114–127.

Mas Bleda, A., Thelwall, M., Kousha, K., & Aguillo, I. F. (2014). Do highly cited researchers successfully use the social Web? *Scientometrics*, 101(1), 337–356.

McMenemy, D. (2007). Ranganathan's relevance in the 21st century. *Library Review*, 56(2), 97–101.

Mehrpour, S., & Khajavi, Y. (2014). How to spot fake open access journals. *Learned Publishing*, 27(4), 269–274.

Merchant, G. (2007). Writing the future in the digital age. *Literacy*, 41(3), 118–128.

Merrill, A. (2011). Library+. *Public Services Quarterly*, 7(3–4), 144–148.

Metzger, M. J. (2007). Making sense of credibility on the Web: Models for evaluating online information and recommendations for future research. *Journal of the American Society for Information Science and Technology*, 58(13), 2078–2091.

Meyers, E. M., Erickson, I., & Small, R. V. (2013). Digital literacy and informal learning environments: An introduction. *Learning, Media and Technology*, 38(4), 355–367.

Microsoft. (2006). *Towards 2020 science*. Redmond, WA: Microsoft Research.

Miliard, M. (2014). Gamification comes to clinicians. *Healthcare IT News*. 17 March, http://www.healthcareitnews.com/news/gamification-comes-clinicians.

Miller, H. (1996). The multiple dimensions of information quality. *Information Systems Management*, 13(2), 79–82.

Miller, R. (2011). Futures literacy—Embracing complexity and using the future. *Ethos*, 10, 23–28.

Mioduser, D., Nachmias, R., & Forkosh-Baruch, A. (2009). New literacies for the knowledge society. In J. M. Voogt & G. A. Knezek (Eds.), *Handbook of information technology in primary and secondary education* (pp. 23–41). Berlin: Springer.

Mohamed, Sh. & Ismail, O. (Eds.), (2012). *Data equity. Unlocking the value of big data*. London: Centre for Economics and Business Research. http://www.sas.com/offices/europe/uk/downloads/data-equity-cebr.pdf.

Monson, J., Highby, W., & Rathe, B. (2014). Library involvement in faculty publication funds. *College & Undergraduate Libraries*, 21(3–4), 308–329.

Mooney, H., & Newton, M. P. (2012). The anatomy of a data citation: Discovery, reuse, and credit. *Journal of Librarianship and Scholarly Communication*, 1(1), 1–14.

Mooney, H., & Silver, B. (2010). Spread the news: Promoting data services. *College & Research Libraries News*, 71(9), 480–483.

Moretti, F. (2005). *Graphs, maps, trees: Abstract models for literary theory*. London: Verso.

Morton, B. (1997). Is the journal as we know It an article of faith? An open letter to the faculty. *Public-Access Computer Systems Review*, 8(2), 6–17.

Morville, P. (2005). *Ambient findability*. Sebastopol, CA: O'Reilly.

Mounce, R. (2013). Open access and altmetrics: Distinct but complementary. *Bulletin of the American Society for Information Science and Technology*, 39(4), 14–17.

Müller, K. H., & Riegler, A. (2014). Second-order science: A vast and largely unexplored science frontier. *Constructivist Foundations*, 10(1), 7–15.

Murray, M. C., & Pérez, J. (2014). Unraveling the digital literacy paradox: How higher education fails at the fourth literacy. *Issues in Informing Science and Information Technology*, 11, 85–100. http://iisit.org/Vol11/IISITv11p085-100Murray0507.pdf.

Nagy, Gy. (2010). PIM - Személyes információszervezés (PIM - Personal information management). *Tudományos és Műszaki Tájékoztatás*, 57(11-12), 458–474.

NAS. (1996). *National science education standards*. Washington, DC: National Academy Press. http://www.nap.edu/readingroom/books/nses.

NSB. (2005). *Long-lived digital data collections: Enabling research and education in the 21st century*. Arlington, VA: National Science Board, National Science Foundation.

Neil, J. G. (2014). New age of reason for academic libraries. *College & Research Libraries*, 75(5), 612–615.

Nentwich, M. (2003). *Cyberscience: Research in the age of the Internet.* Vienna: Austrian Academy of Sciences Press. http://hw.oeaw.ac.at/3188-7.

Newman, M. L., & Sack, J. (2013). Information workflow of academic researchers in the evolving information environment: An interview study. *Learned Publishing*, 26(2), 123–131.

Neylon, C. (2011). It's not filter failure, it's a discovery deficit. *Serials*, 24(1), 21–25.

NFIL. (2015). *A new direction—Information action coalition.* Cambridge, MA: National Forum on Information Literacy. http://infolit.org/a-new-direction-information-action-coalition/.

Nicholas, D., Huntington, P., Jamali, H. R., & Dobrowolski, T. (2008). The information-seeking behaviour of the digital consumer: Case study the virtual scholar. In D. Nicholas & I. Rowlands (Eds.), *Digital consumers: Reshaping the information professions* (pp. 113–158). London: Facet.

Nicholas, D., Watkinson, A., Volentine, R., Allard, S., Levine, K., Tenopir, C., et al. (2014). Trust and authority in scholarly communications in the light of the digital transition. *Learned Publishing*, 27(2), 121–134.

Nicholas, D., Watkinson, A., Jamali, H. R., Herman, E., Tenopir, C., Volentine, R., et al. (2015). Peer review: Still king in the digital age. *Learned Publishing*, 28(1), 15–21.

Nielsen, H. J., & Hjørland, B. (2014). Curating research data: The potential roles of libraries and information professionals. *Journal of Documentation*, 70(2), 221–240.

NMC. (2014). *NMC horizon report: 2014 library edition.* Austin, TX: The New Media Consortium. http://redarchive.nmc.org/publications/2014-horizon-report-library.

Nolin, J. (2007). What's in a turn? *Information Research*, 12(4). paper colis11, http://informationr.net/ir/12-4/colis/colis11.html.

Nolin, J. (2013). The special librarian and personalized meta-services: Strategies for reconnecting librarians and researchers. *Library Review*, 62(8–9), 508–524.

Nolin, J., & Åström, F. (2010). Turning weakness into strength: Strategies for future information sciences. *Journal of Documentation*, 66(1), 7–27.

Norgaard, R. (2003). Writing information literacy: Contributions to a concept. *Reference and User Services Quarterly*, 43(2), 124–130.

Noruzi, A. (2004). Application of Ranganathan's laws to the Web. *Webology*, 1(2). http://www.webology.org/2004/v1n2/a8.html.

Odlyzko, A. (2009). *The future of scientific communication.* http://www.dtc.umn.edu/~odlyzko/doc/future.scientific.comm.pdf.

Okerson, A. (1991). Back to academia? The case for American universities to publish their own research. *LOGOS*, 2(2), 106–112.

Oliver, G. (2008). Information culture: Exploration of differing values and attitudes to information in organisations. *Journal of Documentation*, 64(3), 363–385.

Ondrusek, A. L., Thiele, H. E., & Yang, C. (2013). Writing abstracts for MLIS research proposals using worked examples: An innovative approach to teaching the elements of research design. *College & Research Libraries*, 75(6), 822–841.

Orr, J. C. (2011). *Data governance for the executive.* Colorado Springs, CO: Senna Publishing.

Owusu-Ansah, E. K. (2003). Information literacy and the academic library: A critical look at the concept and the controversies surrounding it. *Journal of Academic Librarianship*, 29(4), 219–230.

Owusu-Ansah, E. K. (2004). Information literacy and higher education: Placing the academic library in the center of a comprehensive solution. *Journal of Academic Librarianship*, 30(1), 3–16.

Owusu-Ansah, E. K. (2005). Debating definitions of information literacy: Enough is enough!. *Library Review*, 54(6), 366–374.

Palmer, C., & Gelfand, J. (2013). Weaving scholarly communication and information literacy: Strategies for incorporating both threads in academic library outreach. In

S. Davis-Kah & M. K. Hensley (Eds.), *Common ground at the nexus of information literacy and scholarly communication* (pp. 1–24). Chicago, IL: Association of College and Research Libraries.

Pauleen, D. (2009). Personal knowledge management: Putting the person back into the knowledge equation. *Online Information Review*, 33(2), 221–224.

Pauleen, D., & Gorman, G. (2011). *Personal knowledge management: Individual, organizational and social perspectives*. Farnham: Gower.

Piez, W. (2008). Something called digital humanities. *DHQ: Digital Humanities Quarterly*, 2(1). http://www.digitalhumanities.org/dhq/vol/2/1/000020/000020.html.

Pinto, M., Cordón, J. A., & Diaz, R. G. (2010). Thirty years of information literacy (1977-2007): A terminological, conceptual and statistical analysis. *Journal of Librarianship and Information Science*, 42(1), 3–19.

Pinto, M., Fernández-Ramos, A., & Doucet, A.-V. (2008). The role of information competencies and skills in learning to abstract. *Journal of Information Science*, 34(6), 799–815.

Piwowar, H. (2013). Introduction altmetrics: What, why and where? *Bulletin of the American Society for Information Science and Technology*, 39(4), 8–9.

Piwowar, H., & Priem, J. (2013). The power of altmetrics on a CV. *Bulletin of the American Society for Information Science and Technology*, 39(4), 10–13.

Potter, W. J. (2004). Argument for the need for a cognitive theory of media literacy. *American Behavioral Scientist*, 48(2), 266–272.

Priem, J., Groth, P., & Taraborelli, D. (2011). The altmetrics collection. *PloS One*, 7(11), e48753.

Priem, J., & Hemminger, B. (2010). Scientometrics 2.0: New metrics of scholarly impact on the social Web. *First Monday*, 15(7). http://firstmonday.org/htbin/cgiwrap/bin/ojs/index.php/fm/article/view/2874/2570.

Priem, J., Taraborelli, J., Groth, P., & Neylon, C. (2010). *Altmetrics: A manifesto*. http://altmetrics.org/manifesto/.

Procter, R., Williams, R., & Stewart, J. (2010). *If you build it, will they come? How researchers perceive and use Web 2.0*. London: Research Information Network. http://wrap.warwick.ac.uk/56246/.

Procter, R., Williams, R., Stewart, J., Poschen, M., Snee, H., Voss, A., & Asgari-Targhi, M. (2010). Adoption and use of Web 2.0 in scholarly communications. *Philosophical Transactions of the Royal Society*, 368(1926), 4039–4056.

Pryor, G. (2012). Why manage research data? In G. Pryor (Ed.), *Managing research data* (pp. 1–16). London: Facet.

Putnam, L. (2011). The changing role of blogs in science information dissemination. *Issues in Science and Technology Librarianship*, 65. http://www.istl.org/11-spring/article4.html.

Qin, J., & D'Ignazio, J. (2010). *Lessons learned from a two-year experience in science data literacy education.* In: Proceedings of the 31st annual IATUL conference, 20-24 June 2010. 2, http://docs.lib.purdue.edu/iatul2010/conf/day2/5.

Rader, H. (1990). Bibliographic instruction or information literacy. *College & Research Libraries News*, 51(1), 18–20.

Rader, H. B., & Coons, W. (1992). Information literacy: One response to the new decade. In B. Baker & M. E. Litzinger (Eds.), *The evolving educational mission of the library* (pp. 118–128). Chicago, IL: Association of College and Research Libraries.

Ramírez, M. L. (2011). Opinion: Whose role is it anyway? A library practitioner's appraisal of the digital data deluge. *Bulletin of the American Society for Information Science and Technology*, 37(5), 21–23.

Ranganathan, S. R. (1931). *The five laws of library science*. London: Edward Goldston.

Rapple, C. (2011). The role of the critical review article in alleviating: Information overload. *Annual Reviews White Papers*, (14). http://www.annualreviews.org/userimages/ContentEditor/1300384004941/Annual_Reviews_WhitePaper_Web_2011.pdf.

Reid, P. H., & Macafee, C. (2007). The philosophy of local studies in the interactive age. *Journal of Librarianship and Information Science*, 39(3), 126–141.

Riddle, J. S. (2010). Information and service learning. In M. T. Accardi, E. Drabinski, & A. Kumbier (Eds.), *Critical library instruction: Theories and methods* (pp. 133–148). Duluth, MN: Library Juice Press.

Ridley, M. (2012). *Beyond literacy: Exploring a post-literate future.* http://www.beyondliteracy.com/.

Rieh, S. Y. (2002). Judgment of information quality and cognitive authority in the Web. *Journal of the American Society for Information Science and Technology*, 53(2), 145–161.

Robinson, L. (2009). Information science: Communication chain and domain analysis. *Journal of Documentation*, 65(4), 578–591.

Royal Society. (2012). *Science as an open enterprise.* London: Royal Society Science Policy Centre. https://royalsociety.org/uploadedFiles/Royal_Society_Content/policy/projects/sape/2012-06-20-SAOE.pdf.

Saat, R. M., & Salleh, N. M. (2010). Issues related to research ethics in e-Research collaboration. In M. Anandarajan & A. Anandarajan (Eds.), *e-Research collaboration* (pp. 249–261). Berlin, Heidelberg: Springer.

Saunders, L. (2011). *Information literacy as a student learning outcome.* Santa Barbara, CA: Libraries Unlimited.

Schiltz, M., Truyen, P., & Coppens, P. (2007). Cutting the trees of knowledge: Social software, information architecture and their epistemic consequences. *Thesis Eleven*, 89(1), 94–114.

Schlögl, C., Gorraiz, J., Gumpenberger, C., Jack, K. & Kraker, P. (2014). Are downloads and readership data a substitute for citations? The case of a scholarly journal. *Libraries in the Digital Age (LIDA) Proceedings*: Vol. 13. http://ozk.unizd.hr/proceedings/index.php/lida/article/view/165.

Schmidt, B. M. (2011). Theory first. *Journal of Digital Humanities*, 1(1). http://journalofdigitalhumanities.org/1-1/theory-first-by-ben-schmidt/.

Schnapp, J., & Presner, P. (2009). *Digital humanities manifesto 2.0.* http://www.humanitiesblast.com/manifesto/Manifesto_V2.pdf.

Schneider, R. (2013). Research data literacy. In S. Kurbanoglu, et al. (Eds.), *Worldwide commonalities and challenges in information literacy research and practice* (pp. 134–140). Cham: Springer International.

Scholz, T. (2008). Market ideology and the myths of Web 2.0. *First Monday*, 13(3). http://firstmonday.org/article/view/2138/1945.

Schreibman, S., Siemens, R., & Unsworth, J. (2004). The digital humanities and humanities computing: An introduction. In S. Schreibman, R. Siemens, & J. Unsworth (Eds.), *A companion to digital humanities* (pp. XXIII–XXVII). Oxford: Blackwell.

Scollon, R. (1998). *Mediated discourse as social interaction: A study of news discourse.* London: Longman.

SCONUL. (2011). *The SCONUL seven pillars of information literacy. Core model for higher education.* London: Society of College, National and University Libraries Working Group on Information Literacy. http://www.sconul.ac.uk/sites/default/files/documents/coremodel.pdf.

Seadle, M. (2012). Library Hi Tech and information science. *Library Hi Tech*, 30(2), 205–209.

Selwyn, N. (2009). The digital native—Myth and reality. *Aslib Proceedings*, 61(4), 364–379.

Shanbhag, S. (2006). Alternative models of knowledge production: A step forward in information literacy as a liberal art. *Library Philosophy and Practice*, 8(2). http://www.webpages.uidaho.edu/~mbolin/shanbhag.htm.

Shapiro, J. J., & Hughes, S. K. (1996). Information technology as a liberal art. *Educom Review*, 31(2), 31–36.

Shenton, A. K. (2009). Search images, information seeking and information literacy. *Library Review*, 58(2), 109–115.

Shenton, A. K., & Hay-Gibson, N.V. (2011). Information behaviour and information literacy: The ultimate in transdisciplinary phenomena? *Journal of Librarianship and Information Science*, 43(3), 166–175.

Shepherd, R., & Goggin, P. (2012). Reclaiming "old" literacies in the new literacy information age: The functional literacies of the mediated workstation. *Composition Studies*, 40(2), 66–91.

Si, L., Zhuang, X., Xing, W., & Guo, W. (2013). The cultivation of scientific data specialists: Development of LIS education oriented to e-science service requirements. *Library Hi Tech*, 31(4), 700–724.

Silipigni Connaway, L., & Faniel, I. M. (2014). *Reordering Ranganathan: Shifting user behaviors, shifting priorities.* Dublin, OH: OCLC.

Smith, A. G. (1997). Testing the surf: Criteria for evaluating internet information resources. *Public-Access Computer Systems Review*, 8(3), 1–14.

Smith, R. (1999). Opening up BMJ peer review. A beginning that should lead to complete transparency. *British Medical Journal*, 318(7175), 4–5.

Smith, S. (2013). Is data the new media? *EContent*, 36(2), 14–19.

Snavely, L., & Cooper, N. (1997). The information literacy debate. *Journal of Academic Librarianship*, 23(1), 7–14.

Spink, A. (2010). *Information behavior. An evolutionary instinct.* Berlin, Heidelberg: Springer.

Špiranec, S., & Banek Zorica, M. (2010). Information literacy 2.0: Hype or discourse refinement? *Journal of Documentation*, 66(1), 140–153.

Springer, C. D. (2009). Avoiding a tragedy: information literacy and the tragedy of the digital commons. *Library Philosophy and Practice.* http://www.webpages.uidaho.edu/~mbolin/springer.htm.

Staiger, D. (1965). What today's students need to know about writing abstracts. *Journal of Business Communication*, 3(1), 29–33.

Steinerová, J. (2010). Ecological dimensions of information literacy. *Information Research*, 15(1). http://www.informationr.net/ir/15-4/colis719.html.

Street, B. (1984). *Literacy in theory and practice.* Cambridge: Cambridge University Press.

Street, B. (2008). New literacies, new times: Developments in literacy studies. In B.V. Street & N. H. Hornberger (Eds.), *Encyclopedia of language and education* (pp. 418–431). New York: Springer.

Stuart, D. (2011). *Facilitating access to the web of data.* London: Facet.

Suber, P. (2003). Removing the barriers to research: An introduction to open access for librarians. *College & Research Libraries News*, 64(2), 92–94.

Suber, P. (2012). *Open access.* Cambridge, MA: MIT Press.

Sugimoto, C. R., Tsou, A., Naslund, S., Hauser, A., Brandon, M., Winter, D., ... & Finlay, S. C. (2014). Beyond gatekeepers of knowledge: Scholarly communication practices of academic librarians and archivists at ARL institutions. *College & Research Libraries*, 75(2), 145–161.

Sundin, O. (2008). Negotiations on information-seeking expertise: A study of web-based tutorials for information literacy. *Journal of Documentation*, 64(1), 24–44.

Sutton, S. C. (2013). Time to step on the gas in approaching the intersections of scholarly communication and information literacy. *Journal of Librarianship and Scholarly Communication*, 1(3), eP1076. http://jlsc-pub.org/jlsc/vol1/iss3/10/.

Svensson, P. (2012). Beyond the big tent. In M. K. Gold (Ed.), *Debates in the digital humanities.* Minneapolis, MN: University of Minnesota Press. http://dhdebates.gc.cuny.edu/debates/text/22.

Swales, J. M. (1990). *Genre analysis. English in academic and research settings.* Cambridge: Cambridge University Press.

Swanson, T. (2004). A radical step: Implementing a critical information literacy model. *Portal: Libraries and the Academy*, 4(2), 259–273.

Talja, S., & Lloyd, A. (2010). Integrating theories of learning, literacies and information practices. In S. Talja & A. Lloyd (Eds.), *Practising information literacy: Bringing theories of learning, practice and information together* (pp. IX–XVIII). Amsterdam: Elsevier.

Tatum, C., & Jankowski, N. W. (2012). Openness in scholarly communication: Conceptual framework and challenges to innovation. In P. Wouters, et al. (Eds.), *Virtual knowledge: Experimenting in the humanities and social sciences* (pp. 183–218). Cambridge, MA: MIT Press.

Taylor, J. (2001). *Defining e-Science*. Talk given at UK e-Science Town Meeting, July, 2001.

Taylor, M. (2014). Altmetrics tell a story, but can you read it? *Library Connect*. 27 May, http://libraryconnect.elsevier.com/articles/2014-05/altmetrics-tell-story-can-you-read-it.

Tennant, R. (2011). 7 words or phrases to never say or write again. *The Digital Shift blog*, March 17. http://www.thedigitalshift.com/2011/03/roy-tennant-digital-libraries/7-words-or-phrases-to-never-say-or-write-again/.

Taylor, R. S. (1968). Question-negotiation and information seeking in libraries. *College and Research Libraries*, 29(3), 178–194.

Tenopir, C., Birch, B., & Allard, S. (2012). *Academic libraries and research data services. Current practices and plans for the future*. Chicago, IL: Association of College and Research Libraries.

Tenopir, C., Sandusky, R. J., Allard, S., & Birch, B. (2013). Academic librarians and research data services: Preparation and attitudes. *IFLA Journal*, 39(1), 70–78.

Tenopir, C., Hughes, G., Christian, L., Allard, S., Nicholas, D. (2014). *To boldly go beyond downloads: How are journal articles shared and used?* In 34th annual Charleston conference: Issues in book and serial acquisition, Charleston, SC, 5-8 November.

Thelwall, M., & Kousha, K. (2014). Academia.edu: Social network or academic network? *Journal of the Association for Information Science and Technology*, 65(4), 721–731.

Tidline, T. J. (1999). The mythology of information overload. *Library Trends*, 47(3), 485–506.

Torres-Salinas, D., Cabezas-Clavijo, A., & Jimenez-Contreras, E. (2014). Altmetrics: New indicators for scientific communication in Web 2.0. *Comunicar*, 21(41), 53–60.

Tsou, A., Schickore, J., & Sugimoto, C. R. (2014). Unpublishable research: Examining and organizing the file drawer. *Learned Publishing*, 27(4), 253–267.

Tuominen, K. (2007). Information literacy 2.0. *Signum*, 35(5), 6–12.

Tuominen, K., Savolainen, R., & Talja, S. (2005). Information literacy as sociotechnical practice. *The Library Quarterly*, 75(3), 329–345.

Twidale, M. B., Gruzd, A. A., & Nichols, D. M. (2008). Writing in the library: Exploring tighter integration of digital library use with the writing process. *Information Processing & Management*, 44(2), 558–580.

Tylor, E. B. (1871). *Primitive culture*. London: J. Murray.

Tyner, K. (1998). *Literacy in a digital world: Teaching and learning in the age of information*. Malwah, NJ: Lawrence Erlbaum Associates.

Ullmann, T. D., Wild, F., Scott, P., Duval, E., Vandeputte, B., Parra, G., ... & Gillet, D. (2010). Components of a Research 2.0 infrastructure. In M. Wolpers, et al. (Eds.), *Sustaining TEL: From innovation to learning and practice* Proceedings of the 5th European conference on technology-enhanced learning. (pp. 590–596). Heidelberg: Springer.

Umpleby, S. A. (2014). Second order science: Logic, strategies, methods. *Constructivist Foundations*, 10(1), 16–45.

UNESCO. (2003). *Prague declaration: Towards an information literate society*. Paris: United Nations Educational, Scientific and Cultural Organization. http://www.unesco.org/new/fileadmin/MULTIMEDIA/HQ/CI/CI/pdf/PragueDeclaration.pdf.

Unsworth, J. (2002). What is humanities computing, and what is not? In G. Braungart, K. Eibl, & F. Jannidis (Eds.), *Jahrbuch für Computerphilologie*: Vol. 4. Paderborn: mentis Verlag. http://computerphilologie.uni-muenchen.de/jg02/unsworth.html.

Uribe Tirado, A., & Castaño Muñoz, W. (2012). Information literacy competency standards for higher education and their correlation with the cycle of knowledge generation. *Liber Quarterly*, 22(3), 213–239.

Varvel, V. E., & Shen, Y. (2013). Data management consulting at the Johns Hopkins University. *New Review of Academic Librarianship*, 19(3), 224–245.

Veletsianos, G., & Kimmons, R. (2012). Networked participatory scholarship: Emergent techno-cultural pressures toward open and digital scholarship in online networks. *Computers & Education*, 58(2), 766–774.

Vilar, P., Južnič, P., & Bartol, T. (2012). Slovenian researchers: What influences their information behaviour? In *E-science and information management* (pp. 46–60). Berlin, Heidelberg: Springer.

Vitae. (2011). *Researcher development framework*. Cambridge: Careers Research and Advisory Centre.

Wai-yi, B. C. (1998). An information seeking and using process model in the workplace: A constructivist approach. *Asian Libraries*, 7(12), 375–390.

Waldrop, M. M. (2008). Science 2.0: Is open access science the future? *Scientific American*. May, http://www.sciam.com/article.cfm?id=science-2-point-0.

Wanser, J. (2014). Documenting and monitoring scholarly communication at a small liberal arts college: A case study from northeast Ohio. *College & Undergraduate Libraries*, 21(3–4), 295–307.

Webber, S., & Johnston, B. (2000). Conceptions of information literacy: New perspectives and implications. *Journal of Information Science*, 26(6), 381–397.

Weber, N. M. (2013). The relevance of research data sharing and reuse studies. *Bulletin of the Association for Information Science and Technology*, 39(6), 23–26.

Weller, M. (2011). *The digital scholar: How technology is transforming scholarly practice*. New York, NY: Bloomsbury Publishing PLC. http://www.bloomsburyacademic.com/view/DigitalScholar_9781849666275/book-ba-9781849666275.xml.

Weller, K., Mainz, D., Mainz, I., & Paulsen, I. (2007). Wissenschaft 2.0? Social software im einsatz für die wissenschaft. In M. Ockenfeld (Ed.), *Information in Wissenschaft, Bildung und Wirtschaft. Proceedings der 29. Online-Tagung der DGI* (pp. 121–136). Frankfurt: DGI.

Wenden, A. (1999). An introduction to metacognitive knowledge and beliefs in language learning: Beyond the basics. *System*, 27(4), 435–441.

Whitworth, A. (2014). *Radical information literacy: Reclaiming the political heart of the IL movement*. Oxford: Chandos.

Wiegand, W. (2005). *Library as place*. In: Presentation to the 56th annual biennial conference North Carolina Library Association. http://www.ncl.ecu.edu/index.php/NCL/article/viewFile/70/88.

Wilde, J., & Wilde, R. (1991). *Visual literacy: A conceptual approach to graphic problem solving*. New York, NY: Watson-Guptill.

Wilkinson, J. (2000). From transmission to research: Librarians at the heart of the campus. *College & Undergraduate Libraries*, 6(2), 25–40.

Williams, G. (2007). Unclear on the context: Refocusing on information literacy's evaluative component in the age of Google. *Library Philosophy and Practice*, 7. http://www.webpages.uidaho.edu/~mbolin/williams.htm.

Williams, P., Leighton John, J., & Rowland, I. (2009). The personal curation of digital objects: A lifecycle approach. *Aslib Proceedings*, 61(4), 340–363.

Williamson, K., Bernath, V., Wright, S., & Sullivan, J. (2007). Research students in the electronic age: Impacts of changing information behavior on information literacy needs. *Communications in Information Literacy*, 1(2). http://www.comminfolit.org/index.php?journal=cil&page=article&op=viewArticle&path[]=Fall2007AR1&path[]=48.

Wilson, P. (1983). *Second-hand knowledge*. Westport, CN: Greenwood Press.

Wilson, C., Grizzle, A., Tuazon, R., Akyempong, K., & Cheung, C. K. (2011). *Media and information literacy curriculum for teachers*. Paris: United Nations Educational, Scientific and Cultural Organization. http://www.unesco.org/new/fileadmin/MULTIMEDIA/HQ/CI/CI/pdf/media_and_information_literacy_curriculum_for_teachers_en.pdf.

Witek, D., & Grettano, T. (2014). Teaching metaliteracy: A new paradigm in action. *Reference Services Review*, 42(2), 188–208.

Wolf, S. (2007). Information literacy and self-regulation: A convergence of disciplines. *School Library Media Research*, 10. http://www.ala.org/aasl/sites/ala.org.aasl/files/content/aasl-pubsandjournals/slr/vol10/SLMR_InformationLiteracy_V10.pdf.

Wong, G. K. W. (2010). Facilitating students intellectual growth in information literacy teaching. *Reference and User Services Quarterly*, 50(2), 114–118.

WSIS. (2013). *Final statement: Information and knowledge for all—An expanded vision and a renewed commitment. Towards knowledge societies for peace and sustainable development. First WSIS+10 review event commitment*. Paris: UNESCO. http://www.unesco.org/new/fileadmin/MULTIMEDIA/HQ/CI/CI/pdf/wsis/WSIS_10_Event/wsis10_final_statement_en.pdf.

Yuwei, L. (2008). Research 2.0. *Qualitative Researcher, 8*. http://www.cardiff.ac.uk/socsi/qualiti/QualitativeResearcher/QR_Issue8_Jun08.pdf.

Zuiderwijk, A., Janssen, M., Choenni, S., Meijer, R., & Alibaks, R. S. (2012). Socio-technical impediments of open data. *Electronic Journal of E-Government*, 10(2), 156–172.

Zurkowski, P. (1974). *The information service environment: Relationships and priorities.* Washington, DC: National Commission on Libraries and Information Science.

# INDEX

Note: Page numbers followed by *f* indicate figures.

Printed and bound by CPI Group (UK) Ltd, Croydon, CR0 4YY

08/06/2025

01896872-0008